GLADYS
and
CAPONE,
the Untold Story
by her son, John Walton

Gladys Walton, *"The Glad Girl"*
Silent Screen Star

The Beginning ... catapulted to Stardom with her very first film at age 16, she quickly finds herself partying with the Stars of the fledgling "Silent Film Industry." Her beauty, wit, and courage in performing her own stunts brings Al Capone to her dressing room door. He just had to meet the "gal with enough grit to parachute outta a plane."

> *"It was his eyes that held me. Power.*
> *Like looking into the eyes of a tiger."*

She was only 19 years old. He was only 23 and already running the Chicago "Outfit" with Johnny Torrio. That was the start of their secret ten-year love affair. Al Capone was her one and only true love, and she sacrificed her career refusing to leave him.

John brings you his mother's poignant story fulfilling
his promise to tell the true story of her early years

WWW.GLADYSWALTON.COM
*Visit John's website in honor of his mother and
her incredible life. Family photos, publicity photos,
movie stills, theater lobby cards and movie posters. Two
of her Silent Movies, "Sawdust" and "The Untameable"
will soon be available on Amazon.com.*

John's two novels are companion pieces.

John Walton's first novel, *Gladys and Capone, the Untold
Story* is Gladys' story. His second novel *Capone's "Fortress
West"* is his step-grandfather's story. He saw Capone far
differently than Gladys did ... he worked for him. A must read.
But It Now!

An exciting, fast-paced story, it provides a glimpse of the
world as it was then and the devastating affects of unintended
consequences. The story of Joe Mayer, Gladys Walton's step-
father—her involvement with Capone affects the entire family.
Joe's struggle with his conscious and the memories of the
horrors of WWI become increasingly more difficult to manage
as he faces the pressures of working for Capone. Jobs "he
can't refuse", while he struggles to care for his wife Ida and
protect Gladys.

As the brutality escalates, Joe walks a fine line trying to
balance the needs of his family and his conscious.

Book Design and Cover Design by Leilani King

In Memory of My Mother
Gladys Walton

As the oldest son in the family of six children, my mother depended on me a great deal. When I grew older we became best friends, kindred spirits. I was her chauffeur and traveling companion, her closest confidant. She regaled me with stories of how she became *The Glad Girl,* with thirty-seven films for Universal and independent companies, as well as many Broadway productions. She shared Hollywood gossip and brought to life for me the age of the Roaring 20's—years of explosive excess, including the intrigue and violence brought by prohibition.

My mother stood only five feet tall, yet seemed to cast a ten-foot shadow. Her essence was imbued as much with her gypsy father's zeal for adventure as her mother's gentle determination and grit. Apart from an unhappy "arranged marriage," mother had boyfriends and companions throughout her life, but only one true love, Al Capone.

I know I inherited her joy of living, and I take pride in being her son and fulfilling my promise to have her story told.

Love,
John Walton

Prologue

Gladys Walton was eighty-nine years old when Crazy Eddie broke into her home in the little coastal town of Morro Bay. Nothing much happened in Morro Bay in the way of crime or violence, even in 1992, so although Gladys had witnessed plenty of both in her lifetime, she hardly expected what took place that evening.

She was in the kitchen with her companion, Barry Hayes, a retired commercial diver and fisherman, a big burly guy who was in excellent shape for a man of eighty. It was a Saturday evening around 6:30, and Barry had just helped Gladys to a chair at the kitchen table. They'd been companions the past six years. Not lovers, companions. Gladys was adamant about that whenever the subject came up.

She'd had only one true love in her life, and that was a long time ago.

Barry was standing at the stove stirring the clam chowder - his own recipe, dug the clams himself down at Pismo Beach - when they heard the front door crash open.

Everyone in town knew Crazy Eddie was crazy. A drinker, a gambler, he showed up at every party, every club. Even introduced himself that way, "Hi, I'm Crazy Eddie. Glad to meet you."

A town joke until that night.

Neither Barry nor Gladys knew that Crazy Eddie's girlfriend finally had enough that morning, packed up their baby son and left, sending Crazy Eddie over the edge. A Chumash Indian of the local tribe, she simply went home to the reservation. No way could he follow her there, no way to knock sense into her this time. He'd have to face her whole damned family, uncles built like fuckin' refrigerators.

Never mind the damned squaw bitch, Eddie told himself when he came home bleary eyed and found her gone. But why'd she have to take his little boy?"

That afternoon, only hours before he showed up at Gladys Walton's house, Eddie strolled into a card palace over in Paso Robles and blew away three dealers. With a pump shotgun. Pandemonium, players scattering as he walked to the first table, leaned over the shoulders of the guests. "You dealt me bad cards, mother fucker!" And fired point blank. Another table and another, two men and a woman, dead and dying. Then he turned and walked out.

Seconds after the front door crashed in, Gladys saw him come through the archway into the kitchen. Not a shotgun now, a .45 pistol. Crazy Eddie had gone home for the hand gun, then made another stop on his rampage, a "friend," another grudge to handle, another body.

Barry looked up, dropped the spoon into the clam chowder and took a step, his fist clenched. That was all. The first shot hit him in the neck, the carotid artery, and he collapsed, blood spraying everywhere, fountains of blood pooling on the linoleum. Like a broken main, which, of course, it was. Enough blood, it seemed, to float him away. He died instantly, but Crazy Eddie stepped forward and fired another bullet into Barry's chest. For good measure.

Then he turned to Gladys.

Old woman, frozen in her chair. She hadn't even screamed. Hand to her mouth, eyes wide. Eyes that, despite her age, still showed the fire of her fabled youth, a kind of defiance as if to say, I will live my life exactly as I choose, grab every last morsel of joy and laughter, no matter what anyone might say. She'd been a flapper, after all. They didn't call it the Roaring Twenties for nothing.

Crazy Eddie walked to her, only a few feet, didn't say a word. He seemed to be thinking, studying her. Why didn't she scream? Tough old bird. Slowly he raised the gun, placed it firmly to her forehead.

The barrel was hot. That's all Gladys could think that first moment, how very hot on her forehead. She could not speak. Could not pull her eyes from Barry, the blood no longer spouting from his neck. Poor Barry. All that blood. He'd been good to her.

She waited, two seconds, three, four...

So this how my life is to end. Eighty-nine years, not bad. Glamour, fame, adventure, lovers, children, grandchildren.

Her throat tightened. How she loved them.

That was the hardest part.

Well, she had lived more than most, that's sure.

Five, six... The barrel burning a circle on her forehead.

Of all the close calls I've had, now this.

Seven, eight... Still staring, her vision blurred, and in her mind she started to see ... how trite, that old saying about your life passing before your eyes. But there it was. True.

In those moments she saw it all, right before her eyes.

The knock on my dressing room door, soft, almost tentative. My face in the mirror. No premonition, no sense that everything from then on would be marked before and after.

His eyes gray as fog. Not pearl gray like the fedora in his hand, darker. He holds a bouquet, two dozen red roses. "Long stem," he would remind me later, laughing, rolling me in his big arms across whatever bed we were in.

His voice. Nothing one might expect. Quiet. Unassuming. Well modulated, my old speech coach would say. A room full of people would go silent to hear him speak.

Even then, when few knew anything about him. Least of all me.

November, 1922. I was nineteen. He was twenty-three.

He stood in the doorway, custom tailored gray suit, shirt pale yellow, silk tie and handkerchief a light plum. The man had a feel for color.

I didn't even notice the scars. Not then.

It was his eyes that held me. Power. Like looking into the eyes of a tiger. Not menacing. At least I never saw that. It had more to do with how he viewed himself and the world. As if he could take it all in his wide hands, good, bad, everything in between and mold it to his desires.

And that smile. The capacity to shut out all else and devour the moment. For the joy of it.

He hadn't killed anyone yet.

Other faces stream by, like old film projected at the wrong speed. Scenes I did in my brief heyday. Elegant parties. Stars I knew. Friends. One especially.

Funerals, too many funerals.

Happiness too. My children, babies I held in my arms. Each precious, none more than the first. Six children. Who would've thought? Different fathers, if they knew the truth.

Only one I regret. Sham of a marriage, more ways than one. Wouldn't do for a star to be pregnant... by a gangster. Gangster. Hollywood never did get much right.

Not Al Capone, that's sure. Not even close.

That even my marriage was arranged.

Al bought the rings, paid for the wedding, such as it was. Almost makes me laugh now.

He moves slightly, surprised, I suppose, this crazy man holding the gun. Pulls me back from the past. I look up into his eyes, and feel my smile fade to anger. Damn fool.

Shoot. Go ahead. You think I'm afraid to die?

His hand trembles.

But in his sick eyes, I see them. And before I can stop, I slip farther back.

Men I tried my whole life to forget.   Ugly.   Men who would put their hands on a child.

Chapter 1

A car was following her. She heard it on the gravel behind and turned. Big black sedan with a flat top, square box on skinny wheels. 1910. She was seven years old. Walking home from school...

No, better to start farther back.

Her mother smiling as she lifted her onto the swing Uncle Tommy had made, climbing the huge elm tree in their backyard. She saw him way up high, testing the rope.

"There you go, Sweetcakes. Swing high like a bird." He'd catch her in his arms. The house outside Portland, Oregon, all green and shady, grass spongy beneath her toes. Chickens clucking in the yard. She saw her Aunt Minnie too.

Gladys never knew her father, her mother "well rid of him" before she was born. He was "gypsy French," mamma said. She loved the sound of that. Half gypsy. It explained a lot, how she'd dance through life to the beat of drums and mandolins. Head back, skirts twirling. Free.

She did not miss having a father. He left her two priceless gifts, an exotic ancestry and the mystery and romance of knowing he was off wandering somewhere. If he had stayed, he would have been a tamed gypsy, and what good was that?

Besides, her mother and aunt were the best parents anyone could want, and Uncle Tommy. "Mamma Minnie," Gladys called her aunt. After two miscarriages, Aunt Minnie couldn't have children of her own. The sisters made a pact, they would raise Gladys together.

Her two mammas gave her everything, ruffled dresses with big sashes, high stockings and button up shoes. Private lessons, gymnastics and dance and voice. Shiny black tap shoes. How she remembered opening the package. She made sparks with those shiny black shoes.

The car was shiny black. She walked faster, not sure why. It drew along side. Two men grinning at her out the narrow windshield...

Her two mammas said she could do anything she wanted with her life, maybe even be in those new moving pictures they were making in Los Angeles. Gladys remembered the penny arcade at the county fair, Uncle Tommy lifting her onto a box. She stood on tiptoe, looking into the little window while Mamma Minnie turned the handle.

It was magic. As if the people were alive right inside the little machine, talking and waving their arms, ladies in sheer dresses with wild hair and black around their eyes. Men with tall hats and mustaches, tapping their canes, pulling gold watches from vest pockets, blowing smoke from fat cigars. Men. Eyes glinting, lips curled in sneers. You couldn't tell what they were saying, except that it was bad.

Gladys begged to watch another and another, the machines in a row.

Later mamma and Aunt Minnie took her to a real movie in a Nickelodeon downtown. Velvet seats like a fancy parlor, only gold lions' feet where you put your hands. A real piano player made music to go with the story. Words came on the screen between the pictures, and mamma read them to her. There seemed something deliciously naughty in these stories of peril, near escapes and love, always centered on the beautiful, young heroine.

What a life that would be!

In the second grade pageant she wore a dress with a hoop skirt and pantaloons, her curls held up with hair pins and powdered white. A dance called a quadrille, stiff and slow. No gypsy dance. She'd rather be home climbing the elm tree or swimming the pond. How tight they laced her dress, and at the end she made a sweeping bow and almost lost her balance when the hoop skirt tipped up. She took the cue from the crowd's laughter, tipping the hoops even farther. Added a flourish and a big grin. She remembered the roar of applause, her mother's smile.

The black car was right next to her. She walked faster.

A week after the pageant mamma called her downstairs early. Mamma's Christmas morning face. "Oh, princess, wait 'til you hear." She led her to the front parlor, the room kept for when they had "company." She'd even taken the dust covers off the furniture.

They sat on the best overstuffed divan. Mamma took her hands.

"Honey, a man, Mr. Allen, saw you in the pageant. He contacted someone he knows in Los Angeles, and we're going. Mamma Minnie and Uncle Tommy too. Oh, sweetheart, they want you to be Dorothy in the Wizard of Oz." She squeezed her hands. "It's a stage play, and they're putting it on film. Who knows where this could lead." Her face grew serious. "You must practice and practice." Then the smile. "But, oh, we'll stay in a hotel and ride the trolley and go shopping. Maybe even take the red car out to the beaches of Santa Monica. Stop over night at a road house on the way. Oh, Gladys you'll be the star!"

Los Angeles in 1910 was a city to fall in love with. Clean and beautiful. Tall buildings, some over ten stories, wide boulevards bustling with traffic, cars and horse drawn wagons, plenty of room for the Pacific Electric Railroad that connected all the way to San Bernardino and Hollywood, biggest electric railroad in the world then. They spent a whole day riding the P.E.R., and Gladys remembered blocks of Spanish style haciendas, each with its own garden. In one area the train passed through a forest of pointy towers, rigs, Uncle Tommy called them, with hammer shaped machines that tipped and rose nonstop, pumping oil. The air smelled of oil, but ocean breezes carried it away.

Los Angeles had more than 300,000 people.

It happened soon after their trip, walking home from school. The shiny black car stopped. She felt like running, didn't know why. The man closest to her got out, the other man came around from the driver's side. They were smiling. Maybe they were lost, just wanted directions. Her heart beat fast, faster than when she walked onto the stage.

Run! But she could not move, like a rabbit when the dogs close in.

The man grabbed her arm. "We won't hurt you, honey. Not if you don't scream."

She shook her head, but he put a hand over her mouth.

The other man opened the door to the back seat. "Go ahead, get on in, girl. It's roomy inside, nice and soft." He patted the thick velvet.

She couldn't help it, her body squirmed and twisted. He lifted her as if she were a doll, set her inside, and both men climbed in, closed the door.

They spoke softly, their voices not matching what they were doing. She was a little girl. What was wrong with them? Touching her cheeks and arms and legs, then up under her dress with their big clumsy hands.

They did not tear her clothes or even take them off. They tied her feet with a cord from the back window curtains, one holding her firmly while the other undid his trousers and forced her mouth open. Gladys somehow knew it could be

12

worse. She knew what grownups did. She'd seen the rooster and hens. Still she gagged and would've vomited if weren't over so fast, grunting like a pig, stupid man.

When the men traded places, she simply went away. Sailing high on the swing, up, up into the branches of the huge elm, whoosh of air, a robin's nest, sun twinkling through leaves.

Even when the men set her outside on the dirt, one straightening the ribbon in her hair, she did not cry.

"If you tell anyone at all, sweetie, we will come back and kill you. You understand?"

"Not just you," the other one added.

And they drove away.

Her legs wobbled, and she plunked down there on the side of the road. Then the sobs came, hugging her arms, her whole body shaking. Minutes passed. And she saw their grinning faces and shuddered. They would like it if she cried.

She stopped. Sat up. She did not go home, but to the pond, stripped off her dress and underwear and stepped in to her waist. Washed her face and mouth. Cupped water in her hands and drank away the bitter taste. They left no bruises, except a slight mark on her arm where he first grabbed her. And a cut on her lip.

She thought of mamma and Aunt Minnie and Uncle Tommy, all they had seen together in Los Angeles. She thought of her gypsy father. He would have cut those men with his gypsy knife! She thought of walking onto the stage, looking out at the smiling faces, the applause, and she felt a sudden relief. She was alive, more alive than those men. Stupid, ugly men. Grunting pig men.

Anything she wanted to be, her mammas said. No, she would not tell. She would not cry. She was half gypsy. She would never be hurt this way again.

Gladys starred as Dorothy in The Wizard of
Oz in one of the Fairylogue Radio Plays.
Her first paid performance.

Chapter 2

Yet the next morning Gladys saw their faces even before she opened her eyes. Felt their hands on her, fingers prying her mouth. She curled into a ball, clenching the covers to her face. How could she go to school? How could she walk that road?

"Princess! It's gettin' up time in the morning," mamma called up the stairs. "And don't forget, today's Madame Ursula."

Gladys curled tighter, touched her swollen lip. Madame Ursula. Eight o'clock. Voice lessons. She had no voice. She could not tell mamma, not anyone at all, they said. Couldn't play sick either. Mamma's thermometer rule.

"The show must go on," she would say. Like before the Dorothy play when Gladys peeked around the curtain and froze. "Just stage fright." Mamma patted her shoulder. "Everyone has stage fright. It's what makes you good. Nothing worth doing is easy, princess."

That was true. She had played Dorothy in The Wizard of Oz! Dancing with the Lion and Tin Man and Scarecrow.

Gladys breathed in, made her voice normal. "I'm awake, mamma. I'm just getting dressed."

That section of road was the worst, the shadowy part where the tree branches almost met in the middle. She sang, practicing her scales and walking as fast as she could, expecting any minute the crunch of wheels on gravel.

She made it all the way to Friday. Then, when she was almost to the lane to their house, she heard a car. She broke into a run. As fast she could, but the car was closing in.

Fine, she thought. Let them kill me. This time I will fight and kick and scream. I don't care!

She stopped running, but the car went right on past.

Uncle Tommy putting along in his Model T! If he stopped he'd have to crank her again, so he just opened the little door and Gladys ran and jumped in, laughing and laughing.

"What's the hurry, Sweetcakes?" Uncle Tommy said, trying not to swerve as she hugged him. "You in training?"

"Training. Oh, Uncle Tommy, yes training." Tears in her eyes, laughing.

"Thought you were gonna be a picture star," he joked, "not the Olympics."

"I am," she said, "I'm practicing for the chase scenes."

After that everything was training. In Junior High she joined the swim team. Diving was her best. In high school she won the championship. Then State, then Champion Girl Diver of the Pacific Coast, two years in a row. And tap dancing. New tap shoes every year. She got so good she could sing and tap and never miss a note. She danced in every talent show and starred in the school plays.

Then, the summer after her junior year at Jefferson High, Uncle Tommy made her a proposition.

"I got a month off from the railroad. What say we all go on down to the city of Los Angels and give 'er a try. Hmm, Sweetcakes?" He winked. "Bet you can't be in movies by September."

Chapter 3

The summer of 1919 they returned to Los Angeles and took a suite at the Roslyn Hotel. Uncle Tommy would escort Gladys to the studios. Their makeshift family was on a mission.

The first morning the women went shopping on Broadway and found the perfect dress, a deep burgundy in the latest dropped waist style. Low slung shoes with square heels and a jewel clasp. No more button-ups. In the lingerie section Gladys noticed a package. *Binding Cloth.* "For the new look. Sleek and flat and sophisticated."

She took it over to mamma and Aunt Minnie who were gazing up at a mannequin in a frothy negligee.

"Please, mamma. The dress will look so much better with this. Don't you think?"

Her mother laughed. "Goodness. Minnie, look. Binding cloth. Twenty-five cents! We could've torn an old sheet."

She glanced from her daughter's breasts to her pleading eyes. "Sure. Why not."

At a beauty shop across from Central Park, Gladys had her thick brown hair cut in the latest style, three neat curls on her forehead. Mamma applied her make-up as she had for every performance, plucked and darkened her brows in narrow arches, outlined her eyes with the new Lashlux, red cupid lips, blushing cheeks. Just the right amount of "glam," Uncle Tommy called it. She wore black silk stockings and Aunt Minnie's long dove-gray beads, perfect contrast.

17

When Gladys walked into the sitting room. Uncle Tommy stood, almost knocking over the chair. "Holy mackerel! Look at them eyes! Like Theda Bara only way more beautiful. You'll knock 'em dead, Sweetcakes." He picked up her packet of photos and clippings, did a sweeping bow. "Miss Walton, your carriage awaits."

She took his arm, giggling. She was sixteen and looked twenty.

They started at the Bill Hart Studio, waited two hours to be turned down cold. In the next days they tried D.W. Griffith and Cosmopolitan, First National, Fox, Paramount. No luck. The studios all had their name stars, Lillian Gish, the Talmadge sisters, Clara Kimball Young, and the great Nazimova, the Russian actress who'd eased from stage to movies. No one did haughty elegance like Nazimova. Gloria Swanson was getting $20,000 a week at Paramount, and Mary Pickford had signed with First National for over a million dollars. To get Mary, they signed her brother Jack too and gave her mother a $50,000 bonus!

But there seemed no interest in an unknown sixteen-year-old from Portland, Oregon, beautiful or not.

"Don't worry, dumpling," Uncle Tommy said. "Plenty more studios. We've barely scratched the surface."

It was true, new companies sprang up overnight replacing those who went bust. Some churned out a film a week, like in the serial craze, Pearl White in the *Perils of Pauline*. Gladys was in sixth grade then.

When they weren't too tired, they'd go over to Grauman's on Broadway. They saw Nazimova in *The Red Lantern* and Lon Chaney in *The Miracle Man.* The theater took Gladys's breath away, gilded and scrolled and opulent, a palace! $2.00 a ticket. You could buy a good coat for $2.00.

Hardly the tiny, dark Nickelodeon in Portland when Bronco Billy seemed about as good as it could get. In those days stars weren't even named. Stage actors didn't want it known they were working in film. Or producers foresaw the salaries they'd have to pay. Gladys vaguely remembered when "The Biograph Girl" was killed in a street car accident and they released her name to the papers. Of course Florence Lawrence didn't die, the first publicity stunt.

Now you had to have a name.

Uncle Tommy sat in the cramped front offices reading the trades, making notes for their next stops as Gladys filled out papers. Now and then she got an actual interview. They left the hotel phone number. Nothing happened. On their way out they'd pass extras and crews waiting around on the back lot.

At Fox, Gladys grabbed Uncle Tommy's arm. "Look." She nodded to a man standing by a door to a set, didn't dare point. Uncle Tommy saw, and they walked nonchalantly past. Tom Mix in his cowboy get-up, hat as big as a horse trough. They passed a vamp that might've been Theda Bara, but they couldn't be sure. There were lots of vamps.

Each evening they returned to their suite and found mamma and Aunt Minnie waiting eagerly. That was the worst. No way to hide the failure on her face. But mamma smiled, took her hand. "Come on, let's get you out of those clothes." She shut the bedroom door, hung up her rumpled dress, unwound the binding from her chest. In the bathroom with its tiny white and black tiles, mamma drew a warm bath and sat on the edge of the big claw foot tub, rubbing her feet.

"Don't you worry, princess. Tomorrow. You'll see."

The next morning they'd start all over again.

Ten days. One more and they had to go back. Lying in the tub, Gladys closed her eyes, slid down until the bubbles lapped her chin. There were other choices. Finish high school, get a nice secretarial job. Maybe marry that George Wilson kid who kept after her. George's dad owned a couple of garages in South Portland.

The thought made her cringe.

That night in the hotel bar Uncle Tommy met a guy who said he knew someone at Sunshine Comedies. He'd make a call.

It was almost to Long Beach. They showed up at 9:00 A.M. and were ushered right in. A fat man sat smoking a cigar behind a cluttered desk, sleeves rolled up, not even wearing a tie. Gladys felt out of place in her perfect dress.

"So, kid. We do comedies here. Cheap comedies, nothin' fancy. Can you make people laugh?" He eyed her dress. It was clear he didn't think so.

She didn't give a damn how she looked any more. She just wanted a job.

"How's this?" She pulled Aunt Minnie's beads up, choking herself, eyes crossed and bugged, tongue out, one finger making a pig nose. It was how she always won Uncle Tommy's silly face contest. And it must've looked even funnier in her perfect burgundy dress, the latest hairdo and "glam" makeup, because the man fell back in his chair laughing, his eyes wide with surprise, big belly shaking.

"Oh my God!" he said, when he could breathe. "You look just like Ben Turpin!" He laughed harder, "without the mustache. You're on, kid. I'll start you at fifty a week. Be here Monday, 6:00 A.M. sharp. Move over Mack Sennett!"

Chapter 4

Mamma stayed, of course. One could not leave a sixteen-year-old girl alone in the city of "Los Angels." Nightmare stories of what happened to girls who left home to be in movies were already circulating.

The next day they moved their suitcases into a "cottage" on the Sunshine Comedy lot. More like a shack, windowless room used for storage, props and flats stacked on one side. A double bed sunken in the middle, an ice box, a sink, a grimy hot plate. The only "facilities," the crew outhouse in back. When Gladys opened the door she gasped, held her nose.

Mamma patted her arm. "We'll get a bed potty," she said, "like when I was a girl."

When they were as settled as possible, Gladys hugged Uncle Tommy and Mamma Minnie.

'You knock 'em dead, Sweetcakes," Uncle Tommy said. "Next time we see you, I 'spect you'll be riding in the back of a limousine." He wiped his eyes with the back of his hand.

"We're so proud," was all Aunt Minnie could say.

Gladys did not cry. She would not stay long at Sunshine Comedy.

Monday at 6:00 A.M. they started. The fat man with the cigar was Ben Steiner, producer, director and camera man.

"I'm making you the star, kid." He chewed his stogie. "Day one. How d'ya like them apples?"

She nodded. "I'll do my best, sir."

He laughed loud. "Sir! I ain't nobody's sir. Call me Ben, kid. Or Mr. S."

He came around the desk, shook mamma's hand.

"Mother Walton. Well, I can surely see where your daughter gets her looks. Ain't often a star comes complete with her own makeup artist. I'd offer you a chair, Mrs. Walton, but we're going out back. Time to get shooting. Catch the light." He stepped past, opening the door. "You're welcome to come and watch."

"I'd like that very much." Mamma grinned.

Start shooting, Gladys thought. She didn't even know the name of the film, much less the plot or characters.

They followed Mr. Steiner across a dirt yard to a canvas awning which shaded an old metal table and six mismatched kitchen chairs. A thirtyish blond woman with tired eyes sat at the table.

A few feet beyond was the set, three black walls open to the sky. A camera and tripod.

"Dottie," Mr. Steiner said, "meet our new star, Gladys Walton, and her mother."

"Pleased to meet you." Dottie shook mamma's hand.

She had a nice smile, but could certainly use a binding cloth.

"Are you an actress, too?" mamma asked.

Mr. Steiner laughed. "Dottie's talents run more toward the behind the scenes area. Ain't that right, Sweetheart? She's my assistant. Costumes, props." He nodded to a rack of clothes at the end of the canopy, an array of materials and styles. A box full of odd hats. Beside the rack was a round curtain attached to the awning, like a temporary dressing room at the beach.

"You ladies like coffee?" Mr. Steiner said. "Get us some coffee, would ya, hon? Now, then..." He looked up. "Hey, here we are."

A woman and two men, or more like one and a half men, were walking toward them.

22

Mr. Steiner rubbed his hands together. "All righty. Let's roll!"

They worked ten hour days making one-reel comedies in which Gladys and the other three scurried back and forth, in one door, out another, gesturing wildly with no apparent reason. Exaggerated, over-dramatic, and always the thinnest story line, which Mr. Steiner took minutes to explain before charging ahead. All that changed were costumes and props, brooms, baseball bats, a fake baby to toss back and forth.

Gladys mostly wore old fashioned underwear, corset and pantaloons, an out-of-style swim dress with striped leggings, her hair a frazzle of curls. Sometimes a clown suit. Lots of pie throwing and running into walls or each other, falling down, legs and arms flailing, always punctuated with a close-up of her silly face.

The best part was working with the other actors, a large boned German woman, Gertrude Vonbraun, the perfect maid or washer woman or prison guard. And George Biggs, not his real name, hardly bigger than a midget. Gertrude would lift George by a hidden harness and fling him across the set. He'd do three somersaults and land on his feet, making faces and razzing the giantess until she chased him off with a broom.

What fun. They could say anything they wanted. Their spoken words never matched the lines that appeared on the screen. The taunts Gertrude and "Big" George flung at each other! "You slimy toad dropping! Piece 'a cow dung!" "Watch where you swing them tits, Gertie. I'll climb up there and braid your mustache, you old Kraut walrus!" And far worse.

She'd glance at her mother watching from her chair. But mamma was having the time of her life.

Then there was Craig Cramer who alternated between handsome-but-fumbling hero and evil nemesis. The third day, Craig took Gladys in his arms for a sweeping kiss. "Your breath is like monkey farts," he said, loud in a foreign accent, eyes full of passion as she struggled to keep a straight face. Then he dropped her flat, onto cushions the camera wouldn't show. She managed to stay in character. Good practice.

But the sensation Gladys felt with Craig's kiss startled her. Prickles down her sides taking her breath. For years she'd had these feelings at night when she couldn't sleep, then she'd see the back seat of that car, those grunting men, and she'd stop her hands. Someday she would have to figure it all out. Marriage and babies. Aunt Minnie and Uncle Tommy were happy, even without babies. Always sneaking kisses and hugs after dinner. More than hugs. Gladys got a glimpse before the kitchen door swung shut.

It wasn't as if she'd never been kissed before. That boy, Freddy something, in fourth grade. And George Wilson once, back stage after the spring talent show. Nothing like it felt with Craig. Craig was twenty-three and full of mischief, with strong hands and arms, laughing eyes. At night she replayed Craig's kisses, but it was hard to recapture the feeling lying next to her mother, trying to stay on her side of the sunken mattress.

Weeks passed filming these two-bit comedies. Once the whole set wobbled and teetered. George and Craig were behind waiting for their cues and scrambled through a door just as all three walls fell in a dusty heap. Gladys and Gertrude burst into laughter. Mr. S kept shooting. Their best movie, actually, which wasn't saying much.

It bothered Gladys, wasting her time on what wasn't even good slapstick. The industry had moved far beyond shoddy one-set productions. It'd been three years since D.W. Griffith's *Intolerance*, almost four hours long and those immense sets. Ancient Babylon, rows of huge plaster elephants, sculptors imported from Italy. Swanson and

Pickford were doing real films, and this new Lillian Gish. *Broken Blossoms*!

Gladys would give her right arm for such a part.

They settled on a plan. One morning, mamma would go and tell Mr. Steiner Gladys was sick. Then Gladys would slip away to put in applications.

"You'll have to go alone," mamma said, "in case he checks on you. I'll tell him you're sleeping. What do you think, princess? Can you do it by yourself?"

Chapter 5

"I'm here to see Mr. Coll." Gladys stood at the gate, clutching her packet of photos, including a few good shots of her work at Sunshine. She had used the phone at the corner diner and managed to get two appointments, Metro and Universal.

The guard eyed her, nodding. "Coll, huh? Building on the left, second floor. Good luck, missy," he added.

Scrolled lettering on the door said, *Frederick Coll, Executive Producer*. She handed the secretary her packet, sat on a high backed chair, smoothing her burgundy dress. The secretary disappeared and returned. An hour passed. She thumbed magazines, her mind drifting back to the set. Would Mr. Steiner go on shooting without her? Did Craig miss her? Silly thoughts.

Finally she was ushered into a huge office, dark wood wainscoting, a large half-circle window looking out at the city, a desk big enough to sleep on. One wall had a full bar, and next to it a plush chaise lounge, purple velvet with gold fringe. Mr. Coll was old, forty-five at least, hair combed over a receding forehead, thin mustache. He wore a dark blue suit, loose and shiny, more like a smoking jacket, silk bunched at his throat, a cravat.

"So, Miss Walton, is it?" He sat at the desk smoking a cigarette, offered her one from a gold case.

"No... I mean, yes, Gladys Walton, but I don't smoke, sir. Thank you."

"Of course not. How old are you, eighteen?"

"Seventeen... in January, sir." As soon as the words were out, she thought better. Should've lied.

"Well, your photos are impressive, young lady. And you're even more beautiful in person." He gestured to one of the leather chairs. "Have a seat."

He chatted with her for several minutes, where she was from, what training did she have? How she liked Sunshine Comedy. Was this her first time in L.A., was she here alone?

She answered, and then told about playing Dorothy in the Wizard of Oz. It sounded childish. She felt uncomfortable. His eyes, the way he looked at her. The way he said Sunshine Comedy, like it was nothing.

True, she supposed. She didn't care. It was fun working for Mr. Steiner. She smiled, thinking of Craig and Gertrude and George. Mostly Craig. Felt her cheeks flush.

Mr. Coll smiled back. An odd smile, she thought, and flushed more.

He stood. "Well, Miss Walton, we'll see if your talent matches your beauty. For the theater you'd read lines, of course, but that isn't much good for the movies, is it?"

"No, sir."

He put out his cigarette, took a paper from his desk and walked around to her.

"So I came up with this." He handed her the paper. "Tests your range of emotions. Let's see what you can do on the spot, Gladys." His leg brushed her skirt. "But why don't you come over here," he gestured to the chaise, "more room."

She looked at the paper. A list of emotions. Merriment, surprise, fear, sadness, anger, embarrassment...

When she looked up, he was right there. She took his hand and stood, felt his eyes behind her as she walked to the chaise, her heart suddenly beating fast. She breathed in. Don't be silly. It's a job, a huge studio that does real movies. She sat on the edge of the chaise.

"Good," he said, pulling the leather chair close. He sat in front of her. "Now, start anywhere on the list. I'll tell you what emotion I see. Go on, relax. Just a little run through."

He was so close. Her hands fidgeted with Aunt Minnie's beads, and she touched her throat. It was hot, probably had splotches! Her hands were sweating. She breathed in."

"Fabulous!" he said. "Embarrassment and fear. Very good. I'm sure we'll have something for you." She hadn't even started. She laughed, but it sounded hollow.

"Yes, merriment," he said. "Go on."

What was he doing? One hand on his crotch. Her eyes widened.

"Surprise, yes! Good, good. Keep going." His other hand now. Unzipping his pants.

She closed her eyes. Little girl again, lifted into the back seat. Don't. That was a long time ago.

When she opened her eyes, Mr. Coll was standing in front of her. He had pulled it out, holding himself, rubbing it.

She looked up at his eyes.

"No," he said, "look at this."

She looked. It was swollen, red and ugly. Hands on her, tying her legs, prying her mouth open...

He stepped closer, rubbing himself. "What does this do for you? Huh, girl? No, don't turn away. Watch. Watch, baby!"

This could not be happening. Mr. Frederick Coll, Executive Producer. He was crazy. She should push past him and run, but she couldn't move. He inched closer. Was he going to touch her with it? Rape her? She shuddered, felt a tightening between her ribs. Gagging, the bitter taste. He was right there, hand flailing.

"Oh, yeah. Almost. Look! Watch, watch it!"

His eyes glazed. His other hand reached to his breast pocket, pulled out a silk handkerchief, covering his thing as it jerked and jerked. A long groan, he stumbled back a step.

Now. She stood, ran for the door, fumbling with the knob. No, don't be locked. Please! The latch gave and she rushed through and past the secretary. At the outer door she stopped. Her packet. He had her packet. It was the only one. She could telegraph, ask Uncle Tommy to send copies, but her appointment with Universal was at one o'clock.

"Are you all right?" the secretary said. "Can I get you anything, some water?"

Gladys couldn't stop shaking. Think. Never mind Universal. She didn't want this. Give up, go home. Marry George. But it wasn't right. Stupid pig bastard.

"Miss Walton, can I help you?"

Gladys turned, blood beating in her ears. She brushed the tears away.

The secretary glanced at Mr. Coll's open door. Then she walked around her desk, all tidy and concerned. Here in her fancy office. She had to know what went on behind that door. It must happen over and over.

Mamma, Aunt Minnie, Uncle Tommy, all counting on her, but what could she do? She was sixteen. Who would believe her?

"Yes, you can help me!" Her voice shrill. She didn't care. "You can go in there and get my packet. I want my packet! Or... I'll get the police. I'll go to every newspaper. I want my packet!"

Chapter 6

Gladys stood outside the door, trembling, tears ruining her makeup. She held her packet to her chest, crying. If only mamma had come with her. She sniffed, wiped below her eyes, trying not to smear the Lashlux, but her fingers came away black. Find a powder room.

Damn him! Anger. Check that off your stupid list of emotions!

She found a Ladies room down the hall, floor and walls white marble, three stalls. When she saw her face in the mirror, she cried harder. A basket of little towels was by the sink. She dabbed the smudges beneath her eyes. Her nose was running. She needed tissue, not these silly towels.

"Here, honey, let me help."

Gladys jumped. Behind her in the mirror was a girl about her age. Taller than Gladys by a few inches, the same hair do, only blond, eyes a soft blue, her dress almost the same shade as her eyes.

The girl lifted a purse hanging from her shoulder.

"Now, I know I got tissue in here. Lordy, what you can pack in one little bag. Finding it is another matter entirely." She looked up, her hand still rummaging.

"You interviewing, too?" She spoke into the mirror. "Tough, ain't it. I just got here last week. Took the train all the way from Atlanta." She laughed. "It was fun, truth be told, but if I don't find me a job soon, I'll be thumbin' down a dern truck to get myself back."

Gladys had to smile. Southern belle accent, words melting like cotton candy. Like that new Tallulah Bankhead.

"Here. Here we go." The girl held out a wad of tissue. "I'm Mabel Huxley."

Gladys turned. "Thanks. I'm Gladys Walton." She blew her nose.

"Oh, that's a great movie name! Probably have to change mine, but don't matter. Never did care much for it. Hey, maybe you can help me think 'a one." Mabel leaned closer, her eyes suddenly serious. "But first we gotta fix up y'all's face. Come on, honey." She took her arm, nodded to an upholstered bench. "Y'all can't even go out the door like that, and I got me a pile 'a makeup right here." She patted her purse. "You'll be good as new in no time."

They sat on the bench. "What happened, anyway? If you don't mind me askin'."

Gladys looked into Mabel's eyes, and then she told about her "interview" with Mr. Coll. She couldn't help it. Mabel was so friendly. A girl her age to talk to.

Mabel listened, wiping her smudges, but when she got to the part where Mr. Coll pulled himself out of his pants, Mabel's eyes widened and her hand went to her mouth.

"Oh, honey, he didn't ra..."

"No, not that," Gladys said. "He just... Well..." She didn't know how to say it. Most girls their age had never seen a male organ, except on babies. Mabel probably didn't even know how big they got, and Gladys didn't want to be the one to tell her.

"Go on," Mabel said, "What'd he do?"

"He... you know..." Gladys looked down, gestured with her hand, like holding a garden hose.

"You mean he abused his self right there in front of y'all?"

Gladys nodded.

"The whole... kit and caboodle?"

"Mm hmm."

Mabel laughed, shaking her head. "Oh, my Gawd!"

Kit and caboodle. Gladys started to giggle.

Then they were laughing and laughing, couldn't stop.

"Men!" Mabel held her sides. "Lordy, what fools they make 'a themselves. If they only knew."

"I didn't know if I should tell you," Gladys said, when she could get the words out. "I mean, I thought maybe you didn't know about..."

"Goodness, honey. I got me six brothers. I change their dang sheets, and they're always goin' on 'bout their night longings."

When their laughter simmered down, Mabel took makeup from her purse and redid Gladys's face. She told about her family back in Atlanta. Her father had a small dry goods store that barely squeaked by. All the boys worked in the store. "But I ain't about to spend my life measurin' out seersucker for them prim ladies."

Gladys smiled. She could listen to Mabel all day. She told how her family brought her down from Portland. How she got a job, such as it was, mamma right now covering for her.

"You've already done movies! Oh, what's it like? Tell me. Tell me everything."

And of course Gladys started with Craig.

Mabel leaned back, watching her. "Girl, look at you, smiling to beat the band. Don't you fall in love, now. That'll kill a career deader than a doornail."

"I'm not in love." A moment passed, then Gladys jumped up. "Oh, I forgot! It must be past noon. I have an appointment at Universal. I'm not even sure how to get there."

"It's easy," Mabel said, "I was there this morning."

"You interviewed at Universal? That's wonderful! What'd they say?"

"They said..." Mabel looked down, her voice almost a whisper. "They said to come back when I lose ten pounds."

She forced a grin. "No more 'n a couple weeks the way I been eatin.' But the place I'm staying is four dollars a month. By then I'll be broke."

Neither spoke for a moment. Gladys took Mabel's hands. "Stand up. Let me look at you. We'll make a plan."

Mabel shrugged shyly, turned in a circle.

"They're crazy. It's just this new skinny look they want." Gladys shook her head. "Maybe you could do something up top. I've been wrapping my..." what, hesitating on a word when a man just waved his damned penis at her? "Breasts," she said loud. "I got a binding cloth down town, but any rag would work."

Mabel stared at her. "Honey, they're wrapped right now so's I can hardly breathe." She laughed. "Never you mind. I'll lose the weight. I ain't spending my life selling dry goods or marrying some man and spill out babies like my mom. Six brothers. Believe me, I know all about wearing yourself out tending to a man."

She shouldered her purse, took Gladys's arm. "But right now we gotta get y'all to that interview. I'll ride over with you. Got nothin' in the world better to do."

Chapter 7

Sitting across the desk from Mr. Howard Thomas, Assistant Director, Universal Studios, it was all Gladys could do to keep a semiprofessional look on her face. She wanted to jump up and do cartwheels! A contract. She'd start the first of December. A four-reel romantic comedy called *La La Lucille*. Five hundred dollars a week!

"There'll be a month of coaching and other preliminaries," Mr. Thomas explained, "publicity photos, costume fittings, makeup and hair consultations. We start shooting right after the holidays. Universal has a whole line of these films coming up, but we were looking for a new face, someone with that certain spark." His lips formed just a hint of a smile. "We think you're it, Miss Walton. We don't often make these decisions so quickly, but your test was exceptional. Mr. Von Stroheim sent the take up to Laemmle himself."

Mr. Thomas was a tall, sober man with thin lips and tiny round spectacles, early thirties, maybe, and Gladys was quite sure he'd keep himself in his pants. Five hundred a week! You could buy a car for that. Make a down payment on a house.

"Of course, *La La Lucille* will be something of a trial film," he went on. "There's a clause in here about that." He slid the contract across the table. "Your father can read through and explain it. There's a place for him to sign too."

"It's just my mother," Gladys said.

"Yes, well, that's fine. And I understand she'll be staying with you. We encourage that with girls your age, and your bungalow has plenty of room. Once we finish here you can go over to Housing. They'll get you all set up. We're geared for production here at Universal City, completely self-contained, you know. Shopping, restaurants, recreation facility. You won't even need to go outside the gates if you don't want to."

He stood, offering his hand. "Welcome aboard, Miss Walton." He actually smiled. "And that was quite a tap dance!"

When the Housing lady opened the door to her bungalow, Gladys almost broke into tears. Sparkling clean, hard wood floors and brand new solid oak furniture, overstuffed chairs, a high backed sofa. Wall paper in a fleur de lis pattern. The kitchen cabinets were that new minty green, and they had windows. There was a Chambers gas stove and an ice box with two doors, twice as big as theirs at home. "Ice is delivered Monday and Friday," the lady said. On the counter was an electric toaster. Gladys had only seen them in magazines. The bathroom had a tub you could lie in and not even touch the end. But most of all, closets. Built in shoe racks. They wouldn't even need an armoire. Think how they could fill those closets on five hundred dollars a week. They'd buy rugs and curtains. And pretty dishes for those see-through cabinets. When mamma wasn't watching the filming, she could spend her days shopping or ordering from Sears catalogue.

Mabel was waiting in the foyer, dozing in a chair. Gladys tapped her arm.

"Oh, honey, y'all did it, didn't you?" She sat up. "It's all over your face! Like a possum eatin' sop."

"Shh," Gladys whispered, "wait 'til we're out the gate." She was a professional now. No jumping up and down, at least not here.

They hurried past a line of people waiting outside to share the behind-the-scene magic of movie making, a policy Universal was already famous for.

When they turned the corner they were two sixteen-year-old girls in pretty dresses, hugging and squealing, twirling in circles.

Gladys caught her breath long enough to tell Mabel the details. "Movies, real movies! And I'm not even starting with a bit part!"

"*La La Lucille*! Oooh la la!" Mabel swung her hip. "Wonder who your leading man will be?"

"And five hundred a week!"

Mabel stared. "Go on. It can't be."

"That's what he said. It's in the contract. Oh, wait 'til mamma hears, and our bungalow. I've gotta get back. Mamma will want to telegram Uncle Tommy and Aunt..."

Gladys stopped. How this must sound to Mabel. Here all alone. It could even be the same job Mabel tried for this morning. Yet all that showed on Mabel's face was happiness for her. They hardly knew each other. No. They may have just met, but they already knew each other. Like finding the sister she'd never had.

Then an idea came to her, complete and perfect. "Come with me, Mabel. We'll go get your things. I'll sneak you in. Mamma won't mind. We'll make you a bed on the floor." She thought of the cushions they used for stunts, stacked there in the room. Better than the sunken mattress.

"Tomorrow I'll tell Mr. Steiner about my new contract. He's a nice man. Only thing he cares about is keeping the camera rolling." She grabbed Mabel's hands. "He'll give you my job. I'm sure he will. He won't have to miss a day." She felt a slight twinge at the idea of Craig kissing Mabel instead, but let it go. Never mind. A door had opened, a huge gilded door like at Grauman's theater, and she would walk right through it and not look back.

"And in no time you'll be at Universal too, Mabel. They said to come back, didn't they?"

Mabel nodded. "When I drop the weight."

"And you will. We might even be in movies together. And no matter what we'll be friends our whole lives. I just know it."

There were tears in Mabel's eyes, but she was grinnin' like that possum.

"Come on," Gladys said. "mamma will worry if I'm not back before dark." They linked arms and hurried toward the nearest trolley.

Mabel laughed. "Just think, honey. If it weren't for that old coot Mr. Coll... waving his dern flag at y'all... we might never 'a met."

Chapter 8

It worked out fine. When Mr. Steiner realized he'd have two girls for the price of one, at least until Gladys had to report to Universal, he couldn't complain. Ten days, five new Sunshine comedies.

The end of November, Gladys and her mother stood in front with their suitcases waiting for the car from Universal. Mamma hadn't stopped smiling since the day Gladys came home, contract in hand. "A Chambers stove," she'd said, "and closets too. Oh, my!"

A long square sedan pulled up. Not quite the limousine Uncle Tommy predicted, but almost. When the driver set their bags in the trunk and opened the door, Gladys asked him to wait a few minutes and ran back.

"Sure, go ahead." Mr. S motioned her onto the set, kept the camera rolling. "Maybe you'll be the new Pickford and I'll get big bucks for this." He laughed and moved in for close-ups. She said good-bye to Gertrude and George Biggs and Craig, who swept her back in a last kiss, her insides fluttering.

"Don't be a stranger," Craig said, and held her eyes. She reached and pulled him to her for another kiss, long and sweet. Sensations shooting through her. "For the camera," she said, laughing to hide her thoughts. Maybe she just stay.

She hurried over to hug Mabel.

"Good luck, honey. I can't thank y'all enough."

"We'll get together weekends," Gladys said, then whispered, "and you'll be there too in no time."

She turned, did a last silly face for Mr. Steiner, then ran across the lot and scrambled into the back seat, wiping her eyes.

Mamma patted her knee. "Here we go, princess. The hardest part is over."

That wasn't true, of course, at least not for Gladys. Her first weeks at Universal were a blur of "preliminaries," rushing from one appointment to another across the 230 acre property, between hours of coaching. How much she was learning! Each night she'd fall into bed exhausted.

Not too exhausted to think of Craig. Alone in her own room, she could not help seeing his eyes, feeling those kisses. *Don't be a stranger.*

She missed Mabel. If she could just talk to her about this. Mabel might say it was just her "night longings." Nothing to worry about. But night longings weren't supposed to be visited by grunting men.

It was hard to find time to visit, Sunshine Comedy way across town. The next Saturday Gladys stood in line at the Housing Office switchboard, and the call actually went through. She left a message with Mr. Steiner's assistant, Dottie, and the next day Mabel met them at Grauman's for an afternoon matinee.

They saw Clara Kimball Young in *Eyes of Youth*. Mabel gasped when a handsome young man with slicked back hair came on the screen. "Lordy!" she whispered, "who might that be?"

"I don't know," Gladys whispered, "looks a little like Wallace Reid."

"Goodness no, that ain't no Wallace Reid! Nothin' sultry about Wallace Reid. Oh, look at him!" She nodded to the screen, leaned closer to Gladys. Neither of them had taken their eyes from the scene unfolding. "That ain't no boy-next-door, honey. Sweet bejesus," Mabel breathed, her voice even lower. "Man looked at me like that, I'd roll over and say, y'all come on in, Honey pie. Hell, I'd find me a dern apron for a man like that'n."

Gladys put her hand to her mouth, but couldn't stop giggling. Neither could Mabel.

Mamma leaned across. "What's so funny, you two?"

Gladys told her, all three of them were giggling until someone behind shushed them.

"Shh." Mabel grinned. "People can't read the words with y'all carryin' on.'

Another burst. The usher shined his light. They quieted then, watching for the handsome man to reappear on screen, but he never did.

When the movie was over, they scanned the poster outside trying to decide which name might be him.

"This one?" Gladys pointed to the smallest print on the bottom.

"Definitely," Mabel said, "fits him to a tee." She sighed the name in a mock accent, "Rudolpho Di Valentino. Oh, Gladys y'all might run into him over at Universal. If you do, honey, tell him you got a friend who's twitchin' like a cat in heat for him." She shimmied her hips.

"Girls!" Mamma glanced at people coming out of the theater. "It's almost dark. We better get you home, Mabel."
They walked down Broadway to the trolley, the street decorated with Christmas garlands and gas lights. Mamma insisted they ride with Mabel, walking her all way to the gate, six blocks each way, and they almost missed the last trolley back.

It was fun that night, but no time to talk alone.

The following week Gladys found an envelope on the floor below the mail slot. Inside was a picture postcard of Santa Monica Beach with its five piers. Santa Claus in his sleigh crossing a full moon. "A California Christmas," it said, signed, "Your new best friend., Alice Andrews." P.S. "How do you like the name Mr. S came up with?"

Gladys smiled, opening the letter folded inside.

"Dear Best Friend And Soon To Be Famous Star,

It was great seeing you and your ma last week. Did I tell you what fun I'm having with these 3 clowns I work with! 4 counting Mr. S. I'm having the time of my life. You saved me from dry goods, honey!

Well, bad news is, as you probably noticed, them pounds ain't exactly melting off, but yesterday I came across a solution. Hope so, anyway. Had me a harrowing adventure getting it, Lord knows. You would not believe stuff they have in that China section over past downtown. Trolley don't even go there, so we bout walked our feet off. But, oh, the sights we seen! Thank goodness Craig was with me. Fitting, since he's the one told me about it in the first place.

You shoulda been there, honey. The shop weren't no bigger than a broom closet. Everything all dusty, burlap bags full of roots and ground up stuff that'd grow hair on the bottom of your feet, by the smell. Oo-eee! And shelves of dark jars with the awfullest looking things inside. Things that moved! We had to explain to this old China man with a stringy beard he coulda tucked into his pants if he'd been wearing any.

Gotta go. Tell you more later. Cross your fingers it works. I'm busting to see you. I want to hear every, every everything.

Love and Hugs,
Mabel (I mean Alice)

P.S. What ya doing for Christmas?"

Gladys read it again. What was Mabel talking about? *Craig was with me.* Craig. She had to sit down. Chinatown. *Shelves of dark jars...* She felt sick. Without Craig at night there would be only those men. Who would make her all right again? But if she lost Mabel...

Christmas. Mabel alone without her family.

Gladys hurried to the front office, but the switchboard couldn't get an outside line. A messenger would run a telegram over to Western Union. COME FOR CHRISTMAS— STOP—SLEEP OVER LONG AS YOU CAN—STOP—UNCLE AND AUNT WILL HAVE GUEST BUNGALOW—STOP—MUST TALK—STOP—ALICE ANDREWS IS PERFECT.

Gladys and Mabel sat on the narrow patio outside her bungalow. They were in pajamas, leaning against pillows, mamma's old crazy quilt wrapped around their shoulders. Christmas night, the air cool and crisp. Through the wrought iron railing, the lights of Universal City and downtown Los Angeles shone as clear and bright as the decade ahead. 1919. The War to End All Wars had been over more than a year, fresh American troops saved the day. A boom was starting, what could go wrong? Especially here in the movie capitol of the world.

Music from the new Victrola drifted from the living room where mamma, Aunt Minnie and Uncle Tommy sat having a Christmas cognac, catching up on the past months. Now and then Aunt Minnie's laughter rose above the music, and Gladys figured mamma was regaling them with Sunshine Comedy shenanigans. Maybe about their first whiff of the crew outhouse in back, how they left the bed potty for Mabel.

The last few weeks mamma had scurried to prepare the house for Christmas. She ordered a "feather" tree from Sears and Roebuck that arrived just in time. What a sight! Made of goose and turkey feathers, all white with artificial red berries and candle holders on the tips of the branches. Fifty-five inches tall, the biggest they had, money no object now. Mamma hung her collection of glass ornaments from Germany, some imitation ones too, since all during the war and even now stores didn't carry a thing made in Germany. She'd found some new drip less candles and a brocade tree carpet for the finishing touch.

That afternoon mamma and Aunt Minnie cooked a turkey with all the fixings in the new Chambers oven. They held hands around the table as Aunt Minnie offered a Christmas grace, thanking the Lord for all their blessings, Mabel adding a loud, "Amen!" Then Uncle Tommy carved "the bird." After dinner they opened presents. A real family.

Gladys adjusted her pillow, pulled the quilt tighter against the chill. "Do you miss your mom and dad and your brothers, Mabel?"

"I do, sure, but this has been so nice." Mabel laughed. "What a hoot, your Uncle Tommy. Them songs. "We're All Going Calling On The Kaiser," and that blowing bubbles one. Must'a been fun growing up with the likes 'a him."

Gladys nodded.

"What happened to your daddy, anyway? If y'all don't mind me askin.'"

"I don't mind," Gladys said, "but I can tell all I know in one sentence."

Mabel listened. "A gypsy. Well, that 'bout sums up most men, truth be told. Some just control it more 'n others. Goodness, look at that sky! Probably a sprinkle 'a snow in Atlanta 'bout now. Or maybe not. Colder 'n here. That's sure."

Gladys sat up a little. "Mabel... what's this about Chinatown? What'd you find there?"

Mabel gazed at the stars a minute more, then she said, "Got me a live-in companion, y' might say. A worm." She drew out the word, eyes wide, voice all spooky.

"A worm!"

"Yep, tapeworm. Workin' already, I think." She grinned. "Although it'll take him awhile to get through your Ma's turkey dinner. Little bugger's got his work cut out for 'im, 'specially them yams."

"Mabel, be serious. What'd you do, swallow it?" The thought made her shiver.

"Weren't hard. I swallowed oysters twice as big. Oh, Gladys, don't look like that. It ain't nothin.' Lots 'a people are doin' it. Now come on, tell me all about yer job. What's it like?" She gave her a nudge. "Y'all seen that dream boat Valentino yet?"

Gladys laughed. "No, but he's here at Universal. Mr. Thomas said he's doing a film with Dorothy Phillips."

"Mmm, lucky gal." She sighed, looked down at her belly. "Hurry up, worm!"

Gladys laughed, shaking her head. "Oh, Mabel."

Music in the next bungalow. Laughter and talk, the pop of a cork, glasses clinking.

"Oh, a party!" Mabel got up, leaned over the rail. "Come on, Gladys, let's put on somethin' pretty and sneak out. I bet they're dancin.' Who knows who we might meet."

Gladys glanced at the open doors to her bedroom, the living room beyond. "Wait 'til they're asleep," she whispered. "When Aunt Minnie and Uncle Tommy go to the guest bungalow, mamma will check on us. I know she will." She wondered what mamma would do if she found out they snuck away to a party, even if it was next door. There'd be adults, men. The biggest stars didn't live on property, but this Valentino wasn't big. Gladys didn't find him that exciting.

Still, a party, dancing! "Yes," she said, "let's go! Soon as mamma's asleep."

"Ooo it's chilly!" Mabel snuggled back under the quilt, and they settled down to wait, listening.

In a few minutes Gladys said, "Mabel, if I ask you something, would you be serious?"

"Of course, honey."

Gladys wanted to tell her about the men in the car when she was seven, and how her thoughts turned ugly at night when she was alone.

Instead she said, "Have you ever let a boy touch you? You know..."

"Hmm..."

Gladys didn't have to look to know Mabel was smiling.

"Let's just say, if you ask me that in a week or two, I'll probably say yes. Craig and I..."

Gladys swallowed. Bird wings beating against her ribs. She wanted to cover her ears.

"We, well... we've been spending time together. I've been tryin,' really tryin' not to fall in love, but he's just so sweet. He's got the gentlest hands. Lordy! Calls me his flower. Petal by petal, he says." She laughed. "Don't mean I'm forgettin' that Valentino, though."

Mabel yawned, curled up in the quilt.

"My, what a day! Y'all promise to wake me if I fall asleep."

Long moments passed. Mabel's breathing slowed.

It's okay, Gladys thought. Mabel was alone. Her best friend.

Anyway, she hardly knew Craig. The kisses weren't real, just playing.

Then why did she feel so empty?

Gladys remembered Aunt Minnie's prayer about all their blessings. True. In eight days they'd start shooting *La La*

Lucille. She'd be too busy to think. She'd find another man to make her all right.

Mamma touched her cheek. "Come on, my two Christmas girls. Wake up. It's nearly three o'clock. Let's get you inside where it's warm."

Rudolph Valentino

Originally, he was unable to find a studio that would take a chance on him ... and then, overnight became America's Heartthrob with the release of the "Four Horsemen of the Apocalypse"!

"The Sheik", released in 1921, confirmed his stardom and had women fainting in theaters, and he was soon known as the "Latin Lover".

August 23, 1926, Valentino died at the young age of 31 from complications of appendicitis and a gastric ulcer for which they operated. Unfortunately, peritonitis had already set in, he lapsed into a coma and died.

More than 100,000 people filled the New York Streets, requiring more than 100 mounted police to manage the crowds. Windows were smashed and a full day of rioting occurred on the 24th.

Chapter 9

The day after New Year's Mr. Thomas called Gladys into his office.

"Well, Miss Walton," he looked at her over his wire rimmed spectacles, "I've had good reports from your acting coach." He tapped a paper on his desk. "'A frolicsome yet virginal sexuality, not so much a vamp as a chaste tease." He smiled. "Mrs. Skevington can turn a phrase, can't she?"

Gladys laughed, blushing. Virginal sexuality. Good for the screen, maybe, but she was almost seventeen and eager to get past the virginal part. A technicality, anyway. If not Craig..."

She gave Mr. Thomas a "chaste tease" smile, but he didn't seem to notice. He might not be thirty, after all, she decided. Nice hair, light brown and slicked back, a few strands straying from the part, hazel eyes. Tall and lanky, still the way his suit fit his chest and arms...

He leaned back in his chair, eyes serious again. "I just came from a meeting with Von Stroheim and your director, Reeves Eason. We decided to postpone *La La Lucille*. A new script came in. Thalberg wanted Norma Shearer. She's about your age, but didn't test well."

He swiveled, looked directly into her eyes.

"They think it's perfect for you, Miss Walton. It's called, *Pink Tights*. Better launch. You play a tightrope walker in a circus, and there's a parachute scene. A little tricky for your first film. We could probably get Lightning Hutch, but we're hoping we don't have to hire a stunt man. Audiences want realism. They can tell a glass shot or studio fix. We want gasps not chuckles. Pearl White does all her own stunts." He leaned forward. "Think you can handle it, Gladys?"

He'd never called her by her first name before.

"Yes, sir. I'm not at all afraid of heights. I was a champion diver, you know." She kept her voice professional, wouldn't mention climbing the giant elm in their yard in Oregon.

Inside she was bouncing. She'd read the scenario for *La La Lucille* and found it bland.

Pink Tights. Her debut film.

"Good, then. Here's the shooting script." He handed her five or six pages. "They put a rush on the sets over the holidays. Had to build a church tower we could burn down. Mazie, your character, rescues a boy from the flames."

"I do that?"

"Oh, don't worry. We've done it before. The crew will be right there ready to put you out."

She laughed. She wasn't worried. A parachute scene *and* a burning building!

"You've got a good head on your shoulders, Gladys, I can tell."

"Thank you. I don't think anyone ever said that before, at least not in Hollywood." She tried her 'chaste tease' smile again, but he stood, went on with his speech.

"So I'll tell you something up front. We're not aiming for *Birth Of A Nation* or *Broken Blossoms*. He paced a few steps. "No, this is straight forward no-risk business. Now days people flock to whatever comes out, low budget, high budget, doesn't matter. Boys upstairs have it figured to the last dollar. Which means sending you right to the top, fast as possible. They won't wait to see how *Pink Tights* does. Full steam ahead. You're going to be a star, Gladys. Don't doubt that for a moment."

He paused, then his eyes softened. He offered his hand, and she stood. "They're waiting for you over in Wardrobe." He walked her to the door, smiled. "Gotta get you fitted for those pink tights."

"I'll do my best, Mr. Thomas, thank you." She thought he might tell her to call him Howard. Why was her heart fluttering? Because she was going to be a star or the touch of his hand?

Her very first film at age 16 catapulted Gladys into instant stardom. She amazed and startled everyone by doing her own stunts, making a perfect parachute landing on a roof in her starring role as Mazie.

Chapter 10

Not afraid of heights! Gladys stood on the wing, clinging to the strut with one arm, her other hand holding the rip cord. She'd had two days training with "Skeets" Elliot in his Spad XIII biplane, now she was two thousand feet up in her full Mazie Darnton costume, a tight fitting top with a short skirt that flared out over ruffled petticoats, all bunched up by the parachute straps between her legs, and of course she was wearing those pink tights. The wind whipped against her, and she held on as Skeets maneuvered the plane in a wide turn for their third pass, bright circus banner streaming behind.

"Don't look down," Skeets had said, "just keep your eyes on me. I'll get you through." She watched Skeets now as he straightened out of the turn. He pointed off to their left, nodding. She looked. The camera plane was moving into position. In seconds it was along side, not twenty yards away. Her cue. Skeets tipped the wing slightly, and she did a big circus smile, let go of the rip cord just long enough to wave and do a sweeping curtsy for the cameraman. The muscles in her left arm almost cramping from holding on so tight.

Mazie Darnton, "Queen of the air," fearless aerialist for Mr. McKeen's circus.

Well, Mazie might be fearless, but Gladys Walton's heart was hammering. She found the ripcord again, gripped it. Below circus wagons, elephants, white horses, acrobats, clowns, a troop of performers in full three-ring regalia paraded into the little Massachusetts town on Universal's back lot. Besides scores of extras playing the good townsfolk, a crowd of a hundred or so tourists had gathered to watch the shooting.

51

Mamma was there too, praying. But Gladys did not look down.

In the back seat of the other plane the cameraman motioned, he'd gotten the shot, and she turned to Skeets. He gave a thumbs up. Now. She took a deep breath, oh, dear God! and jumped.

The roar of the plane passing above. Five, four, three... Falling, stomach in her throat. The ground rushing up. On one, she pulled the cord. And felt herself jerked upward as the chute billowed out. Only then did she breathe again. Floating. Alive, still alive. The camera plane did another pass, and she smiled and waved.

Now only the landing.

In the story, Mazie lands on the roof of the Reverend Jonathan Meek's house, her pink tights causing a scandal with the congregation, but all Director Eason wanted were the air shots. For the rest they'd just film her on the roof getting out of the parachute.

Gladys looked around. Now that she was off the plane, there was no breeze, just a gentle swinging. Glorious! A clear, crisp California day. She could see snow on Mount Baldy. She could see Central Park and downtown, tiny black cars and here and there a horse drawn wagon, the red roofs of the trolleys, the road east to San Bernardino, train tracks running beside. She turned and saw the hills of Hollywood and west, the ocean stretching out forever.

She looked down. She was drifting over the naked backs of the false buildings on the set, crowd gathered in the street, circus parade at one end, all heads turned up, watching her. Now the church, the preacher's house beside it. She noticed some activity in the church yard. Mr. Eason in a frenzy, waving his hat, yelling at a cameraman waiting on the roof for the staged shot of her getting out of the parachute. They had expected her to land in the open field on the other side, a crew there to drive her around, but she was drifting right toward the church.

Maybe two hundred yards away now. The man on the roof scrambled to get his camera in position, aimed up at her, started rolling. The parachute was dropping her straight toward the church roof. A hundred yards. Gladys did not know what came over her then, the crowds, the circus, Mr. Eason looking up, stunned and grinning, the camera rolling. She spotted Mr. Thomas standing by her mother. Mamma waving to beat the band.

And suddenly she *was* Mazie Darnton, Queen of the Air. She stretched her arms out straight for a moment, then up, grabbing the parachute straps, and she pulled herself up like a gymnast, legs straight in those pink tights and black ballerina shoes, toes pointed, then she swung her body in a circle, legs back horizontal with the ground.

Fifty yards, twenty.

Twice she did the move, and at the last second she shifted and her feet brushed the roof. "Lean back, away from the drag, and pull hard on the straps," Skeets had said, "so you don't go head over heels." With all her strength she leaned and pulled and fell back on her ruffled petticoats, bounced twice down the slope beside the church steeple and came to rest on the Reverend Jonathan Meek's roof, not ten feet from Mr. Eason and the cameraman, the parachute making a canopy between the house and the church.

The crowd cheered and cheered.

"Keep shooting! Don't stop!" Mr. Eason shouted. "Perrin, where's Perrin?"

Then Jack Perrin appeared at the top of the ladder, adjusting his clergy collar, slipping on his black frock coat, and looking as stunned as any small town preacher would be if a beautiful young woman dropped out of the sky onto his roof.

Perrin scurried over to her, and although they weren't supposed to shoot this scene until later, he kept in character. The Reverend Jonathan Meek gazing at Mazie sprawled in her circus costume, skirt and petticoats pulled up by the parachute straps, revealing even more of those shapely legs in pink tights. Then, with full dramatic effect, Reverend Meek looked around, worried. What if someone from his congregation saw? The film title would read something about having to hide her until after dark. If the church people found out there'd be scandal for sure.

But what Jack Perrin said as he helped Gladys out of the straps was, "Holy shit! That was some entrance, baby. How the hell did you do that?"

Chapter 11

As the scenario went, members of Reverend Meek's flock pay him a surprise visit, and little Johnnie Bump discovers Mazie hiding in a closet. Then, just as the scandalized church folks are about to ride Mazie and her pink tights out of town, the fire bell rings. The church tower is in flames. And Mazie, Queen of the air, saves Johnnie Bump from the inferno.

Unfortunately not without catching her petticoats on fire.

The moment Gladys handed Johnnie to the fireman on the ladder, she was quite sure she would be remembered more as a blazing candle on the church roof than for yesterday's parachute jump, but she covered her face with her arms and slid down the shingles onto the mattresses below where the crew smothered her with blankets. She came through with only singed arms and first degree burns on her thighs and hips where the petticoats melted onto her skin.

Not bad enough for a day off, apparently.

She was lying naked under a sheet in the infirmary, a nurse rubbing salve on her arms, when Mr. Thomas tapped on the open door and came in. His face more serious than usual, he didn't speak but waited as the nurse finished wrapping her arms in gauze.

"There, all set, Miss Walton," the nurse said, pulling a notepad from her pocket. "And, Miss Walton, I'd surely appreciate that autograph. What a scene, I'll never forget it! I'll come back..." she glanced at Mr. Thomas, "or you can just leave it here on the tray."

"Of course," Gladys said, "I'd be happy to."

The nurse nodded to Mr. Thomas and hurried out, closing the door behind her.

The tall assistant director just stood there staring.

Gladys blushed. Could he see her nipples outlined beneath the sheet? She didn't dare look. Her breasts were covered, but her bare shoulders clearly announced she was naked. Well, except for patches of gauze on her thighs and hips.

Finally he spoke. "Are you in much pain, Gladys?" His glance seemed to settle on a spot just below her throat.

Gladys thought she sensed a shift in him, some difference in his eyes. In everyone's, as if she had transformed over night. No, not over night. One step off the wing of Skeets Elliot's plane. Crowding around her after the scene, clamoring for autographs, even Laemmle grinning like a kid. Odd, to think a single step could set forces in motion, affect her whole life, maybe, yet she could no more control it than the drift of that parachute. She felt an odd sadness, like watching the girl she had been fly off to a different future. A simpler one, probably.

Her head felt fuzzy. Must be the medicine. For a moment she imagined Mr. Thomas walking to her, kissing her. The rest of her body suddenly as hot as the scorched parts. Silly. She pushed the thoughts away. What did he ask just now? Oh, yes, pain.

"It's like a bad sunburn, that's all." She had to form the words carefully, her mouth suddenly bone dry. "They gave me a shot. Mamma went to... get my dressing gown... then I'll go sleep." She couldn't stop a yawn. "But I'll be on the set tomorrow morning, Mr. Thomas... don't worry."

"Oh, I'm not worried," he said quickly. "If it were up to me you wouldn't have to go at all. Anyway, no need to be early. We're shooting the scene where the circus owner dredges the lake for your body." He smiled. "Mazie's body, I mean. They'll cut that in. Then the final takes."

Yes, Gladys thought. When Mr. McKeen finds out Mazie is alive and saved the day, he proposes marriage, naturally. McKeen was played by Dave Dyas, and burns or no burns, she wouldn't miss that!

"Better fix my costume," she said, nodding to where it lay crumpled on a chair. "It's a bit charred, especially the petticoats."

She yawned again, her eyes heavy.

"Of course. I'll take it to Wardrobe myself." Mr. Thomas picked up the costume, folded it over one arm. "We're ahead of schedule," he went on, "but after yesterday, Laemmle's putting an extra rush on this." He paused, looked into her eyes.

She blinked, tried to focus.

"Gladys," he said, "you were amazing. I've seen stars twice your age who couldn't handle those scenes with such... style and wit, and... panache. Yes, panache, that's the word." He nodded, pleased with his choice. "And, well, I've been thinking I'd like to spend some time with you, get to know you better. You are an intriguing gir... young woman, and I was wondering if you would have dinner with..."

There was a sound from the hallway, and the door opened.

"Here you go, princess." Mamma bustled in. "I brought the lavender one you like and slippers... Oh my..." Her eyes widened, and she glanced from Mr. Thomas to her daughter, then back at the door, which certainly should not have been closed.

"Mrs. Walton. I... I was just leaving." He lifted the costume. "Have to get this over to Wardrobe. But I'm glad you're here. It's been quite an ordeal for our... rising star." He smiled. "And I was just asking if... the two of you would do me the honor of having dinner with me some evening."

Mamma's look changed instantly. She beamed. "Why, Mr. Thomas, we'd be delighted! Wouldn't we, princess?"

Gladys nodded, smiling through closed eyes. She could no longer keep them open, and anyway, she was quite sure it was all a dream.

"It is all in the day's work of a cinema actress to be perched in perilous positions. Here we see GLADYS WALTON sitting on the roof: JACK PERRIN is also in the picture."
(Caption for newspaper article photograph)

Chapter 12

She was having trouble concentrating. They were on an interior set shooting the final scene in Reverend Meek's home. The part where circus owner McKeen played by Dave Dyas rushes in, finds his star aerialist, Mazie, alive and proposes marriage. But Gladys' look of delight was closer to a grimace. Partly the pain. It wasn't easy pulling those tights over the gauze wrappings, although the skirt of her costume hid the bulges. Mamma had helped.

Beyond the lights, Gladys could see mamma now, talking with Mr. Thomas, planning where they'd go to dinner, probably, the three of them. It occurred to Gladys that if Mr. Thomas was indeed over thirty, he was closer to mamma's age than hers. And mamma was still a very attractive woman, even if she was closing in on forty.

The thought didn't help the queasiness in her stomach. But what bothered her more was that other man. Standing a few feet from the camera was a tall, portly gentleman in a finely tailored pinstripe suit. He just stood there staring directly at her. What was he doing on the set? No tourists were watching today, just him. He hadn't budged. And the look in his eyes. It reminded her of Mr. Coll rubbing himself in front of her that day in his office, only this man was older and fatter. Made her skin crawl. All she needed with the lights heating up her blisters.

"Take three," Mr. Eason called. "Relax, Miss Walton. Let's try it again. Places everyone. Ready Dave?"

"Any time." Dave Dyas nodded, awaiting his cue.

They hadn't even gotten to the kiss yet, but it was no use. Gladys shaded her eyes from the lights, walked off the set and over to the director.

"Mr. Eason," she whispered, "could you please ask the... portly gentleman to leave. I cannot concentrate with him staring like that."

Mr. Eason glanced over her shoulder toward the man, hesitated. "Well," he said, "if that's what you want, Miss Walton. We'll take a short break. You need makeup, anyway. Your forehead's moist. That was quite a scorching yesterday. You okay?"

"I'm fine," she said, "or I will be."

Mr. Eason called the makeup girl over, then went to talk to the man in the pinstripe suit.

The scene went well after that. Mazie smiled delightedly, accepted Mr. McKeen's proposal. The church folk applauded, the scene ended with a kiss. Flat, nothing like what she'd felt with Craig, but her first real movie was ready for editing.

The cast was barely off the set when the crew got to work transforming it. Push back the walls, add posh furniture and accessories, and Reverend Meek's modest home became an uptown hotel suite for *La La Lucille*.

Gladys went to thank Mr. Eason.

He chuckled. "That 'portly gentleman' you had me order off the set was William Randolph Hearst, young lady."

"Who?" Gladys looked blank.

"Hearst!" Her mother hurried to them. "Oh my word! William Randolph Heart is a very powerful man, princess. He owns half the newspapers in the country! He ran for President, you know. Gladys, you must apologize. How can we contact him, Mr. Eason?"

"He's in the executive lunch room," Eason smiled. "He wants to talk to you, Gladys. Said any sixteen-year-old girl who'd give him the bum's rush was someone he had to meet."

Seventeen in March, Gladys almost said. The whole thing irritated her. One day everyone treating her like a star, the next having to apologize to some pompous ass. She could see Mr. Thomas directing the crew. He turned and smiled, gave her a thumbs up, mouthing, "You did good, kid."

Mamma linked her arm. "I'll go with you, honey. William Randolph Hearst! Oh my! You know, he's building a huge mansion up in San Simeon."

But when they reached the studio door, Gladys stopped. "Mother, if you don't mind, I'd rather do this myself. I'm not a little girl."

For a moment mamma looked as if she'd been slapped. She nodded. "Of course. You go on. I'll... I'll be at home. And... I was thinking we'd better cut those tights off you. Might pull your skin off."

"Good idea," Gladys said. She touched her mother's arm. "Mamma..." She didn't want her mother tagging along on her very first dinner date either, but couldn't bring herself to say it. Mr. Thomas only included mamma because she happened to walk in just then. At least, Gladys hoped that was true.

"It's okay, honey. I understand."

"I'll only be a minute. I'll apologize, but frankly, I don't give a damn about Mr. William Randolph Hearst."

She hurried out the door and across the lot. *Sixteen year old girl. Bum's rush.* Laughing at her, rich old fool. When she reached the entrance to the executive lunch room, she wished she'd thought to wear a robe over her costume. Oh, well.

"Miss Walton, what an honor!" The doorman grinned. "I saw that jump the other day." He looked up at the sky.

61

"Sailed right over my head. Magnificent! Can't wait to see the movie." He reached to shake her hand.

'Thank you." She smiled, gave his hand an extra squeeze. "Is Mr. Hearst still here? Am I allowed in?"

"Why, of course, Miss Walton. I believe he's waiting for you." He held the door open.

My, my, she thought, Mr. Eason sent a messenger? Or did the pompous ass simply assume she wouldn't dare affront him without apologizing? She was beginning to see the significance of what she'd done. And she liked it. She liked it very much. She decided to play this scene as Mazie Darnton.

The room was dimly lit, solid wood tables and leather chairs, dark wainscoting, like a gentleman's lounge, which of course it was. Whoever heard of a female executive? He was sitting at the bar smoking a fat cigar, his jowly face and thinning gray hair reflected in the mirror. Gladys sauntered past the few men sitting at tables, their eyes following her pink tights. Her heart suddenly beat faster. Hell, if she could step off the wing of an airplane, she could do this.

Smiling, she spoke into the mirror. "Mr. Hearst, it was so kind of you to leave me to my work. But I was sure a man of your profession would understand. You don't run a newspaper empire without concentrating, now do you?" She held out her hand. "Anyway, I'm pleased to meet you, Mr. Hearst."

He turned and seemed speechless for a moment, then set his cigar in the ashtray and took her hand, his eyes drifting to her neckline and down.

"I enjoyed your performance, Miss Walton, what I saw of it. Eason told me what I missed the other day. Guess I'll have to wait for the film." He glanced at the drink in front of him. "Would you like a martini? Prohibition doesn't start until Friday."

She gave a laugh, hand to her chest. "Oh my, no. Law or no law, I'm much too young to drink. And I only have a minute, anyway. So what is it you wanted of me, sir?" There, she thought, take it right to him. It felt good to be Mazie, Queen of the Air.

"I wanted to ask you to have dinner with me," he said. "You're not too young to have dinner, are you?"

"Mmm." Gladys shook her head, did a disappointed pout. "Oh, I'm afraid I am. Or at least my mother thinks so. She lives with me, you know. Watches my every step. Awful way for a girl to live in 1920, for goodness sake, but I owe everything to my mother. I love her beyond words."

Mazie had turned into Mary Pickford's Pollyanna, but she was having too much fun to stop. Could hardly wait to tell Mabel.

"You know, Mr. Hearst." She touched his arm. "William, can I call you William? My mamma would love to have dinner with you. She'd be tickled pink. She really would." Gladys nodded toward the door. "I'll go get her right now, if you want..."

"That's all right." Hearst grabbed his cigar. "I'll take a rain check."

"Well, thanks, anyway. I'll be off then. Gotta change, start preparing for *La La Lucille*. They hardly give me time to breathe." She took a few steps, felt his eyes on her behind, then gave a last wave and smile over her shoulder. "It was nice to meet you, sir, and I'm sure our paths will cross again."

She did not add, when I'm older.

Chapter 13

As soon as they turned east off Alameda, Gladys wondered if dinner in Chinatown was such a good idea. The streets were unpaved, and they bumped along ruts in the packed dirt, Mr. Thomas steering his new Model T Sedan around the worst pot holes.

Gladys gazed down narrow alleyways lit only by the occasional glow of paper lanterns and thought of Mabel and her worm. She'd sent Mabel a letter all about her Mazie escapades and how she gave Mr. William Randolph "Pompous Ass" Hearst the bum's rush, that she was going on her first real date with the assistant director!

If you could call this a date, mamma in the back seat gasping "Oh my" every half block.

They passed the Chinese Opera Theater, people gathered in the flicker of gas lamps. A temple with tiered pagoda roof, rows of tiny houses, shops with apartments above, all in a state of decay. They passed an open market covered with tarps, a man unhitching a horse from a rickety wagon. And the smell. Even the chill winter air didn't mask the stench of rotting vegetables and sewage, pungent smoke curling from dark parlors.

"Oh my," mamma said again, "are we safe here?"

"Sure," Mr. Thomas said, "those opium den stories are mostly for tourists." He winked at Gladys. "The Red Dragon is in better shape, and the food's excellent. I know it's here somewhere. I'll find it." He turned another corner

"The land has been sold," he went on, "they'll tear all this down soon as the litigation's over. Southern Pacific is putting a main station here."

"But what about the people?" She could see families in upstairs windows. On almost every corner an open door, men huddled over smoky tables, gambling.

"They'll move, make a new Chinatown somewhere. Ah, here it is."

Curved above an elaborate entrance was a red Chinese dragon, its scales chipped in places, white plaster showing through. One of its green glass eyes was missing. Gladys looked back along the street. Litigation. A whole settlement displaced, homes and businesses sold from under them.

Mr. Thomas handed a boy two bits to watch the car and came around. He put his hand on her back, and she felt tremors up her sides.

Only a few other diners were in the restaurant, all Chinese. They ate in a private cubicle with dark wooden walls and a door that closed, food she couldn't name except for a whole fried fish staring up from a platter of Chinese noodles. Odd dumplings, chunks of pickled eel, impossible with chop sticks. They gave up, laughing, no one to see them use their fingers.

The waiter brought plum wine and tiny porcelain tumblers. Prohibition apparently didn't apply to Chinatown. Mr. Thomas looked across at mamma, permission to pour one for Gladys.

"Of course," mamma smiled, "we're celebrating. We even got new dresses."

She lifted her glass to Gladys, smiled. "Isn't she beautiful? Plum is her color. We decided that today when we were shopping, didn't we princess?"

Mr. Thomas put his hand on hers. "Beautiful, yes. In any color."

Gladys blushed. She felt the warmth of his body. Here in this private cubicle. If only they were alone.

"So, Mr. Thomas, tell us about your family," mamma said. "How long have your people been in California?"

"Howard," he said, "call me Howard."

Then he went on about how his grandfather had come out from Pittsburgh for the gold rush then drifted down to Los Angeles with his small fortune. "Very small," he laughed, "but Grandpa bought a few acres out in Pasadena, and he and dad went into banking. Wanted me to join them after university, but ever since I saw my first Nickelodeon all I wanted was to make movies." He squeezed Gladys's hand. "Never thought I'd discover a star."

When the waiter brought candied chicken feet for dessert, they drew the line. They made their departure, retracing their path through the maze.

At the studio, Mr. Thomas walked them to their bungalow.

Mamma thanked him for the evening. "It's chilly out here," she said, pulling the collar of her new coat higher. "Don't be too long. Can't have our star catching a cold."

When mamma was inside, Mr. Thomas moved close and his eyes changed, suddenly younger the way he'd looked that day in the infirmary.

"What torture!" He removed his spectacles, folding them into his pocket. He laughed. "I don't mean your mother. She's charming, but... I wanted to be alone with you."

"You did?"

"Oh, man!"

He glanced at the bungalow windows, pulled her to him, a bit awkwardly. He was so tall, even in heels her head came to the middle of his chest. Still, it felt good to be in the arms of a man, assistant director.

"Mr. Thom... Howard..." She wanted to tell him about Mabel, ask if he could maybe get Mabel a part in *La La Lucille*, but the way he was clutching her back...

"I'll make this night up to you, Gladys." His voice was husky. "I wanted to talk to you, but your mother..." He breathed in. "This might not be proper, but may I kiss you? I really want to kiss you. Oh, I can be patient, of course. And I was thinking I can take you and your mother to the movies. You should see the new releases, professionally speaking, I mean. Chaplin is doing one with this new Jackie Coogan kid, sure to be a hit, if they ever finish it. And I'd like to accompany you... and your mother to the opening of *Pink Tights*. We'll be able to go places alone after awhile. Parties, I get invited to lots of parties and...

"Yes," Gladys said, standing on tiptoes. If she didn't interrupt him, he'd keep talking until mamma called her in.

"You'll go with me?"

"Of course. But I meant, yes, you can kiss me." She smiled up at him. "Stop talking, Howard, and kiss me!"

He laughed, lifted her to him, her feet almost off the ground. He kissed her softly, then harder. Not at all what she'd felt with Craig. But something.

Chapter 14

Patience, Gladys thought later in her bed. She did not want to be patient. She wanted to know. Get it over with so she could be rid of the grunting pig men who crept into her mind at night. She tried to push them away. Like after a nightmare, simply go back to sleep, dream a different ending. Think of Howard, imagine him opening the car door, lifting her out. He'd carry her to the pond, lay her on the soft grass... and what? She had nothing to pin her thoughts to, no other ending.

Besides mamma, the problem was time, weeks passing in a blur. Her next work made the shooting of *Pink Tights* seem leisurely. The studio executives wanted five Gladys Walton films in current release by midyear. *La La Lucille*, *The Secret Gift*, *Risky Business*, ten hour days, Saturdays too when they were behind schedule, always scurrying from costume fittings to make-up to the set, and in between, publicity shots, appearances. "Indefinitely," Howard said when she asked how long this would go on. Sometimes he'd steal a kiss behind a door or curtain, but she had to stop that, ruined her concentration.

They were calling her "The Glad Girl" now, postcards, calendars, autographed photographs. By March Gladys was sure she could do a glamour pose in her sleep. For one series, they simply draped her in yards of black velvet just covering her breasts, the chair draped too. Lips slightly parted, she sat holding one knee, feet bare, legs showing several inches above her knees, her skin powdered creamy white for more contrast.

"Seductive, yet innocent," Howard teased, standing beside the camera, the black cloth over the photographer's head, "you know, virginal sexuality." She stared directly at Howard, head tilted, the slightest smile. She wet her lips, and even in the glare she could see Howard's face flush. She loved toying with him. He'd take off his glasses, wipe them with his handkerchief.

But he seemed content with all this playing. Too content.

She lived for Sundays. Sundays she slept until noon, then she and mamma would meet Howard at the gate and drive downtown, or take the trolley. They'd stroll through downtown Los Angeles. Between Main Street and Grand everything was in walking distance, wide streets, solid square buildings, all about the same height, ten stories. Some with column facades and ornate trim, others plain, no-nonsense, built before the turn of the century. New buildings were going up on almost every street. They'd start at Blackstone's or the Broadway, window displays of the latest fashions.

"Goodness, mid-calf," mamma said one afternoon, gazing at the new dresses for spring 1920. "When I was a girl we didn't dare show an ankle. Skirts getting shorter, waists dropping. Pretty soon the waist will be the hem! Oh, but look at that hat! There, that cool green with the feathers fanned in front." Mamma linked Gladys's arm. "Come on. I must try that hat!"

69

They'd lunch at the Woolworth's counter or Cole's in the Pacific Electric Building on Spring Street. Then take in a matinee, often an evening movie too, Grauman's, the Belasco, the Pantages just opened on 7th. They saw Babe Ruth and Jack Dempsey. "Parlaying sports careers into film," Howard said, shaking his head. And Will Rogers, lovable no matter how clumsy his acting. They laughed at the Talmadge sisters and Mabel Normand, Chaplin and Harold Lloyd, Buster Keaton. When they saw William Farnum in *If I Were King,* Gladys wished Mabel were here to giggle and nudge. The way that suede tunic fit across his chest, boots all the way to his thighs. She missed being silly with Mabel.

Howard sat between, so serious with his must-see list. He'd lecture about camera angle and lighting and acting techniques while she tried to read the captions. In D.W. Griffith's *Way Down East* he leaned close, whispering, "See, each frame is a perfect composition. Griffith never uses a script. Takes days doing 'work up' shots for stuff like this."

"Shh, Howard, please!" Gladys glanced over, tears on mamma's face.

He drew back, arms folded.

Stuff like this. On the screen, Lillian Gish held her dead baby, a long close up of her anguished face. Poor Anna, tricked into a phony marriage, pregnant, the baby dies and she's sent away to live with a farm family.

Howard sulking because she'd shushed him.

Gladys kept her eyes on the screen. Anna cast out in a snow storm, drifting on an ice floe. You could feel the cold, everything stark white except winter trees and shards of black river where the ice opened. Richard Barthelmess struggling through the storm, knee deep snow, to get to Anna in time. *Stuff!*

Still, she didn't want Howard to be angry. What if he got tired of dragging around a sixteen-year-old and her mother?

Plenty of girls to choose from, girls willing to do just about anything for bigger parts.

But they weren't stars.

"There," Howard said, nodding to the screen, "that's a running shot. The Griffith trademark." He put his arm around her, and she breathed again.

When the movie ended there was a stunned silence, then the entire audience was on its feet, whistling and stomping.

The next week they saw John Barrymore in *Dr. Jekyll And Mr. Hyde*, and Gladys gripped Howard's arm, pretending to be scared. She expected another tedious lesson, makeup and camera effects. Head him off at the pass. She pulled him to her, not caring what people behind them thought, kissed him hard, mouth open, searching for his tongue, hand behind his neck. He seemed shocked at first, then kissed her back, and she closed her eyes, felt it all the way to her toes. "Please Howard," she breathed, sure mamma couldn't hear over the music. "I'm tired of being patient! Think of something!"

"I have," he whispered. "It's a surprise."

She opened her eyes. Mamma was staring at her over Howard's shoulder.

He cleared his throat, stretched his long legs, adjusting his trousers.

Gladys met mamma's stare. What do you expect? her look said.

Mamma nodded, a touch of sadness in her eyes. When they turned back to the movie, Mr. Hyde was Jekyll again, and they looked at each other and smiled.

Later that night Gladys got up from her bed and went to mamma's room, snuggled beside her. The only light, a sliver where the curtains parted. It seemed easier to talk in the dark.

"Mamma, I... I get confused sometimes." She'd never told about the men in that car, couldn't now.

71

"Of course." Mamma was facing the wall. Her voice had an edge. "Yes, you're becoming a woman, Gladys, everything's new and exciting. I'm proud of you." Her words said one thing, but the tone was stern, almost harsh. She turned. "You must be careful, Gladys. It's easy to get caught up in all this glamour." Her laugh was short, bitter. "Oh, I know, these modern sophisticated times, but some things don't change. We worked hard for this, Minnie and I and Uncle Tommy. You think it was easy finding money for all those lessons and pretty clothes? Well, it wasn't. And now one wrong step..."

She sat up, her eyes sharp even in the darkness. Her voice lowered, slow and deliberate. "If you get... pregnant, this will all be gone. All of it. It isn't a game, Gladys. It isn't a movie. And being a star won't protect you. Unmarried women just scrape by or worse. Far worse."

"I know, mamma."

"No, you don't know!" She shook her head. "Men. My own father, your grandpa Rolf. When he came from Germany, he brought his housekeeper too, his mistress. Right there in the same home with my mother. You didn't understand. How could you? But women do what they have to, that's all. So if you're thinking about Howard and his... needs, don't. There are places men go for that."

She was quiet a moment, then her tone softened. "You're still my little girl. I don't want you to get hurt." She paused again. "Are you in love with Howard?"

"No... maybe. Oh, I don't know." Gladys felt a tightening in her chest, didn't want to cry. Little girl. She was not a little girl! And she wasn't interested in love. There was no time for love. *One wrong step. Places men go.*

She snuggled closer. "Were you in love with my father, mamma?"

"Hmm. I guess, in the beginning. He swept me off my feet, that's sure. And he gave me you."

She could hear the smile in mamma's voice, but it didn't erase the other. They lay quietly for some moments. Gladys thought of her gypsy father, his blood in her, and how lonely her mother must be, living only for her all those years. Or to be the mother of a star, a bungalow in Universal City, handle the finances. No, don't think that. Complicated enough without that, one minute wanting mamma to disappear, the next wanting her to hold her and call her princess.

Still, she had to live. Had to find out.

"Sometimes I think of my life back in Oregon," Gladys said. "I'd be finishing my senior year at Jefferson now, getting ready for graduation with my friends."

"And then what?" Mamma turned on the lamp, looked into her eyes. The edge was back. "Then what? Be a secretary? A clerk in cosmetics like I was? Marry one of those no account boys? You were meant for more, Gladys. At least I thought so. You don't miss that, do you? Good Lord, Gladys, what your friends would give to trade places with you for even one day!"

They sat looking at each other, tears filling their eyes. Gladys felt the changes. It was true, everyone wanted what she had, but that didn't mean she had to be alone...

"Oh!" she said suddenly. "Oh, how could I forget!" She was up on her knees, excited. "Mamma, when Howard said goodnight he invited me to a party. Saturday after next, and not just any party. A lady named Fannie Ward is having a gala, a grand house warming. She was a stage actress before the movies. She and her husband built an Italian villa, a mansion. Everyone in Hollywood will be there!"

She was making the bed bounce. Mamma laughed, wiping her eyes.

73

"Howard said we can bring Mabel and Craig, and you, of course. Everyone in Hollywood! Now we really have to go shopping. Gowns, mamma, we'll need gowns!"

Mamma was quiet. She hugged Gladys, held her at arm's length.

"No. It's time I left you alone. I'll go home soon. You're strong, you'll manage. Just be careful, and..." Her voice caught. She took a breath, her hands tightened on Gladys's shoulders. "Remember our talk... when you first got your monthlies? It's very, very important, honey."

"I remember. Don't worry, mamma. But the party. Are you sure you don't want to go?" She tried to look disappointed. There was more to the surprise, but Howard wouldn't say what.

Mamma smiled. "Well, to tell the truth, I met a nice man in props the other day. We're having dinner that evening. But we'll go shopping for your gown, princess. You know I'd never miss that."

Chapter 15

The week of the party she still hadn't heard from Mabel. Gladys got to the set early, found Howard. "I know she'd want to go. I don't understand, and we still have to get dresses. My scenes aren't until later. Can you take me, Howard? The trolley's too slow."

Howard checked his pocket watch. "Come on. What the heck, I am the assistant director."

They hurried through the Sunshine Comedy gates, but at the edge of the set, Gladys hesitated. Mr. Biggs and Gertrude and Craig were there, but who was the black haired girl in the maid's outfit about to throw a pie?

The girl turned to see what the others were looking at, and Gladys recognized those blue eyes. She was so thin! Gladys walked right onto the set, sure Mr. Steiner would work it into the story.

Mabel dropped the pie. "Gladys!"

"I missed you so much." She tried not to let the shock register. "Are you okay, Mabel?" How different she looked. Her face no longer round, voluptuous curves gone. Alluring in a waifish sort of way. Just what directors wanted.

"I'm fine," Mabel said. "Oh, I was a mite puny awhile back, but I'm fine now." She leaned close. "It worked. Don't need no binding now, that's sure."

The smile was the same, and that smooth as cream Georgia accent, and Gladys knew why she hadn't answered. She had nothing to wear. "Mabel," she whispered, "come with us to the party. And shopping. My treat. We'll celebrate the new you. Please don't say no. I don't want to go without you."

Mabel met her eyes. "Honey... well, all right. It's just so good to see you. I'd 'a been over to visit, but time just gets away. You know." Mabel nodded at Craig, then took Gladys' hands. "Oh, but y'all are feast for sore eyes. And goodness, *Pink Tights*, we saw *Pink Tights*! You were wonderful! We'll celebrate that too. Everybody's talkin' about it. When I saw y'all up there on that wing, I was fit to be tied. Wasn't I, Craig?" She gestured to him. "Craig, come say hello to Gladys."

The other cast members were standing back out of camera range.

"Go on, all of you." Mr. Steiner waved, still rolling the camera. "We'll make it a reunion. Long lost cousin back from Hollywood. Rich husband to boot." He included Howard in his sweep, and Howard joined the others, introductions all around.

"Husband," Gladys laughed, "hardly." She'd thought it might feel awkward seeing Craig again, but the attraction was gone, like last year's coat suddenly outgrown. Besides, even in their glances she sensed Mabel and Craig might have something rare, like Aunt Minnie and Uncle Tommy. She wondered if she would ever find that.

"Hey, don't block her," Steiner yelled. "Get around behind. You know what I can sell this for with Gladys Walton in it? Few more months afloat." He grinned. "Kid, you just saved my Sunshiny ass!"

They could see the glow of lights from blocks away. The Fannie Ward estate took up half a street between Santa Monica and Sunset Boulevard, and a line of limousines filled the circular drive as they pulled in behind. Gladys and Mabel sat side by side in the back seat, Howard and Craig facing them, elegant in tuxedo and top hat.

Gladys took Howard's hand, stepped from the limousine, careful with her gown which formed a slight train in back. She wore a short coat of black chiffon velvet, her dress a soft taupe, sleeveless, the thinnest silk over a satin chemise. It reached just above her ankles in front and had a headpiece to match the beading and pearl trim on the low V neckline and the band at the hips. Her shoes and purse had the same beading.

They stood beside low steps that wound up through a columned portico to the mansion. Globe lamps lined the walkway, and light glowed from every window and open door. Couples in full evening dress strolled toward the entrance, music playing above the talk and laughter. A photographer had set a wooden tripod on the lawn, his head under the black cloth, a poof and flash when he clicked the cord. A rounded balcony curved out from the upper story, filled with guests. A cool spring night in Los Angeles.

"Oh, Howard, what a dream, even more than I imagined!" Gladys clung to him, as if without his arm she might billow up into the sky. Sophisticated, act sophisticated.

"Lord, lord, y'all can take me now!" Mabel said behind them, stunning on Craig's arm. Her blond hair in the latest bob framing those blue eyes, ethereal in a gown of pale lavender Charmeuse, its straight lines softened by sashes of tulle flounced at the hips. She wore an ostrich feather stole and satin headband, one small plume fastened with an amethyst in the middle.

Howard nodded toward a couple getting out of the next limo. Gladys and Mabel stared, managed not to squeal. Douglas Fairbanks and Mary Pickford! No mistaking those long curls. Only farm girls wore hair past their shoulders now. Her gown a creamy organza with high neck, ruffles all the way down, it actually tied at the waist. A little girl dress. Only

Mary Pickford. The nation's sweetheart, if she ever changed her Pollyanna image there'd be rioting in the streets. How perfect they looked together, Fairbanks with his athletic build.

"I'm surprised they're here," Howard whispered. "Rumor is they're getting married next week and leaving for Europe. Something of a scandal. She got one of those quick divorces in Nevada few weeks ago."

They stood back for the royal couple to pass, but Miss Pickford walked right to them.

"Gladys Walton," she said, "that parachute scene everyone's talking about?"

Gladys could only nod.

"I've done my share of stunts," Miss Pickford said, "but nothing like that." She shook Gladys's hand. "It's nice to meet you, and I hope Laemmle gives you vehicles worthy of your talent. You tell him I said that." She looked toward the house. "I'll tell him myself if I see him."

"Thank you, Miss Pickford." Sophisticated. She'd be lucky not to faint!

"I hear they're calling you the 'Glad Girl.' They called me that too. My name was Gladys. They said it wouldn't work for movies." She laughed. "Shows what they know."

That Pickford smile, the only one in Hollywood with no hidden meaning.

There was a pause. Mr. Fairbanks glanced back at the line of cars, and before Gladys could introduce the others, he said, "Shall we go on up, Mary? I didn't think Charlie would be here, but now I'm sure." He nodded to the four of them. "Have a nice evening."

Mabel squeezed her arm, grinning. They followed the couple through the portico toward the mansion.

"What was that about?" Gladys whispered to Howard.

"The Great Nazimova," he said, bending close. "She's behind us. Don't look. Fairbanks is a good friend of Charlie

Chaplin. They formed a new company with Griffith. Chaplin's getting a divorce. In court he accused Nazimova of seducing his wife."

"No, you mean...?"

"Mm hmm. Chaplin's wife claimed he's a sex addict." Howard laughed. "Probably truth to both stories. It gets ugly. They lost their baby, and now Chaplin's pouring everything into the new film with Jackie Coogan. Come on, let's have some fun." He kissed her cheek. "Don't forget, I have a surprise later."

At the door a butler checked their wraps and the men's hats. Fannie Ward greeted them, beautiful in a gown of gold lamé, Hollywood matron, her husband, John Dean beside her.

"She's forty-eight," Howard whispered when they were inside. "Claims to be forty and plays parts much younger. Dean was her leading man in one of her Lasky films. Divorced her rich husband to marry him. Hubby was a diamond broker worth fifty million, they say." He glanced around. "That's where all this came from."

The floors were marble. Gilded Italian furniture and white statues, Greek and Roman, fit for a museum. The entry opened onto a ballroom, a sweeping staircase at one end. A twenty piece band played jazz and ragtime, couples dancing the fox trot. Upholstered benches lined the walls, but Gladys and Mabel preferred to stand. So many gowns to appraise, so many hair dos and jeweled headpieces, not to mention plunging necklines. They stood between Craig and Howard, chatting and sipping champagne from crystal goblets on silver trays. Prohibition had only become law in January. No one thought it would last.

All these dazzling people in one place, Gladys thought, the women anyway. The men more like props in tails and white tie. Nothing could be done with faces like Ben Turpin, Buster Keaton or "Fatty" Arbuckle.

"Look what Pola Negri's wearing," Gladys whispered. "And Theda Bara. Doesn't she know the vamp days are over?"

Mabel laughed. "Can't say I blame her. If I ever got as big as Theda Bara, they'd have to drag me out 'a town with a dern rope." She leaned across Gladys. "Howard, honey, maybe y'all can tell us, is Gloria Swanson pregnant? 'Cause if so, she's my idol, comin' out to an affair like this with her belly showin.' My, my, what they'd say in Atlanta! But then this ain't exactly a cotillion, is it?'"

Howard laughed, sputtering, almost spilled his drink. "Could be. I believe Miss Swanson got married last summer. You girls..." He shook his head, then pulled Gladys closer. "Why don't we go up on the balcony. It's a beautiful night. We can look at the real stars..."

"No siree, not this tomato." Mabel grinned, took Craig's arm, her hips moving to the music, which had cranked up a notch. "Come on, dance with me, Daddy. Y'all said you would." She nodded to the dance floor. "What's that they're doin' now?"

"The Texas Tommy." Craig laughed. "I'm game. Saw it once at the Fairmont in Frisco." He gave her a spin right where they stood.

There was a sudden flurry of laughter, and through the archway swept Nazimova with her ladies in waiting. A half dozen beauties in full glimmer and glam shimmied out, dancing with each other, Nazimova with her favorite of the moment. Nazimova was producing her own movies now, had her own casting couch too, apparently. Or wanted people to think so. She danced barefoot, a gown of metallic bronze mesh, white skin showing through, eyebrows like slashes, her thick black hair a frenzy of curls and no headpiece at all. Couples moved away, some actually left the floor. Women danced together all the time, but not like this.

Mabel shrugged. "Don't make no never mind to me." She took Craig's hand and they danced onto the floor, their version of the Texas Tommy.

Gladys watched. They were good. She'd never seen Mabel dance. Why, she herself hadn't danced since coming to Los Angeles. How could that be? She loved to dance. Years of lessons. So caught up in her work. She felt the music, her body pulsing, Gypsy blood. Shoulders moving with the beat, she smiled up at Howard.

"Well, good looking?"

"I'm afraid I don't dance," he said.

She stopped moving. Her disappointment hung in the air. Didn't dance! What was she doing with someone who didn't dance?

He read her eyes. "But I imagine that fellow over there would dance with you." He nodded toward the far wall. "I noticed he's danced with several ladies tonight. Fannie probably hired him for that. He's a professional dancer, down on his luck, if it's who I think it is. Did some bit parts for Universal last year and something with Clara Kimball Young."

Gladys looked. Her eyes widened.

"It's okay, I wouldn't mind, Gladys," Howard added, "if that's what you want."

She wasn't listening, already walking across the room. She should tell Mabel, the way she'd carried on about him that time at the movies. But Mabel was happily dancing with Craig.

The man was standing at the foot of the staircase, dark hair slicked back just like in the movie. But much more handsome in person. *Down on his luck.* That won't last long, she thought, and then he turned and looked at her with those intense Italian eyes.

"Mr. Valentino," she said, "would you dance with me?"

Chapter 16

How they danced!

Gladys fastened her train to the clasp at her wrist and simply followed, her feet moving with the music, barely skimming the floor when he held her. A master, this Valentino. Guiding her with the slightest touch. No, just his eyes, like telepathy, a puppet without strings. These Italians and their magic.

They danced apart for the Texas Tommy, the Fox trot. He'd pull her to him, twirl and dip, his hands holding hers, then her waist and back. Then gone, on her own again, fixed to those magnetic eyes. They danced face to face, arms to their sides, fingers splayed, shimmying their shoulders, then he'd sweep her up, lift her over his head. Amazing. Oh, if Miss Myers could see her now! She laughed. Songs changed, *Tiger Rag*, *The Georgia Grind*, the next and the next, the room a blur.

She saw Mabel, grinning at her over Craig's shoulder, mouthing, "It's him. It's him!"

Then the sound of bongos and marimbas, a Latin section had set up beside the main band, and without a word he swept her into the *stance*. She thought of protesting. She'd only tried a tango once when Miss Myers was upstairs with the juniors. Viola Desmond put on a record and they exaggerated the stiff moves, giggling. Thirteen year olds. But this man was hardly Viola Desmond! How could she refuse?

"Do not worry," he said, reading her thoughts, of course. "The tango is a story. If you think of the story, it will take you." He smiled. "You will like it." And he started her in that rigid walk.

Couples stood back, watching. No one else was dancing. The whole room watching, studio executives, the biggest names in film. A story, she thought, think of the story. Of passion... with a stranger. A handsome out-of-work actor, a dingy hotel... on a beach, waves crashing. A woman pays him to...

Such insistence in the beat, she felt it in her chest, her stomach, let it take her. A story of love without surrender. To have it all. Why, she wondered, had Nazimova and her beauties strutted off the floor when she and Valentino started dancing? Hollywood intrigue. His hand firm on her back, elbows up, they made the turn. Again. This dress, the way the silk formed to her legs, perfect for the tango.

"Make your arms stiff," he whispered, closing his hands over her fists. He lifted her high, then let go and caught her waist, let her body slide slowly down, their lips almost touching, then her head against his chest, and just as she thought she might swoon, he swung her again into the walk.

But at the end when he dipped her all the way to the floor, then back into his arms, hard, there was a silence, awkward. She looked around. Couples were whispering, staring. Had she broken some rule? She blushed.

Then a voice called out, "Stunning, magnificent!" Mabel.

"Bravo!" Craig added, and they clapped and started scattered applause.

The band played a simple slow dance, *After You've Gone*, and couples again filled the floor. She leaned against his shoulder and breathed. Cologne as exotic as his skin. His body, slim and perfect. The body of a dancer, and just tall enough, she didn't have to strain on tiptoes.

Howard, she'd forgotten all about Howard. She didn't care.

"Mr. Valentino," she said when she could speak, "do all men in Italy dance like this?"

"No, not quite." His eyes mock serious. "There's that one in the Vatican, and... I met a man in Genoa once who did not dance, but he had no legs."

"Go on!" She laughed, and he laughed too.

"Call me Rudolpho. Rudolph. Or Rudy." He sighed. "My name, it is getting less and less here. Soon I fear it will be nothing."

"Oh, I doubt that. What was it to begin with?" How she loved his accent.

"You promise to not tell?" He shrugged. "But it does not matter. No one in Hollywood uses their real name."

"I do."

"Yes? It is?"

The way his brow arched. Expressive eyes, yet sad, in a way. Like looking at a mask, one that hid things perhaps better not to know. Her heart beat faster, and not from the dancing.

"Gladys Walton," she said. How dull it sounded. She'd ask mamma her grandmother's name, the Gypsy French side.

"Ah, yes, I thought I have seen you." He nodded. "Mazie, Queen Of The Air. For this you dance so good. And because you are a star, at what, sixteen?"

"Seventeen."

"Well, me, I have twenty-five... old years. Rudolpho Di Valentina Guglielmi." He laughed. "I was a count for awhile, an Italian count, what else? Why I tell you this, I do not know. But I am tired of these stories. These little parts they toss at me. I am thinking to go back to my village..."

"No, no, you mustn't, Rudy." She teased, "Stay and dance with me. Why, I could dance with you forever! You're not... married or anything?"

"Yes, for a fact I am. But that is not real either. Nothing here is real. I carry a curse, I think."

"Nonsense..."

The music had stopped. They were standing in the middle of the floor, only a few other couples remaining. She moved out of his arms. Married. What did he mean, married but not real? Gladys could feel the stares, raised eyebrows again. So, it was one thing to dance, another to spend time laughing and talking with a man hired as part of the entertainment. Or was it because he was Italian and down on his luck? In the east they hated Italians, but this was Hollywood. Weren't they all paid to entertain?

Valentino offered his arm, and they walked off the floor.

She looked for Howard, but he was gone.

A hand touched her shoulder, and she jumped.

"Gladys, honey, if y'all don't introduce us this very instant, we will never speak to you again." Mabel grinned, holding Craig's arm. Then she smiled up at Valentino. "Magnificent. You were magnificent! We saw you in *Eyes of Youth*, you know."

He bowed slightly, recited his full name and shook their hands. Mabel introduced herself as Alice Andrews.

"What are you working on now?" Craig asked.

"Well," Valentino said, "there is some talk, a film of the Spanish novel by Vicente Ibañez," he smiled, "but I do not count chickens. And now I fear I have, how do you say, shirked my duties. But who could resist such a beautiful dancer?" He took Gladys' hand and kissed it. "I hope to see you again, Miss Walton. We can dance and be friends, can we not?"

"Yes, of course. Absolutely."

She watched him walk away. The slight sinking she'd felt at the word "married" was gone. To be friends and dance, what could be better? If his wife didn't mind. Wife. A marriage that wasn't real. She had to find out what that meant.

Mabel linked her arm. "Come on, let's find a powder room. Oh, honey, I'm about to bust with all I got to tell you."

Chapter 17

"Wait, gotta get more bubbly."

Mabel lifted two glasses from a tray, handed one to Gladys. They hurried out to the hallway, almost bumping into the Talmadge sisters. On either side of Fatty Arbuckle, the sisters were struggling to hold him up long enough to drop him on a bench.

"Nice dancing," Norma said, or maybe it was Constance. Gladys never could get them straight. Constance was the funny one.

Fatty looked up, blinking. "Would ya getta load 'a this," he slurred. "Who might you lovelies be?"

Ignoring him, Gladys tried the nearest door, but it was locked.

"Use the stairs at the end of the hall," Norma said, "guest rooms all have W.C.s."

"Watch out for the bodies," Constance added, laughing.

She wasn't kidding. When they reached the stairs, a man was sprawled out cold at the bottom.

Gladys whispered, "You think he needs help?"

"Oh, he needs help all right," Mabel said, stepping over him, "but nothin' we can do."

Gladys followed. "Where's Howard?"

"Last I saw he was out on the big balcony." She shook her head. "You got some mendin' to do, honey. After a few numbers, he walked on out. We went after, and that's what I got to tell you." Upstairs, Mabel stopped at the first door. They could hear rustling and murmurs inside.

"Lord, these folks don't have a pig's sense of what's fittin.' Whatever breedin' they had, they left behind the barn." Mabel bounced from one foot to the other. "Oh, but I do need me a privy!"

"Here, let me have that, you'll spill." Gladys took Mabel's drink, couldn't help but laugh. Mabel in her beautiful gown, bouncing like a little kid.

The next room was empty. Mabel hurried past a four poster to the bathroom. Gladys sat at the dressing table, touching up her hair in the round mirror, an array of perfumes and powders, ivory handled combs and brushes there on the vanity. She leaned closer to the mirror. Her face rosy and happy. Dancing. She could hear the couple through the wall. "Pull yourself together, sweetheart." She thought of Howard and his surprise. If there was still a surprise. At least he didn't see the tango. She smiled, emptied her glass, felt the warmth wash through her.

"So what's the news, Mabel?" she called, "I need to go find Howard."

The toilet flushed, and in a moment Mabel appeared in the doorway.

"Honey, looks like I'm gonna be at Universal after all, part time anyway. Howard introduced me to Mr. Von Stroheim. He said he might have a part for me in *The Secret Gift*, maybe some others. Small, but a start. I'm meetin' with him Monday, and I know he wants me." She laughed. "More ways 'n one, undressin' me with his eyes. I sure don't understand. Back home this skin 'n bones body'd hardly be worth tossin' to the hounds." She shrugged. "But I ain't complainin'"

"What about Craig?"

"Oh, we'll stay on at Sunshine meantime, but we all know Steiner's gonna fold soon. Not much market for two-reelers anymore. Craig'll find work. He wants to get married and move closer in, but you know how I am." She shuddered. "Marriage. Scares the bejesus out 'a me. I didn't come to California to get hitched. Move over, honey."

She sat beside Gladys on the little bench, their eyes met in the mirror. "Honey, you were sensational. I didn't know you could dance like that, and I've never seen you so happy." Mabel grinned. "Maybe it's love at first sight. Even if it ain't, I wouldn't let that Valentino get away."

Gladys laughed. "I'm afraid he already did. He's married."

"No! Go on! Oh, that's a cryin' shame. Man like that has no right to be married!" Mabel turned to face her, as if searching for any sign of heartbreak. "Well, then it must be the dancin.' That's something else I wanted to tell you. I've been doing these musical revues over at the Ambassador. Man named Shubert produces 'em. I'm just in the chorus line, but it's fun and another fifty dollars a week. I know you don't need the money, but look at y'all glowin' like a firefly. Honey, you need to be dancin'."

Gladys smiled. Musical revues. It would be good, to be with Mabel and free of the studio at least some evenings. "Maybe," she said, "yes, I'd like that, if I can fit it in. Mamma's going home soon. You can have her room, if it works out. But, Mabel, don't lose Craig. It isn't worth it."

Mabel hugged her. "I know, but I'm eighteen. I got time."

"Time. Goodness. What time is it?" Gladys stood. "I have to find Howard and do 'some mendin'"

"Well, don't do too much. 'Cause Howard ain't your type. Anybody can see that." Mabel laughed, following her into the hallway. "Y'all need to burn, not just toast yer toes by some cozy fire."

They'd only taken a few steps when the door to the next room opened and a man came out, adjusting the cummerbund to his tuxedo over his paunch. A blond, clearly beyond tipsy, clung to his arm. She groaned, her knees buckled and he caught her, holding her like a rag doll.

"Isn't that Marion Davies?" Mabel whispered. "Drunk as a skunk and him old enough to be her grandfather!"

"Shh." Gladys was hoping to pass unnoticed, but Mr. Hearst looked up. He recognized her, she could tell. To turn away now would be worse.

"Mr. Hearst, would you like us to get help?"

"No, no. It's quite all right. She just needs to lie down a little longer." He hefted Miss Davies in his arms, backed into the room and kicked the door closed.

Gladys found Howard on the balcony. He was in the shadows where the railing met the house, checking his pocket watch. He slipped it into his coat as she approached.

"It's a full moon," he said simply.

"Yes, beautiful."

A moment passed. The balcony was large, a half-circle jutting out from the house like the prow of an ocean liner. Couples stood along the railing, talking, sipping champagne, a louder group at the far end. Inside, the band was playing a waltz. People were dancing on the lawn.

"Howard, I... I forgot how much I love to dance, and the time got away. Then Mabel had to tell me about Mr. Von Stroheim..."

"You don't have to explain, Gladys."

"No, but I want to thank you. It means a lot to Mabel... and to me."

"He's a gigolo, Gladys, a taxi dancer, a two-bit actor. He worked in clubs in New York. I heard he had to leave in a hurry, some scandal. The guy's all wet, Gladys. Trust me, he won't amount to a thing."

"I know," she said, although she did not believe that for a minute. A man could hardly be expected to understand what Valentino had. Not just looks. It wasn't easy to explain. But she didn't blame Howard for being irritated. She was lucky he hadn't left. Or maybe not. The thought almost made her smile. Better not think what might've happened if Howard had left.

"Anyway, Mr. Valentino is married."

"He told you that?"

"Yes."

"Well, I haven't heard of it. Hardly seems likely."

She managed not to smile. Did he think he could know the marital status of every *two-bit* actor in Hollywood? But he'd find out now, she'd bet.

"Howard," she said, "that isn't exactly the lie men go around telling, now is it?"

He looked at her, then away. "No, of course not."

She touched his arm, stood on tiptoes, kissed his cheek. "Howard, sweetheart, why don't we get more champagne and go out on the lawn? We could take off our shoes and waltz slow or just watch the shenanigans. There's lots of shenanigans going on tonight." She brushed her finger over his lip. "You still have a surprise for me, don't you?"

His laugh had a slight harumph to it. "I suppose, if that's what you want."

Chapter 18

"Shh, stand still. Stop giggling."

Howard twisted his handkerchief, trying to tie it over her eyes. "Gladys, do you want your surprise or not?"

She put a hand to her mouth, couldn't stop laughing. It's just that as soon as he'd said the word blindfold she'd pictured... oh, what she pictured! Nakedness. Like those postcards men collected. She'd found a stash in Uncle Tommy's tool shed once. But this was hardly the place. They were standing at the door to Studio Five on the back lot. All this time she'd had the wrong idea about the surprise? Too bad, because she really wanted it. This lovely champagne making her all warm and bubbly.

"Gladys, you're spilling." Howard stood back, crossed his arms. "All right, let me know when you're ready. You're going to like this, if you ever settle down." He was laughing too.

After dropping Mabel and Craig at Sunshine Comedy, the limo delivered them right to her bungalow, but Howard waited until the car was out of sight then walked her through the dark streets of Universal to this building. Blindfold? The air chill on her flushed skin, she pulled her coat closed, took a last sip. She handed him the glass, and he set it by the door.

"Okay." She made her face serious. "I'm ready."

He tied the handkerchief over her eyes, turned her toward the door.

She heard a lock click, the door open.

He guided her in. "Don't worry, I'm right here."

He stopped a moment, to turn on a light, she supposed, her eyes closed under the handkerchief. She could feel the draft of the space above as they made their way deeper into the building. No sound but their footsteps. She didn't think she'd ever been in this building although it wasn't far from where they were shooting *The Secret Gift*.

"All right." He positioned her just so. "Now stay here, just a second."

Gladys waited. In a moment she heard the sound of water splashing against stone. Water? Then he was back, untying the handkerchief.

She blinked, her eyes adjusting to the low light. It took several moments to absorb what lay before her. She didn't speak, just stood taking it in. Another time and place, faraway, exotic. She'd only seen such things in books and paintings.

At her feet was a shallow pool tiled in turquoise and mother of pearl, water flowing from the mouth of a stone sphinx. The sound echoed. To her left, ochre walls formed a series of arches all patterned and scrolled in arabesque. The actual pool was only ten or twelve feet wide, but the wall and arches were painted to look as if it went on and on, a vaulted Turkish bath.

Directly across from where she stood, low steps led up to... she glanced at Howard standing there watching her, then back... it was an alcove the size of a bed but walled on three sides. Persian carpets covered the steps, tapestries on the walls, and inside were large cushions, silk and damask and brocade in deep shades of red and gold, a leopard skin draped at one end. Sheer curtains tied up with cords. Behind the alcove was a high wall with windows of latticed wood like in Arabia.

A harem. My God! She could almost hear the laughter of girls dancing with veils, bells on their ankles, the air filled with incense. The light through the windows cast intricate patterns on the floor. Just the sight of that enclosed bed made her want to stretch her legs, naked, feel the lushness.

She looked up at Howard.

He smiled. "It's that Priscilla Dean film," he said, "*The Virgin of Stamboul*. Big production. They're breaking it down Monday after the last editing." His eyes clouded then. "Gladys, I... I know we're not so well matched, and I understand, but if this is your first time, I thought it should be, well, memorable." He paused. "Do you like it?"

"Shh. Don't talk. It's too perfect for talk." She did not want to think of it as a set, did not want to think of anything. Only to feel.

He stepped to her, his voice a whisper. "Just one more thing. Don't worry about... precautions. I'll handle that. No one understands the importance better than..."

"Shh, Howard."

She stood on tiptoes, pulled him to her, kissed him hard, holding him, afraid if she stopped he'd start talking again, break the spell. There *was* passion in him after all.

She felt him ignite, clasping her, leaning her back, quick hungry kisses, her mouth, her throat, his breath hot below her ear. He lifted her in his arms, carried her around the pool and up the steps, set her on the cushions. He drew the curtains, tugging at his coat, his tie.

In moments they lay naked, enclosed in this pleasure chamber, Howard gazing at her body, her skin pearl white against red and gold and leopard. They were in another world where eyes met boldly, pleasure the only purpose. She stretched and turned, luxuriating, looking up at him with Sheba eyes. Their silent agreement, no words.

Watching her, he breathed deeply as if remembering something, and she looked away as he handled the "precautions." He took his time then, touching, kissing, slowly, slowly, and when he finally entered her, it was smooth, only a little pain. She'd heard older girls talk about first times and knew not to expect too much. But this, my God! He moved steadily, slow, even thrusts, and it was... glorious! Nothing on earth could be so delicious. She wanted it to last and last, no one to hear her moans as she arched against him.

She closed her eyes, sure the childhood visions would not dare intrude. Replaced by a bed of soft cushions, the sound of water and Howard's breathing. But when the sensations began to shudder through her, she was surprised what came to her mind. Those dark eyes holding her in the tango. She bit her lip, but the name escaped, "Valentino."

Chapter 19

In the next weeks Gladys saw Howard only on the set. They never spoke of their night in *Stamboul*. How could she explain what it meant? Her childhood monsters were not imaginary, yet he had chased them away, replaced the ugliness with... enchantment. Her first time should be memorable, he had said. If he only knew! The Turkish bath and harem bed were gone, flats painted over for another film, yet the images would stay with her forever.

Still, when she imagined spending her life with Howard, it fell flat like a missed note. He knew, of course, even before she murmured Valentino's name - my God, had she really done that? It made her cheeks flush whenever she remembered. Yet Howard seemed to hold no resentment. He had a job to do. And that job was making her a star.

Risky Business would soon be ready for editing. By late summer there would be four Gladys Walton films in current release, and the studio planned twice as many for 1921. Already bringing her new scripts. Always a spunky, clever girl who foils the villain's scheme, saves the day and finds wealth or love (usually both) through some final twist. Her favorite so far was *Rich Girl, Poor Girl*, a Prince and Pauper variation in which she'd play both parts. *All Dolled Up* had an actual fight scene. Humble but feisty salesgirl, Maggie Quick, pummels some crooks trying to snatch a rich lady's purse. What fun! The million dollar reward catapults Maggie up the social ladder, yet she remains down-to-earth and likable. Audiences loved that.

On the last page was a hand written a note: "Laemmle's found gold in this one. Every shop girl in America will lap it up. Now, if we can get our hands on another circus movie." The initials, H.T.

Gladys felt a twinge. That was all? Howard had nothing more personal to say? It was also a relief. He had given her a night that could as easily have been a dream. And for once Howard must've realized words would only detract.

It was Fannie Ward who explained about Valentino's marriage. Monday after the party Gladys had a studio driver take her to the mansion and wait while she hurried up the marble steps. She'd return the crystal goblet she'd pilfered that night, simply hand it to the butler with her apologies, but Miss Ward appeared behind him. In a flowing satin dressing gown of the palest pink, matching strand of pearls, hair and makeup as perfect as those red cupid bow lips. Even lounging at home, a star must always be a star.

"My dear, that wasn't necessary," Fannie said, "but how very thoughtful. Come in, come in. We'll have tea." A slight British accent from her years on the London stage.

They sat at a small table on the back verandah. On the lawn a servant was exercising Miss Ward's Afghan hounds. "Pathé and Lasky," she smiled, "our studio dogs."

Gladys laughed, careful not to clink her cup and saucer.

"Have a tea cake." Fannie nodded to a tray on the table. "Deliciously decadent." She laughed. "So much rum in them I'm sure our cook will be arrested soon. We'll have to send someone to Tijuana when the last bottle is gone." She shook her head. "Prohibition. Whoever heard of such a thing? Silly women on their high horses. Americans fancy themselves such Puritans." She sipped her tea. "Imagine the Brits closing their pubs. Or the French, good Lord! It's absurd!"

"It is," Gladys said, remembering the champagne. "Your party was wonderful, Miss Ward." With the silver server she lifted cake onto two tiny plates, handed one to Fannie.

"And how beautifully you danced, my dear. Charming young man, Valentino. I saw him at Grauman's last year. He and Carol Dempster danced a stage prologue for one of Griffith's films. I told D.W. he should've given Valentino the lead. Far more sultry than Richard Barthelmess." Fannie leaned forward, smiling, her tone confidential. "Oh, if I were younger... Do you plan to see him again?"

"Well, he spoke of being friends," Gladys said, "but I don't know how to reach him, and... he's married, you know."

"Oh, that." Fannie waved her hand. "It's nothing. One of Nazimova's nymphs got a hold of him." Fannie brushed crumbs from her gown. "I heard there was a dinner party, a restaurant out in Santa Monica. The great Nazimova with her girls and some bigwigs from Metro. Someone who knew Valentino in New York invited him at the last moment, and when he walked in Nazimova flew into a rage, called him a gigolo and a pimp in front of everyone." Fannie drew herself up like a queen, mimicking. "'How dare you approach my table!' The woman's a Medusa! Poor man. They say he had tears in his eyes as he left."

"No." Gladys put a hand to her mouth. So cruel. Yet how lovely having tea on the verandah, gossiping with a woman who'd been a star before movies were even invented.

"So who did he marry?" And why did he say it wasn't real? she wondered.

"Her name is Jean Acker. Little nothing, calls herself an actress. But it isn't a marriage. She was at the dinner that night and felt sorry, invited him to another party. Then they spent a few days together, horseback riding and such. Valentino is as splendid on horseback as he is on the dance

98

floor, I hear." Fannie sighed, took another bite of rum cake. "At any rate, on a lark they got married in someone's parlor, and when they returned to her room at the Hollywood Hotel, little snip locked him out. Changed her mind. Left him waiting in the hall. His wedding night!" Fannie made a tsk tsk sound. "My friend Pauline Frederick told me. Her driver's wife runs the switchboard at the Hollywood Hotel. But I doubt we've heard the last of it."

"You think they'll work it out?"

"No, not that. Two hundred a week won't pay for fancy dresses and furs, much less a suite at the Hollywood, and heaven knows Nazimova's whims change faster than the tides. No, I think Miss Acker is calculating what she can get if... *when* Valentino makes it big."

"Goodness, I never thought of that."

"No, you wouldn't, my dear." She patted Gladys' hand. "But you'll see soon enough. This town. Like sharks tasting blood. Show people aren't exactly the most refined. But who is, underneath?" She laughed. "And when you add large sums of money... Oh, if I'd known that bitch Nazimova would show up at my party, I'd have canceled the whole thing!"

"Well, I'm glad you didn't." In the afternoon light Gladys noticed the lines around Fannie's eyes, the slight slackening in her cheeks. What a battle it must be, always trying to look ten or twenty years younger.

They sat watching Lasky and Pathé snarling over a stuffed burlap doll until the trainer pulled it away, tossed it again. Gladys felt almost light headed. These Hollywood stories. In a hundred years they'd never sort them out.

She stood, thanked Miss Ward for tea and her *illegal* cakes. "I'd better be going. The studio car is waiting."

"Of course."

Fannie walked Gladys through the house, their footsteps echoing on the marble floor.

At the front door she took her hand, brushed a kiss on one cheek, then the other. She spoke just above a whisper. "By the way, dear, Mr. Valentino has an apartment at Grand and Fifth. You can find him most afternoons at the Alexandria Hotel Bar down the street. Everyone goes there. Elegant yet informal. They say some of the biggest movie deals are made on the lobby's 'million dollar' carpet. Fannie smiled. "Well, I haven't been since this prohibition nonsense, but I imagine they've found a way around that, upstairs salon or something."

"It's been most charming," she added, "and do tell Rudy I said hello."

Chapter 20

When Gladys returned to her bungalow, she found Mabel in the living room. No lamp was on, and in the dim light she thought Mabel was asleep, leaned back in the wing chair. She was wearing the same pretty blue dress as the day they'd met. It looked as if it'd been taken in, yet still way too big. Like a little girl in hand-me-down. The interview with Mr. Von Stroheim was today. If Gladys had known she would've gotten Mabel a dress when they went shopping for the party.

It didn't make sense. Mabel had been at Sunshine since December and doing musicals as well. An extra fifty dollars a week. Was she sending money home to her family? But if her father owned a store in Atlanta and she had all those brothers... In Hollywood it seemed there were the stories people told to remake themselves, and then there was the truth.

But Gladys knew all she needed to know about Mabel.

She stepped closer. Mabel wasn't asleep. Her eyes open, staring out the darkening window. She'd been crying, makeup smeared, her hair mussed, her dress. Gladys knew the look. She'd seen it on her own face in the mirror, felt it. She remembered Mr. Cole. And those men lifting her into the back seat as if she were made of paper.

Gladys touched her arm. "Honey, what ha...?"

Mabel jumped, let out a yelp, which made Gladys do the same, laughing.

Mabel put her hands to her chest, breathed. "Land sakes, y'all 'bout scared the puddin' outta me. Sneakin' up like a derned Indjun." She wiped her eyes, grinning. To hide what happened.

Gladys knew about hiding what happened. She would not question her. She scrunched beside her in the big chair, hugging her close, and in minutes Mabel stumbled out bits and pieces.

"Mr. Von Stroheim forgot, I guess. He was in a meeting. Secretary didn't know a thing, like I just walked in off the street. I waited and waited... finally she sent me over to casting... Mr... oh, it don't matter. Disgusting man." She shuddered. "Gladys, that wasn't me. I never thought I'd let that happen. I thought I was strong..."

"You are." She held Mabel's shoulders. "Look at me. You are! You came all the way out here by yourself. You are strong."

"I 'spose..." Mabel's eyes filled again and she looked down. "He said he'd find me some parts... but if I made a fuss I'd never get more 'n a walk-on, not anywhere, he'd see to it. I thought of all I done for this, swallowin' that God awful worm, and..." She sobbed, closing her eyes tight. "I never told y'all, but..." Her voice broke.

Gladys touched her cheek. "It's okay. You don't have to tell me anything."

She held Mabel as she cried, and when she quieted, Gladys turned on the table lamp, reached a hanky from her purse, wiped the smudges below Mabel's eyes.

Moments passed. She blew her nose. When she spoke again, it was barely a whisper. "I have me a baby, Gladys. My Aunt Dora's got him over in Monroe. He just turned two. Nathan Andrew. He's so beautiful." Her eyes glowed for a moment, and she smiled. Then she looked away. "Craig don't know."

Gladys stayed still, fighting her own tears. A baby. It explained everything, but she would not let the slightest reaction show.

"This mornin'... somethin' just snapped inside me, I guess." Mabel's voice was different, hollow, like a screen door banging on an empty house. "You weigh it quicker 'n a blink. Make a fuss or let it slide on by. What the hell, it's only sex. Don't mean nothin.' Nothin' at all. That's true, ain't it?"

Gladys nodded. "Yes."

Mabel was quiet for several moments, and suddenly she untwined herself and sat up.

"No. It ain't sex. It's somethin' else entirely."

Gladys had to smile. She could almost see the thoughts churning, Mabel's voice no longer hollow.

"Oh, I know what sex is, believe me, and it ain't one bit what that little peanut of a man thinks he done to me." She turned, her eyes fierce, bluer than her baggy dress. "No, Gladys. It's... it's to remind us who's in charge. It's to break us so we'll be happy for... anything we can get. *Find me some parts.* Bastard! Why, it's like... like the plantation owner puttin' his brand on his darkies 'cause he can." She sniffed, shook her head. "Oh, if I'd a see'd it before... But that's how it is. You gotta walk through fire to burn the scales off 'n yer eyes."

Mabel paused. Her voice softened. "But I can't look at Craig right now. Not yet. Can I stay here tonight, Gladys?"

"Of course. As long as you want." A baby. But Gladys wouldn't ask. Give her time. Then she remembered. "Where's mamma, anyway?"

"She went to dinner with her new gentleman friend. Said to tell you not to wait up." Mabel smiled. "Your mamma. She must'a tried on a dozen hats decidin,' ended up changin' to another dress. Good thing, 'cause she didn't notice me lookin' like somethin' the hounds drug in. She's so cute."

103

"I know. The other night I was worried what she'd say about me coming in late from the party, and she wasn't even home yet. In the morning all she could talk about was Joe Mayer. That's his name. Even when I told how Miss Pickford made a point to come and talk to me, mamma went right back to her evening. Joe Mayer this, Joe Mayer that. He fought in the battle of the Marne but made it home, thank goodness. He has a little house in Pasadena. I never even got to tell her I danced with Valentino." Gladys smiled. "But I'm happy for her. Mamma needs something in her life besides me."

She wanted to tell Mabel about Howard's surprise, a night to hold the rest of her life, and how she lay in her bed thinking about it, decided she'd take love, or even just sex, whenever she chose, as long as it was her decision and there were precautions. Why not? Life was to be lived. And she'd never felt so alive...

Hardly the time to say that to Mabel. Instead Gladys told about having afternoon tea with Fannie Ward. About Nazimova and what Jean Acker did to Valentino.

"Poor Rudolpho. It ain't right." Mabel thought a moment. "But that Nazimova might be smarter than people think."

Gladys sat up. "How can you say that? She's... she's a bitch."

"Exactly! Maybe that's the best thing to be. That woman oozes power just walkin' into a room. Makin' her own movies, defyin' everybody. Barefoot!" She laughed, her eyes fierce again. "Men 're scared 'a her. Just move outta her way. She don't need a man for nothin.'"

Gladys smiled. "Well, that's true, more ways than one."

They sat a long time cuddled in the chair, and after awhile Gladys said, "Mabel, I don't mean to pry, but if you ever need anything for... your baby, anything at all, just tell me."

"Thanks, honey. That means a lot, but... I reckon I'll manage. I wire something every few weeks." Then her voice changed. "I tell Craig it's for my grandma's doctor bills. I hate that. But what if he didn't understand?"

Gladys nodded. "Do you have photographs of Nathan Andrew?"

"One. I keep it under the linin' of my suitcase. I'll show y'all someday."

She didn't say more. And Gladys saw how spoiled and coddled she must seem. An only child, mamma, Aunt Minnie and Uncle Tommy giving her the best of everything. Living free and easy now on her star's salary. What Mabel had gone through, pregnant, sent away, probably. Her family must be poor. Scraping to wire money for her baby. A baby she couldn't even hold. And now her rich friend offers to help. It felt awkward, a gap forming between them.

To live with such a secret.

She'd been keeping her own secret way too long. She turned, looked into Mabel's eyes. "There's something I've never told anyone. It was a long time ago when I was little, and I'm over it now, pretty much, but I think it'd be good if one person in the whole world could know."

"Of course, honey." Mabel's eyes filled with tears, but she smiled. "Lord, do I know what that's like. Y'all go on. Then I'll swap you how I met Nathan Andrew's daddy. There's a story. But one thing about a baby..." Her smile widened. "Y'all look at that little face, and every last regret just flies off like a flock 'a snow geese headin' south."

Chapter 21

He was there, standing at the bar.

Even with his back to her, she could tell it was him. Those shoulders and arms that held her in the tango. Not the least of Valentino's attraction was his body, lean and straight and proportioned. Impeccable in that finely tailored tweed suit. So European. Slicked black hair, not a strand out of place. If he was down and out, he still managed to dress the part.

She remembered the cushioned alcove from her night in *Stamboul*, but instead of Howard she imagined Valentino's naked body, olive skin and dark eyes far more fitting for a Turkish harem. No wonder she whispered his name. Her cheeks flushed, a tingling below her waist.

Silly girl, standing in the archway staring at his back, the grand lobby of the Alexandria Hotel behind her. Walking through felt like floating, all that scrollwork set off with bronze and marble. Soft green walls above carved wainscoting, white marble pillars, gilded settees, a forest of potted ferns. Crystal chandeliers straight from an Austrian palace and the famous "million dollar" Turkish carpet. All it needed was one of those huge rococo paintings, nymphs and satyrs cavorting in a glen.

She'd chosen the perfect dress, a drop-waist just past her knees, sheer organza over silk, frothy, the color of cream. Matching hat, ostrich plumes curved gently onto her shoulder. Heads turned, whispering. "Isn't that Gladys Walton, the *Pink Tights* girl? And *La La Lucille*. She's even prettier in person."

The bartender brought Rudolph a plate. They chatted a moment. Then Valentino turned toward a table where two other young men were seated, and it was as if her eyes drew him, or the silly beating of her heart. He looked up, and the slight melancholy that tinged his dark eyes vanished. He smiled.

The smile snapped her out. And some subtle clue. The brush of his hand on the other man's sleeve? The jeweled stick pin in his lapel? A ruby that size could not be real. He was wearing one of those flashy new wristwatches Uncle Tommy wouldn't be caught dead in. Sissified, Uncle Tommy would say, like wearing a bracelet. Was there more to this Valentino?

Friends. That's what he'd said at the party. It was enough. She adjusted, relieved, actually, to see him as a real person instead of the fantasy she'd been building. If he waged secret battles of his own - and who in Hollywood did not? - they would only have more in common.

Gladys walked forward. He set the plate on the table, met her half way.

"Miss Walton, how nice. You look stunning. Like a cloud." That certain quality in his voice, as if nothing in the world mattered but standing here. If sound could caress... And that accent.

He seemed about to touch one of the plumes on shoulder, then glanced behind her. "You are perhaps... meeting someone?"

"You." She laughed. "Fannie Ward told me where to find you. She said to say hello. But it took weeks to get up my nerve." No reason not to flirt.

"Come, sit with us. We are honored." He directed her to the table.

Nothing sissified about his hand on her back, tingles again. What a mystery, Valentino.

He introduced the two men, names she would not remember, pale attendants grinning, like boys from Kansas compared to Rudolpho. One with sandy hair and freckles, the other tall and thin. They stood, shook her hand across the table. She felt the camaraderie, soldiers laughing it up between battles.

"We are brothers," Rudy smiled, "of the... what is the word...?"

"Notch," the tall one said. "Brothers Of The Notch."

What was he saying? Counting conquests? "I'm afraid I don't..."

"As in belt." The man laughed, patting his waist. "You know, tightening, taking it in a notch. We are the starving actors club."

"Ah," she laughed, "I see."

Rudy seated her beside him. "And this is our kitchen." He swept his hand, indicating the room and the three small plates on their table. "I can offer you a ham sandwich? They are hot," his eyes twinkled, "and free." He smiled. "We dine here often, but today is special, a celebration."

"Then, of course I'll have a sandwich," she said, and the freckled man hurried to the bar. "What are we celebrating?"

"These weeks I was in New York with a Dorothy Phillips film." Valentino waved his hand in dismissal, "same nothing character, Italian Count up to no good." His voice rose. "But one day I got a call... oh, that day!" He looked around, lowered his voice, but the excitement was in his eyes. It seemed to thicken his accent, and Gladys leaned forward, listening closely.

"It was to meet Mr. Rowland at Metro, the New York office. He told them they must hurry my scenes so I can return. I just came yesterday. It is the Ibanez book, *Four Horsemen of the Apocalypse*. Big production. Serious, full of war and sorrow, and..." his voice almost broke, "and they want me. June Mathis writes the script. She is the best, and the director Rex Ingram. Miss Mathis saw *Eyes of Youth*, insisted they give me the part. Can you believe?"

She touched his hand. "I am so happy for you, Rudy. Who do you play?"

"Julio, the Argentine gaucho. In love with Alice Terry. It could not be more perfect. They put in a tango scene. It is a role with teeth, as they say." He grinned. "And the best? I get to die."

"Oh, how wonderful!" She clapped her hands. "If only one of my characters would die."

The boys from Kansas laughed. "So much for the Brotherhood," the tall one said, "your notches will go the other way now."

"Tell her what you did." The one with freckles laughed harder. "I wish I'd seen it."

Valentino looked down, blushing. "I did not..."

"But you were about to." Freckle face turned to Gladys. "He tried to kiss Mr. Rowland's hand. Top executive at Metro, guy about fell out of his chair." He slapped his knee, laughing.

"It was nothing," Rudy whispered, his dark eyes flashing. "We do this... in the old country. Gratitude, no more. I should never have told you."

Then the irritation was gone, and he looked quickly at his wristwatch.

"Madre mia, I am late. I must go." He sat forward. "Gladys, you will come with me? You did not drive here?"

She shook her head. "No, I took the Red Car."

He stood. "Come, then. We wrap the sandwiches, eat them in the car. Such a car! Wait 'til you see. I will give you a ride you will not forget."

Her eyes widened. "That car outside is yours? What is it?"

It was parked in front, where the doorman could keep an eye on it, probably. Like no car she'd ever seen. She'd walked around it twice so she could tell Uncle Tommy. Bright yellow and so long it had six wheels, two axles in back. Huge engine compartment, like a limousine and speedster combined. The front where the chauffeur sat was completely open air, a convertible top for the distant passengers. A car for kings and emperors and Hollywood stars.

"Hispano Suiza," Valentino said, "made in Barcelona." He laughed. "But sadly she is not mine. I borrowed her from friends. Italians. They have a mechanic shop on Sunset. I help sometimes." He saw her eyes, smiled. "Yes, a dancer who can hold a wrench. Someday I will own many such cars. Do the work myself."

He took her hand, and she stood. "Then I will come take you for rides. What do you think? Even when we are old and forgotten, we will drive fast with the wind. Our hair will be silver, and we will wear..." he touched his neck, drew his hand out to the side, "what is it called?"

"Scarf." She smiled.

"Yes. Our scarves blowing. Would that not be fine?"

"Very."

Leave it to someone from the old country to have dramatic visions of the end when he's just getting started. It would be so easy to fall in love with him, if she could ever decide who he really was. Maybe that's what was so captivating. Innocent, almost childlike, yet she sensed a kind of aura shrouding him, layers and layers.

He touched the ostrich plume by her throat. His eyes held her. "For our ride you must take this off. It is a hat far too beautiful to risk. Like you, I think."

HISPANO SUIZA VICTORIA TOWN CAR
6-Cylinder 6-Wheel Model H6A
Barcelona, Spain

The Hispano Suiza was very popular as a sports car as well as a glamorous luxury automobile. In their time they were the most expensive cars in the world and were fitted with the most elegant bodywork of the period. They became the favorite of Royalty in Europe and India as well as wealthy celebrities. Hispano Suiza set a standard of quality, innovation and performance that no others could match.

Sometime during the 1930's, a Hispano Suiza was bought by the Hollywood director D.W. Griffith for $35,000, and used in several of his films.

Chapter 22

On their way through the grand lobby, a slight, dapper man in a dark three-piece suit approached them. His hair was wavy, and he looked familiar twirling a pearl handled cane, but Gladys could not think where she'd seen him. He appraised her a bit too long before turning to Rudy.

"Well, chap," he said in a British accent, "you're looking considerably more cheerful than last we met, and I certainly see why." He stared at Gladys, held out his hand. "And who might this beauty be?"

"Sir Charles Chaplin," Rudy said, "may I introduce Gladys Walton. The new Glad Girl for Universal."

"Ah, yes, the parachute scene." He shook her hand. "Quite a feat. A fetching costume too."

"Mr. Chaplin, it's an honor. I didn't recognize you, but everyone must say that."

"Yes, yes they do." He laughed. "But I'm not always such a tramp, whatever the newspapers print." The famous Chaplin wink. "Well, I won't keep you." He glanced at Valentino then again at her. He patted Rudy's arm, a kind of congratulations. "You take good care of her, now. A gem, yes, indeed."

She felt his eyes on her as they walked away. When they reached the gilded doors Valentino leaned close and whispered, "Do not worry, Gladys, you are much too old for Charlie Chaplin."

He held the door, and they walked out to the Hispano Suiza.

Behind the wheel, Valentino seemed to make yet another transformation, and she with him, grinning, carefree, absorbed in power and speed, the thrust of the massive engine, the long, sleek lines, all that car behind them. Like riding the shoulders of a yellow dragon.

Late or not, he took a detour down the long empty stretch to Santa Monica, past acres of bean fields, the gauge edging past eighty, ninety. How could human beings go so fast? A speed to chase away all thought, all yearnings. As fast as an aeroplane.

"It is the engine of the Spad VIII they flew in the war," he said, reading her mind again, leaning close so she could hear over the wind.

"Like Skeets Elliot's plane." She nodded, felt the slightest brush of his lips on her ear, breathed his cologne, a faint scent of tobacco, his skin.

Friends, she reminded herself.

He parked on a cliff in Malibu, and they watched the sunset tracing flares across the waves, a red ball on the horizon. She wanted to pull him to her, feel his perfect body against her. She wanted him to look at her with that fire she'd seen in *Eyes of Youth*, but she thought of what he'd said, *too beautiful to risk*. If only she were older. He thought she was a virgin, probably, and with his old country beliefs... How could she tell him? She was tired of this sweet young thing image, in her movies too, only playing at seduction while the Hollywood life seemed to swirl just out of reach. Even so, he was still married. She breathed the chill air, trying to still the fluttering in her chest.

"So when do you think we will dance again, Rudy?"

"Now."

"Here?"

"Why not?" He smiled, opening his door. "One dance, then I must return our carriage." He got out, swept his arm in a slight bow. "Mademoiselle, comme tu desire."

She scooted out, laughing, her heels sinking in the soft grass. She slipped off her shoes, and he twirled her in a Viennese waltz, wide circles there on a grassy cliff overlooking the sea, the light fading around them.

"You speak French too?" she said.

He nodded. "My mother was French. I spoke it as a child."

"Really. My father was French, a Gypsy."

"Ah yes."

And he spun them faster, no longer a waltz. "The dance of my village," he said, "the tarantella. They say it cures the tarantula bite if you spin fast enough... and drink enough Sambuca." He saw the question in her eyes. "A drink of my country, the flavor of licorice. I love licorice almost like I love spaghetti. I will cook it for you sometime. Spaghetti with meatballs. I am a master of this dish." He grinned, dipping her low. "Come, it is late, little Gypsy princess." And he kissed her, once, as light as the breeze.

On the way back he drove even faster, and she closed her eyes, thinking, to die now might not be so bad. And yet, to miss what lay ahead?

They pulled into the shop on Sunset Boulevard just as his friends were cranking down the metal door. The two men hurried toward them, talking loud in Italian, cursing, she thought, but their anger vanished when Valentino introduced them to the *Pink Tights* girl. They bowed and kissed her hand, talking excitedly.

"They ask for a photograph," Rudy said. "With your name signed. I told them you will bring one." He patted the man's shoulder. "Otherwise Luigi makes me work one week for free."

"He said that?"

"No. I joke."

"Tell them I'll bring movie passes as well."

He translated, and their faces lit up more.

Waiting with her at the nearest trolley stop, Rudy stood in the light of the gas lamp and wrote his address and the switchboard number on a card. He had moved to a small apartment not far from the mechanics shop. "Morgan Place. Across the street is Wallace Reid," he said. "He wakes me with his saxophone."

She slipped the card into her purse. They stood silently for some time. The night clear, studded with stars. Valentino lit a cigarette and offered her one, she shook her head.

In another moment he said, "Have you been out to the desert yet, Gypsy?"

"You mean Palm Springs? Goodness no, I've had no time. I could only come today because they canceled the afternoon shoot. Something with one of the cameras. It's been hectic lately."

"What is this word, hectic?"

She smiled. "Busy. Too many things happening. My mother has been staying with me, and now she's going back home, so she's skittering around packing and all this shopping. Things she can't get back in Oregon. And mamma keeps postponing because of this man she's seeing." She looked up. "She's been alone all these years. My father left when I was a baby."

He nodded, his eyes sad. "Of course. Gypsies do that."

"But this new man is nice. I like him. He was in the war, and he seems to love my mother very much already. She'll visit and... What is it, Rudy?" Tears. What had she said?

He tossed his cigarette, pulled the handkerchief from his breast pocket, wiping his eyes.

"No, you must not..." his words choked, "I am sorry..." He sniffed, tried again. "You must not let your mother go. Oh, if I could bring my mamma..." He sobbed.

She touched his arm. She had never seen a man cry, certainly not her German grandfather.

"Why don't you bring her, Rudy? Now that you have this new film, you can."

He closed his eyes tight, drew a deep breath, his voice a whisper.

"She is dead. A letter came from my brother. Two years, five months... but I feel it like yesterday. She was everything. She and my sister... they went to France to help the wounded, and she grew sick..." He paused, got control. "I saw her last on the dock in Naples. She paid my ticket. And more. I was eighteen." He looked away. "I was not a good son. But here I thought to show her..."

Gladys waited, searching for what to say. She wanted to take him in her arms and rock him. A man with such feeling. "She knows, Rudy. Don't you think?"

"Mmm, perhaps. I hope." He took out another cigarette, lit it, taking long draws, and his eyes gradually calmed.

"The Red Car is late," she said.

He nodded. "They break sometimes."

She looked at the scattered lights along Sunset, the glow from Hollywood Boulevard.

"So tell me about this desert of yours."

"Ah, it is a strange beauty. Not much there. Palm Springs is a village, few hotels, bungalows, but it's growing. Ten miles to the train. A watering stop, that's all. I went early this year with... someone I met."

He dropped his cigarette, crushed it with his shoe.

"You feel the emptiness, and... it is a place to see the truth of things, I think. Alone, yet not alone. Critters. Lots of

116

critters. I learned that word. Lizards and coyotes and funny birds that run." He looked up. The smile was back. "We will go some day. I will teach you to ride. A fast horse is almost better than the Suiza. There the palm trees have long beards. We will find an oasis and dance the tango for the owls."

Chapter 23

Gladys didn't see Rudy for a long time after that. Weeks and months were swallowed up in work, glamorous and fun, but still work. Even before *Risky Business* wrapped, they started "prelims" for *The Secret Gift*. Both films were for fall release, and by late summer they'd start the list for 1921. Five scripts were lined up, Acquisitions was looking for more. Like dime novels, the same thin story line, characters and plots dolled up with different names and settings. *All Dolled Up* was number three on the list, in fact, between *Desperate Youth* and *Short Skirts*, then *High Heels, Playing With Fire*.

What did she care? She was seventeen. Plenty of time ahead for more important roles. Anyway, for one of those serious, work-of-art films, she'd have to change studios. Universal didn't make movies like *Way Down East* or *The Four Horsemen of the Apocalypse*. Carl Laemmle was the Henry Ford of the film industry, it seemed, whisking her and others like her along the assembly line. Still, five hundred dollars a week and nothing but star billing wasn't bad. Rudy had struggled for years for a film like *The Four Horsemen*, and his offer was three-fifty a week, and most likely his name would appear in the credits no bigger than anyone else's.

Yet sometimes when Gladys came home to the bungalow she felt an emptiness. Exhausted, she slumped into the wing chair. Mamma was out with Joe Mayer. Mabel shared Gladys' room now, but they rarely saw each other. During the day Mabel scurried between sets for bit parts in several different movies, or took the studio bus out to location to be an extra in crowd scenes. Evenings she'd hurry off to dance in whatever show was playing at the Arcade or Lowes. Saturday mornings mamma would bring coffee and breakfast, and they'd stack the pillows and catch up.

Gladys sat too tired to move. She thought of that evening dancing barefoot on that grassy cliff. She thought of Fannie Ward's party and the night with Howard. She missed Howard and his lectures, in a way, their Sunday afternoon movies. Maybe she'd made a mistake.

When she went to the Alexandria a few weeks after their ride in the Suiza, Rudy was not there.

"Are you okay, Princess?"

Gladys opened her eyes.

Mamma stood beside her making tsk, tsk sounds. "Terrible, isn't it? How they let such a thing happen, I'll never know. Both dead." She shook her head. "Well, come on, I'll draw you a bath..."

"Dead?" Gladys thought of Uncle Tommy and Aunt Minnie driving down from Oregon. They were due tomorrow or the next day.

"Who, mamma? What happened?"

"You didn't see? They were filming at night. There was a crash. It's in the evening paper. I left it here on the table for you. I didn't know Mr. Elliot was a lieutenant."

Gladys took the paper, read quickly. A scene for *The Skywayman*, a Fox Production, shot over oil fields near Los Angeles, a plane plummeting from five thousand feet. Unusual to film at night. Phosphorous flares on the wings to make it look like the plane was on fire. On the final spiraling dive the ground crew was supposed to kill the searchlights to signal when the pilots should pull out. They never did. The plane crashed in the pool of an oil well. Lieutenants Ormer Locklear and Milton "Skeets" Elliot died instantly.

Her eyes filled. The date on the paper was August 2, 1920. Six months ago Skeets had talked her through the parachute scene that launched her career. "Don't look down," he'd said. "Keep your eyes on me."

She blinked, wiped her eyes. There was more to the article. It did not surprise her. The cameras caught the entire scene. Fox was rushing to release the film. Ten percent of the profits would go to the families of the men who had died. Of course.

Chapter 24

At lunch the next day Gladys had the driver take her down to Lucille's dress shop on Hollywood Boulevard. They had started shooting *Desperate Youth*, same basic story but set in post Civil War Alabama, and she was in full makeup, her hair a cascade of ringlets. On the streets of Hollywood it wasn't unusual to see actors in cowboy or Indian or swashbuckler garb waiting for the Red Car or lunching at a corner diner.

She hurried into the shop and bought a black hat and veil, a simple black sheath. It would become her "funeral" dress. She could not know how many times she would wear it in the next few years.

She was back with her packages in time to find Howard in his office.

"Of course," he said when she asked for time off to go to the services. He stood, removing his glasses. "Terrible accident. I could go with you, if you want."

She hesitated. Howard looked older and still bland, but maybe that was better than her... illusions. How many Valentinos could there be? Even Rudy must have his own not-so-handsome realities.

"Uncle Tommy will be here," she said, "I'm sure he'll take me." She turned, half regretting the words. But it was a funeral. Better to go with her uncle. Fewer whispers.

"And Gladys..."

She turned back.

"I've been meaning to tell you. I have an offer from Lasky, a full directorship."

"That's wonderful. Congratulations. You deserve it."
Her tone didn't match the words. It wouldn't be the same
without Howard. "When?"

"End of next week. And there's something else...
you'll like it. I was waiting until the deal finalized." He came
around the desk, walked slowly to her.

His draw-it-out smile, like a drum roll that goes on too
long. If Howard was an editor her films would be three hours
long.

But when he took her hands she remembered other
moves he had drawn out quite nicely, and the memory of lying
naked on those cushions washed through her. She couldn't
help it. She pulled his hands behind her back, stood on tiptoes,
kissed him.

"Gladys, I don't think..." He freed a hand to check his
pocket watch, but she stopped him, grinning up at him. Her
Mazie Darnton look and a dozen other teasing scenes, harmless
seduction that ended with only a kiss.

No cameras now.

"A quick good-bye," she breathed, "that's all. Come
on." She kissed him again, tugging at his belt, nodding toward
the divan. She was pouring herself into an adult career,
earning adult money. Why not? These were new times, the
old rules didn't apply.

He seemed to hesitate, not much of a kiss, then he drew
back.

"Gladys, not here. The secretary might..." He looked
at his watch. "We need to get back to the set."

She looked up, felt her cheeks flush. So serious, his
voice stern. What was wrong with him? It would be fun. Who
cared if they were a little late? Embarrassing... No, it was his
problem. She shrugged. Mabel was right, Howard was not her
type. She needed to burn, not toast her toes.

"I think we should've met five years from now," Howard said, tucking in his belt. "Maybe then you'll be ready to settle down."

She forced a smile. "In five years I'll be twenty-two, Howard. Hardly a spinster."

She re-pinned a stray ringlet. All right, she thought, work. Go by Wardrobe, change into her *Desperate Youth* costume. Check her makeup and hair. Then she remembered what else she wanted.

She turned, straightened his bow tie. "Howard, sweetheart, could you at least do something for me?"

"Mmm." He didn't look at her.

"Well..." She put her hands on her hips. You had to be firm in this business. "If I'm doing the same silly movie over and over with no say in the matter and making them all this money, they could at least let me go a bit early Fridays and Saturdays so I can do something I want."

He raised an eyebrow. "I'm afraid to ask what that might be."

Dance, she almost said, but best not to remind him how she'd left him alone while she tangoed with Valentino. Was that what this was about, punishing her?

"Musical reviews," she said. "They're casting one next week. Oh, Howard, Mabel says it's the cat's pajamas. No waiting around for crews or someone else's scene. No re-shooting. Would you talk to Laemmle? Please?" She touched his cheek.

He shrugged. "I'll do what I can. Now let's go, Gladys. We're late. Where did I put my glasses?"

She brought them from his desk.

At the door she stopped, remembering how he'd walked to her, took her hands. His drum roll look. Something about a deal being finalized.

"You were going to tell me something, Howard. Before. You said I'd like it."

"Ah, yes. We found your circus movie. They'll shoot early next year. Harry Harris is going to direct. You will like it, fits you to a T. It's called *The Lion Tamer*. Kitty Horrigan, star of the big top." He smiled. "You'll be working with real lions."

GLADYS WALTON
As Kitty Horrigan in "The Lion Tamer"

Gladys, at only 17, was working with live lions on this set.
Circus movies were in great demand during the 20's.

Chapter 25

"Are you okay? What are you doing?"

The bathroom sounds had wakened her. Then drawers and cabinets opening in the kitchen, the clank of utensils.

Gladys rubbed her eyes, blinking into the light. It was almost 3:00 A.M.

Mabel stood at the counter trying to crush something in a bowl with a spoon. She was trembling and pale, her hair matted, face glistening with sweat, although the night was cool. November.

"Pumpkin seeds," Mabel said. She didn't look up, just kept working the spoon.

"Pumpkin seeds?"

"Yep. Gotta grind 'em real good, 'most to a powder. Mix it with milk." She nodded to the quart bottle open on the counter. Her voice was flat.

Gladys moved closer, trying to understand. Pumpkin seeds? In the bowl, she could see it was more stirring than crushing, seeds slipping from under the spoon, only a few breaking in pieces.

"Lord 'a mercy! This ain't easy." Mabel adjusted her grip, her thumb in the hollow of the spoon. Shoulders hunched, she pushed harder, trying to hold the seeds in place with her other hand, but some spilled over the edge. She scooped them up, started again.

"Need one 'a them things they use at the drug store... That'd work." She shook her head. "Should 'a thought... Stupid. Stupid no 'count girl."

She ground harder, but then the bowl slipped, knocking the bottle over, milk splattering on the scattered seeds.

Gladys grabbed the bottle, set it up. "Don't worry, there's still plenty. I'll clean it..." She stopped.

Mabel was staring, hands to her mouth, and the look in her eyes... It was almost terror.

Gladys should've seen. Mabel's dancing had been off tonight. It wasn't like her to miss steps or struggle to keep up.

"Come on, honey." Gladys put a hand on her shoulder. "You're shaking. You need to sit down. In the morning I'll call the infirmary."

"No! Not that!" Mabel drew back, pushed her hand away. "Promise. Gladys, you have to promise. I mean it. They can't know... I'm just scraping by, and I... I have to send more money. My aunt needs more money." Her voice choked to a whisper. "I... I need... a towel... could you get me... please..." She covered her mouth, trying not to retch. Then her legs buckled, and she sank to her knees, vomiting again and again.

Gladys ran to the bathroom, grabbed towels, soaked one with water, was back in seconds. She knelt and wiped Mabel's mouth and hands. She was crying, her eyes and nose streaming, and Gladys held her, there on the floor, swallowing her own tears, trying not to grimace with the smell. Or to look too closely at what had come out of Mabel's stomach. What did a tapeworm do to a person? Who could she ask?

"It's all right, I'm here. I'll take care of everything. Don't worry, you'll be fine. You look better already."

"I do?"

"Absolutely."

She wiped Mabel's face again, handed her the towel. Her eyes did look clearer. It always helped to throw up. Maybe it was just the influenza, but the thought made her cringe. No one said "just the influenza" any more. Not after 1918.

She felt Mabel's forehead and cheeks. She didn't have a fever.

In a few minutes Gladys helped her stand, got her to the bathroom. She drew a warm tub, but when she took off Mabel's soiled robe and lay it on the chair, something fell from the pocket. Gladys picked it up. A photograph.

When Mabel first moved in she had pulled a photograph from the lining of her suitcase and showed her. A baby in a woman's arms, his face almost hidden by the blanket. Even then it was hard to comprehend. A baby. But this was a toddler standing on chubby legs, holding onto a chair, delight in his eyes. He was dressed in a little white tunic, a wide collar crocheted at the edges, shiny black shoes, white leggings with buttons all the way down, his blond hair combed to the side. Nathan Andrew.

Gladys looked up. "He's beautiful. Look how he's grown!"

Mabel smiled. "He took his first step, my aunt said. Last month. The letter came yesterday."

"Oh, Mabel, you must be so proud."

Mabel nodded, bit her lip.

Their eyes held a moment, and Gladys tried to think of something more to say. What else was there?

"Well, let's get you cleaned up. At least tomorrow's Sunday." Gladys slipped the photograph back into the pocket of the robe, then pulled the nightgown over Mabel's head, but when she saw the corset, she couldn't hide her surprise.

Mabel shrugged. "It's my belly. Beats all, don't it? Pencil thin 'n I get a dern paunch. That's what them seeds 're for. Somethin' in pumpkin seeds a worm don't like. Least that's what the China man said. Craig took me yesterday. Paralyzes 'im so's I can get my strength back 'n not be running

127

to the W.C...." She looked down. "I'm sorry for wakin' y'all, honey. It's just, I get to thinkin,' this... creature inside me." Her hands went to her abdomen. "My stomach makes the slightest gurgle and I imagine it flappin' its tail, dining on my innards, maybe hatchin' out younguns..." She shuddered, her whole body shaking. "I get nightmares, and... whew-ee, I stink like a dead polecat, don't I?" She laughed.

There was no better sound in the world than Mabel's laugh.

Gladys pulled her close. "Nothing to be sorry about," she whispered, "nothing at all." She made her voice lift. "I've never seen a polecat, much less smelled one. But, yes, you most definitely do stink. Let's get you in the tub."

She retrieved the robe, wrapped it around Mabel's shoulders, started unhooking the corset. A long process. Even without having to will your hands not to tremble, eyes not to blur. Paralyze, she thought. Why not kill? There had to be a way to get rid of it.

She helped Mabel in. "There, warm bath, you'll be like new, then you can get some rest. Lean back, we'll wash your hair too." She lathered and rinsed, forcing herself not to glance again at the bulge in Mabel's abdomen. "I'll tackle those pumpkin seeds," she said. "That crystal perfume bottle mamma forgot must weigh a pound or two. It's a Hoya. It'll grind those seeds to dust. We'll get you in bed, then I'll bring you a pumpkin milkshake."

Chapter 26

Gladys stepped into the ring, cracked the whip, and a dozen big cats loped in a circle around her. One by one they rose on their haunches, snarling, pawing the air. The crowd cheered, and Gladys turned and bowed low. Kitty Horrigan, her favorite roll since Mazie. No flammable skirt this time, but a high collared jacket and snug pants, bright red with plenty of gold braid, a cap to match.

There'd been no real circus scenes in *Pink Tights*, but for *The Lion Tamer* Universal set up a huge big top, and for the week of shooting her lion scenes filled it with thousands of tourists from eight hundred cities, every state and many foreign countries. The gate man kept track. What a treat to work before such an audience, energy pulsing the air.

Aunt Minnie and Uncle Tommy made the trip again and had special seats, mamma too, holding Joe Mayer's hand. Craig was there, mainly to watch Mabel in her bit parts. Mabel wore a ballerina costume and rode bareback on a fancy white horse with a silver plume, then she scurried to change to a trapeze outfit and ran around the back in time to end the parade.

Mabel seemed better, tired and a little weak sometimes, but no more bouts like that night. The pumpkin seeds must be working.

Each day the cameras rolled as Gladys put the lions through their paces, big old tired beasts, gentle as pussy cats, really, trained to act ferocious at the snap of a whip. Learning the whip had been her main challenge, but she finally got the

129

knack, and Bart Bundy, the real trainer was never far away, disguised as clown.

The best part was when the lecherous circus owner corners Kitty Horrigan behind a wagon and tries to force himself on her, but Kitty struggles free, runs and grabs her whip.

"Back, Mr. Delmar, back, you randy old goat!" Gladys yelled, snapping the whip a little too close to his curled mustache, but of course the words on the screen would be different.

On the last day in the big top, the lions must've sensed their job was almost over because they outdid themselves, shaking their mangy ruffs, showing more fang than usual, their growls sending a wave of lion halitosis. With her final bow the applause was deafening. She thought she heard a thud behind her, and the crowd hushed. She turned, gripping the whip, half expecting to be mauled in front of two thousand fans, but the lions hadn't moved from their wooden blocks... except the big one on the end. Goliath.

He had tottered off his perch, apparently, and lay on his side in the sawdust, tongue out. Gladys glanced at the crowd, thought a moment. Then she walked to the big cat, knelt and petted him, the whip ready in her other hand. Eleven lions a few feet away. Murmurs and gasps from the stands. "Holy cow! What is she doing?" She leaned and gave Goliath a big hug, her head on his chest.

Listening for a heartbeat, actually.

Then she stood with a wide grin, arms up, flexing her muscles, one foot on Goliath's back. The audience went wild, hooting and whistling, stomping their feet, shaking the stands. The cameras kept rolling. For the film they'd cut in another lion getting up, make it look like part of the act.

But poor Goliath was a goner.

Gladys *and* Capone, *the Untold Story*

By spring of 1921 there were five Gladys Walton films in current release. She attended premiere after premiere at Los Angeles theaters, each time stepping from the limousine in a different stunning gown on loan from Universal. She signed souvenir photos and spoke to reporters from *Photoplay, Motion Picture World, The Examiner*. She went to opening night parties on the arm of one leading man after another. She left with someone else, usually, but at least she made the proper entrance.

In April she took the train east for the New York and Chicago premieres. A pleasant break from filming, but when she returned, she'd hardly unpacked her bags before they started work on next year's list. *The Guttersnipe, The Girl Who Ran Wild, Lavender Bath Lady, Top O' The Morning, The Wise Kid*. In *Second Hand Rose* Gladys would play the character from the hit song made famous by Fannie Brice in the Ziegfeld Follies.

Each film ended with a proposal and that magic happily-ever-after kiss, a far cry from her real life. For awhile she dated one of the writers, if you could call dinner and a night in his cramped apartment dating. Then a director of photography and a few of her leading men, but they were hardly more interesting than the characters they played.

She had money, anyway, and bought an armoire for her overflow of dresses and gowns, evening wraps and headpieces, and most of all shoes. Like mamma with her hats, Gladys decided you could never have too many shoes.

Every few weeks she offered to help Mabel with money for Nathan Andrew, but Mabel always refused. "I'm managin'" she'd say, "it's gettin' better."

Gladys bought a huge Packard Touring car, big enough to transport half the cast out to location, although she rarely used it for that. She drove it herself or Craig would drive and escort Mabel and Gladys to Hollywood parties or dance halls

131

and late dinners at Musso and Frank's. "A princess on each arm," he'd say, "if that ain't the berries!" Craig was their anchor. To Gladys, he seemed the brother she never had. Quiet and steady, but always that twinkle, and when you least expected, he'd come out with a one liner that set the whole table laughing.

When Sunshine Comedy folded, Craig decided the Hollywood life was best experienced from the fringe, and he took a job selling automobiles at a dealership on Wilshire, and within weeks was assistant manager. It was Craig who got her the deal on the Packard. His plan was to run a chauffeur business on the side, build a fleet of limos, starting with a half-interest in the Packard. In time he'd buy her out, find her a jauntier car.

"I'm thinking of investing in a few of those 'encyclopedia lots' over in Huntington," he told her the day she picked up the Packard. "We're in an oil boom, you know. Besides the land's gotta be worth something sooner or later, and for the price of a set of encyclopedias, might as well. No sense letting these out-of-towners grab 'em all up."

Craig and his schemes. Gladys wished she could tell him about Nathan Andrew, but you never knew how a man would react, and it wasn't her place. Craig adored Mabel, anyone could see, but he didn't pressure her to accept his standing marriage proposal. On the dance floor of one club or another, Gladys would hear them playing their will-you-marry-me game, "Now, honey bee?" he'd say. "Anyway you like, justice of the peace or the whole shebang."

And Mabel would laugh. "Nope, not yet, but y'all 'er welcome to keep tryin'."

"Well," he'd grin, "no hurry. Plenty of years for making babies. We'll keep practicing." And later Gladys would hear their murmurs through the wall. When Craig stayed they slept in mamma's old room.

No hurry. They were living in the best possible time to be young. Everyone felt it. The War To End All Wars was fading into the past, along with senseless rules. What morality dictates the length of a hem while a million young men die in one battle? Prohibition was just a joke. A remnant of by gone days, like bustles and lace collars.

In the weeks between musical revues, the three of them would start early on a Saturday night and search out one of these new speakeasies sprouting up all over. They'd just get in the Packard and drive, Culver City and Santa Monica, at first. Then they ventured farther, the more remote the better. A town might not have a gas station but always a speakeasy. In places like El Monte or Topanga or Chino, Gladys might spend a whole evening with no one recognizing her. In Riverside they played cards in a back room and drank homemade beer. In Anza they went to a barn dance, farm boys with muscles bulging under their flannel shirts, the night rich with the smell of alfalfa. When the music stopped, they could hear the horses tied outside, shifting and blowing air.

She was a star, a flapper, yet her nights of drinking and having fun weren't all that often. If a man were interested he soon realized her work came first. She was not wife material.

It was in New York that she finally saw Rudy again, at the Biltmore Hotel. She was having tea and reading a newspaper. After Lieutenant Elliot's funeral she rarely passed a day without at least glancing through the paper.

"May I?" he said simply.

The voice, the accent. Even before she looked up she felt her cheeks and throat redden.

"Rudy, how nice. Yes, of course." She folded the paper. "I... I looked for you at the Alexandria. More times than I should say, I'm afraid." What was it about this man that suddenly turned her to pulp? Tailored suit and silk tie, sideburns, that cologne. She glanced down, Italian leather shoes, spats!

No, his eyes.

"I am flattered," he said, setting his felt hat on the table. He sat beside her. "You look as beautiful as our day in the Suiza, Gladys. I think often of that day. And your movies, they are everywhere!" He teased, "Gladys Walton in *High Heels*, Gladys Walton *Playing With Fire*. And *The Rowdy*. What is this word, rowdy?"

She laughed. "Wild, rambunctious."

"Ram...bunc... Hmm, sounds like something you need medicine for. But I saw *The Man Tamer*." He nodded. "Most impressive. Congratulations."

He looked so happy, like a boy holding some treasure, a robin's egg, a puppy with six toes.

"Thank you, but... Goodness, Rudy, have you seen the paper? *The Four Horsemen* is all over the entertainment section. They're calling it a masterpiece! Look." She opened to the page, found the line. He leaned in. "'...beyond anything as yet achieved by the drama,'" she read. "And here. It says fifteen hundred people were turned away at the Lyric. They expect it to break the record set by *Way Down East*."

The blend of his cologne with the musk of those Abullah cigarettes he smoked. She steadied her hand. "You did it, Rudy. You're there!"

He beamed, nodding to the paper. "I can have this? I saw other articles, but not this. I only hope it lasts. And you, Gladys? Did you like *The Horsemen*?"

There, that look. She didn't think he was even conscious of it, something instinctive, animal. That a glance could suggest some rare and mystic bond.

She looked down. "Rudy... I haven't seen it yet. Those long lines. People recognize me, and..."

"Ah, yes, I know."

Women at other tables were staring, tittering together, and they both knew only her presence was keeping them away.

"Well," he said, "in two weeks you must come to the Mission Theater in Los Angeles. We will protect you, put you in the front row. You will be in L.A. in two weeks?"

"Yes. I leave tomorrow."

"Good then." He nodded to the small band playing in the corner. Every large hotel had a dance floor in their tea room now. "No we will dance," he smiled, a slight nod toward the tittering women, "and you can protect me."

But before they could stand, a woman approached their table. She was tall and wore a straight, ankle length dress and one of those stylish new turbans. Low-heeled shoes! It seemed more a costume than a dress, sumptuous purple fabric draped just so, its sheen accented by scarves and layers of clunky jewelry. How exotic she looked, bohemian, her pale skin, coils of black hair peeking from under the turban, blue eyes outlined with kohl, lips sculpted a deep red. Formidable, icy. She walked like a ballerina, never moving her head.

Gladys had only seen the style in magazines, the Paris designer, Poiret. A look to make anyone next to her seem a frump, which was exactly how Gladys felt. Reminded her of The Great Nazimova. In fact, she thought this woman might've been in Nazimova's retinue that night at Fanny Ward's party.

But most surprising, almost beyond belief, was how this woman's presence could make Rudolph Valentino change the moment he saw her. He seemed shorter, as if he were shrinking, and for the first time Gladys noticed his right ear was crinkled on top. His magnificent film had opened to rave reviews, thousands and thousands lining up at theaters across America to see it, but as he stood, his aura simply vanished.

"Rudy, darling," the woman said, "I hope I didn't keep you waiting too long."

"Not at all. I was just chatting with... Gladys, may I introduce... Natacha Rambova."

His tone, that little pause, as if she were an empress. It took several seconds for Miss Rambova to unfurl a gloved hand. And Gladys could not stop the thoughts. Was she supposed to kiss it? Maybe click her heels and bow?

She stayed seated, smiled, shook the Ice Queen's hand. "It's so nice to meet you."

Yet how striking they were together, magnificent, each complimenting the other with a unique style and grace, as if posed for a portrait. The perfectly matched couple, physically, anyway.

"Miss Rambova was the art director on *Camille*," Rudy said. "Her work is stunning, the sets, costumes," he smiled at Natacha, "pure genius. The release is next month. You must see it, Gladys."

They're having sex, Gladys thought, no doubt about it. Divorce or no divorce. She'd probably had sex with Nazimova too. The Bohemian crowd. But Rudy had seemed more old fashioned. At least she'd thought so.

"I definitely will," Gladys said. She'd read about *Camille*, all Art Deco and stylized, a camellia blossom motif in almost every scene. The entire production an avant-garde background for Nazimova, who produced and starred in it, called all the shots. Why she bothered to hire a director no one knew. Even Rudy seemed a mere decoration to enhance her. Not to be upstaged, Nazimova had cut his best scenes.

Gladys stood. "Well, I'm afraid I must go. I have an appointment." She nodded to Natacha. "It's an honor, Miss Rambova. I hope we meet again."

Then she turned, smiled. "Take care, Rudy," and walked away.

He hadn't even said her last name, hadn't mentioned a single one of the dozen films she'd already made for Universal.

More films than the Ice Queen would make in her lifetime, she'd bet.

But she didn't blame Rudy. Even the king of passion and romance needed love. So this was the flaw, his not-so-handsome reality.

She stepped through the Biltmore's gilded revolving doors into a warm spring day. April in Manhattan. Yet she felt a shiver. How fleeting it all was. Beginning to fall the moment you reach the top. These few enchanted meetings with Rudy, then to see him change before her eyes. The mystery all but gone. Part of her wanted to run back, pull him away, shake sense into him, but, of course, that was impossible.

Chapter 27

She did have an appointment. Dr. Herbert Eisington, Internal Medicine, his office a few blocks past Grand Central Station. She turned down Madison Avenue, found the address, took the elevator.

Dr. Eisington peered at her over wire rim spectacles. With his neatly cropped beard and white coat, he looked a little like this Dr. Freud everyone was talking about.

"Hmm, tapeworm," he said, "and you say your *friend* ingested this voluntarily?"

"Yes." Gladys nodded, ignoring his slight emphasis on the word friend. "The studio told her to come back when she lost ten pounds. She needed the job." She had explained Mabel's symptoms, diarrhea and vomiting, but none lately.

"And it wasn't in pill form," he went on, "not one of these mail order things that claim to have worm heads or segments? Because those are nothing but fraud, you know."

"It was in a jar. She got it in China Town."

"I see." He raised an eyebrow, his hands forming a steeple. "A segment, perhaps, although that too seems unlikely." He leaned forward. "And... Miss Walton, is it...?"

She nodded.

"Well, this... *friend*. Is she also a star out there in Hollywood? Is she as beautiful as you?"

"No... I mean, she is very beautiful, and she works in the film industry, but..." What did that have to do with it? And his tone. There were people who thought movies the work of the devil, but she didn't expect that in New York. She shouldn't have worn makeup.

138

Dr. Eisington pushed back his chair, walked across to a book case, scanning the rows. He was only an inch or two taller than she. Weasely man.

In a moment he unlatched the glass door, pulled a tome from a lower shelf, returned to his desk. He didn't open the book, but removed his glasses, studied her, cleared his throat.

"Miss Walton, how old are you anyway, sixteen, seventeen? Hard to tell, but younger than you look, I imagine."

He leaned back, and his eyes were filled with... contempt? No other word for it.

"I wonder, did you even finish high school? And this *friend*, is she a relative, sister perhaps? If so, where are your parents?" He made a harumph sound. "That is, I believe, the most significant matter here. Without supervision, young girls are susceptible to all forms of... indecency. And you do realize that even if this *friend* is indeed you, a girl underage must have the consent of..."

"Dr. Eisington," she stood, "I just want some information." She should've known. Doctors. Like stern fathers, you made your bed, now lie in it.

"And I am happy to pay you." She drew two one hundred dollar bills from her purse, set them on his desk. "If you could just explain what we're dealing with and how to get rid of it. There must be a way to get rid of it. The... someone told her to take crushed pumpkin seeds mixed with milk. It seems to be working, but..."

He laughed loud, cutting her off. The sound filled the room, and she felt her cheeks burn.

"Pumpkin seeds! If that isn't the most ridiculous thing I've ever heard." He spoke between bursts of laughter. "Pumpkin seeds! Miss Walton, I don't want your... Hollywood money." But he glanced at the bills and made no move to hand them back. Thirty times the fee for a standard office visit, even in the big city.

"Pumpkin seeds." He shook his head, still chuckling.

She breathed in, waited. How rude of him to stay seated. Mocking her.

"Look," he said finally, "I'm no Albert Schweitzer. My practice is in New York City, not black Africa. But I understand tapeworms come in several varieties, some quite harmless. Weight loss, that's all, then they're gone. In those cases the poison used as treatment could be more dangerous, even deadly."

He thought a moment. "So I wouldn't get hysterical. If the thing was in a jar, it most likely wasn't even alive, or not a tapeworm at all." The contempt was back. "People play all kinds of tricks on ignorant young girls, especially those foolish enough to think they can fend for themselves. Which is just an excuse to run wild."

He stared up at her, his eyes drifting to her neckline, then down.

"All this trash spreading out of Hollywood. Young women doing whatever they want. Flappers." He spit the word. "Dancing. Drinking and smoking and fornicating. Precisely what's wrong with this country. You watch, it'll be our downfall. A nation rests on the moral fiber of its women."

He was almost quivering. Brimstone. All this delicious wickedness and lust. The real reason he stayed seated, probably. Like the villains in her movies. How many times she'd played this scene. If only she had her Kitty Horrigan whip.

But it wasn't funny.

"Miss Walton," he went on, "the symptoms you describe sound plain and simple. Pregnancy. Makes complete sense under the circumstances."

She just looked at him. That night was back in November. Six months ago. Mabel was not pregnant.

He glanced again at the hundred dollar bills, tapped the book in front of him. His voice lowered. "I'll have my secretary transcribe the pertinent pages. Just give her the address on your way out."

"Thank you, doctor." She drew a handful of tickets from her purse. "I'll leave these with her too. Your secretary might enjoy watching some Hollywood trash. Especially *Short Skirts*."

She took a few steps then turned, smiling over her shoulder. It took a moment for his eyes to lift.

"And in a few months she can see *The Girl Who Ran Wild*."

Chapter 28

Dr. Eisington's "pertinent pages" never arrived, and Gladys meant to find a doctor in Los Angeles to ask, but maybe Eisington was right. Maybe the worm was gone or had never been. Mabel still drank her pumpkin seed milkshakes every night. Couldn't hurt. It was all so confusing. Sometimes Mabel ate ravenously, sometimes not at all. She was spending more and more time with Craig. And time just flew by. They were all so busy.

Gladys had a vague feeling something more than time was slipping away, but she couldn't put a name to it. Dark threads that seemed to connect, and yet too snarled to work through. She wasn't even nineteen, and she sometimes felt swept along in a world that wasn't real, or at least one she didn't understand. She had stepped off the wing of Skeets Elliot's plane into a new life, and seven months later watched his widow and children toss handfuls of dirt into his open grave.

In September the headlines started.

"ACTRESS DIES AFTER HOTEL FILM PARTY"

And the whole sordid story unfolded. Roscoe "Fatty" Arbuckle was tried for manslaughter in the case of Virginia Rappe who had died after a party in his San Francisco hotel rooms. Besides peritonitis, Miss Rappe suffered a ruptured bladder, bruises on her arms and abdomen. Impossible to sort facts from words weighted to sell newspapers. *Orgy. Rape. Murder. Hollywood Dope Ring.* Even reports of something obscene with a Coca Cola or champagne bottle. But that was the Examiner owned by William Randolph Hearst. The least reliable paper.

Paramount pulled Arbuckle's films from theaters, but the case dragged on, three trials ending finally in not guilty. By then it didn't matter. The comedian of the decade, second only to Chaplin, was finished. But how stupid of him! Gladys never liked Fatty anyway, sloshy three-hundred-pound drunk, although once when she and Mabel and Craig went to a Wednesday night dance at the Sunset Inn in Santa Monica, Fatty and Buster Keaton broke up the room with their antics. Mimicking Gloria Swanson's regal entrance.

At first Gladys followed the stories out of curiosity. None of it had to do with her. Her characters were spunky and tough, yet basically innocent, more like Mary Pickford than Theda Bara. Then she'd remember Dr. Eisington's damning leer. "Hollywood trash."

The scandals started overlapping. Valentino's divorce from Jean Acker wedged on the same pages with what Mabel called, "that damn Fatty story." In January a new murder, Director William Desmond Taylor found in his Alvarado Street bungalow, a bullet through his chest, and reporters fell like hounds on the two actresses "in love with him," Mabel Normand and Mary Miles Minter. According to the press they went to "hop parties where drug addicts gathered." The stew thickened. Taylor not only had another name but a wife and child back east. There were no arrests, but Mary's career ended. Gladys had met her once. They were the same age.

At least Rudy's new film, *The Sheik,* changed the tone for awhile. ATTENDANCE RECORDS SMASHED Within ten days 125,000 people saw it. "Sheik Week" was declared. Women went wild. The L.A. premiere was the same night as *Rich Girl, Poor Girl*, so for the next Sunday matinee Gladys wore a scarf and glasses and her plainest dress and went with Mabel to see for themselves, the frenzy as well as the film.

Then the mocking reviews and cartoons started, Valentino as a sleazy, bug-eyed Arab in flowing robes. "I hate Valentino," a writer for *Photoplay* ranted. "All men hate Valentino... I hate his Roman face; I hate his smile; I hate his patent leather hair... I hate him because he dances too well... because he's too good looking."

Gladys smiled. Reporters were male, ninety-nine percent of them, anyway. Men! Of course it was a silly movie. Did they think Valentino didn't know exactly what he was doing? Silliness was the cover so women could fantasize what they never got in real life. Like her night in Stamboul. Oh, to be abducted to an exotic, faraway place where rules and guilt did not exist. Then ravished. Polite society be damned! And the way Rudy moved in that tent scene, raw and deliberate, like a panther, each gesture and look coiled for the lunge. She'd thought the tango in *The Horsemen* would be his signature, but no, it would be the tent scene.

She also knew Rudy would not be able to shrug off the ridicule.

In May, 1922, Gladys was on the train to New York for the premiere of four films when she read, RUDOLPH VALENTINO JAILED ON BIGAMY CHARGES. She gasped, glancing at the couple across from her in the dining car. How she loved the train, the posh dining car, private compartment with plush seats of burgundy velvet, the porter coming to fold down the bed. The most rest she ever got, it seemed, and she'd brought a stack of newspapers and trades to catch up. Now this. Rudy had married the Ice Queen. She folded the paper, pushed aside her plate and hurried back to her compartment.

In her compartment she settled onto the velvet seat and read. Valentino had just finished *Blood and Sand*, another perfect part for him. Gallardo, a brooding, conflicted and

144

doomed Spanish bull fighter, lured from his wife by Nita Naldi. So absorbed in the roll, Rudy spoke his close up lines in Spanish for those in Spanish speaking audiences who might read lips.

He had won his divorce case and paid Jean Acker a settlement, but didn't wait the year for the divorce to be final. Settlement! Gladys fumed as the train clacked along somewhere in Indiana. They never even lived together, and it was no secret Jean Acker was having a lesbian affair with Grace Darmond.

Rudy and Natacha had gone to Mexicali for their wedding, the mayor hosting a grand celebration. Days later Valentino was arrested. The Los Angeles District Attorney vowed to make an example of the flagrant star. Right, and snatch fame for himself, Gladys thought. Rudy in jail! Two days. She in Chicago, and now stuck on this darned train! *The Four Horsemen* made a fortune for Metro, *The Sheik* was still breaking box office records and his new studio refused to post bail. Ten thousand dollars cash! For bigamy with the divorce already granted? Had they gone mad? Friends in the film community pooled resources to get the distraught actor released. Miss Rambova left to join her parents in the east, declining all interviews.

How could a studio ignore its biggest star?

Gladys stared out the window, cows and fields against the darkening sky, the wheels clacking. She turned on the lamp and noticed a smaller headline. "ACTOR WALLACE REID ENTERS SANATORIUM FOR MORPHINE ADDICTION" She read quickly.

Why? Why would they print only that? Craig had told her the real story. Mr. Reid and his wife Dorothy Davenport had engaged his chauffeur services. A servant took Craig aside. The studio doctor gave Mr. Reid morphine when he was injured in a train wreck on the way to location. The doses continued way past what was safe, but kept him working. Of course, Gladys thought, must stay on deadline.

She leaned back, closed her eyes. Studios protecting themselves at all costs. Valentino she could understand, in a way. He was foreign, after all, although what difference should that make? But Wally Reid was the all American hero, number one leading man ever since she could remember. No one worked harder than Wally Reid. Ten years churning out more than a hundred films. Like her own movies, fun and entertaining, no masterpiece except *The Birth Of A Nation*. One hundred! By the end of this year she'd have nineteen. At this rate she might catch up.

Studio moguls had appointed Will Hays as a "czar" to clean up the industry. Presbyterian Elder and Post Master General in Harding's cabinet. "Dictatorship of virtue," they called it. "Morality clauses" inserted in contracts, which could be canceled with a mere accusation.

Morphine addiction, sanatorium. Damn them! Tears. She pressed her fingertips to her eyes. Now even when Wally recovered, his career would be over.

The porter knocked, and she went out to the corridor while he prepared her bed. She stood at the open window, the wind blowing her hair. Maybe she was just tired. And a little lonely. Well, get through the premieres. Representatives from the New York offices would meet her at Grand Central. She could send Rudy a telegram care of Lasky.

No. That would just embarrass him more.

Gladys was still seething when she returned to Los Angeles. Daily articles for fuel. The Valentino trial a charade, armed guards to control female fans. Defense claiming the marriage was never consummated; at a friend's cottage in Palm Springs Miss Rambova had taken ill. The D.A. called witnesses. Witnesses, for Christ sake! A maid saw the couple

146

breakfasting together. Natacha's purple silk pajamas were entered as evidence. Front page photos of pajamas. Jesus! Like a disease. Get close to a star, people become imbeciles.

Right now in Boston those poor immigrants, Sacco and Vanzetti, were facing the death penalty. Protests in Europe. And here, pajamas!

Gladys stepped from the train before it even rolled to a stop. A chauffeur waited by the Packard. Bless Craig's heart! She'd send the driver back for her bags.

At Universal she marched straight to Mr. Laemmle's office, didn't wait for his niece, the secretary, to announce her. Uncle Carl, everyone called him. "Uncle Laemmle had a big faemmle." As many relatives as Laemmle hired, it seemed impossible there were any who did *not* work for Universal. Maybe back in Germany, little town he visited each year.

Well, he was not her uncle!

Laemmle looked up. "Gladys, what a surprise. Have a seat. We have much to discuss."

He stood, indicating two handsome chairs across from his desk. A kind man, actually, but make no mistake, he'd probably figured the dollar amount for every hair on her head.

And she would not sit. Would not let him throw her off, acting all chummy.

"Mr. Laemmle..."

"So how was New York?" He grinned. "Heard you took the town. *Lavender Bath Lady, Second Hand Rose.* Best yet. I knew it! High time I gave you a raise, wouldn't you say?"

"No. I don't want a raise!" My God, did she say that? Standing eye to eye, Laemmle who was not a breath over five foot. Like a stout elf, but a giant of film.

"You don't? But..."

"No, I don't. I want a vacation," she said. "A month, no less."

Chapter 29

They stood at the railing on the top deck, drinking in the ocean breezes. A clear morning, not a wisp of fog. The blue Pacific as far as you could see, all the way to China.

"Lordy!" Mabel grinned, stretching her hand high. "If this ain't the whole platter 'n a piece of pie! My entire life I never felt so glorious." She glanced at Craig, squeezing his arm. "Well, not quite never."

He laughed. "And the ship hasn't even left the harbor!"

Mabel hadn't let go of Craig since they boarded, and Gladys could see a sadness behind his smile. Missing her already. Yet Craig knew it was just what she and Mabel needed, and he couldn't get away to join them.

Uncle Carl's niece had booked their passage on the steam ship, *The City of Los Angeles,* its maiden voyage, September 11, 1922. Perfect timing, since Laemmle insisted Gladys finish shooting *The Town Scandal* before she left.

The City of Los Angeles would be the largest American ship in Pacific waters, a regular connection to Hawaii. LASSCO, the Los Angeles Steam Ship Company could finally compete with San Francisco's Matson line, a milestone for the city, and the Los Angeles Chamber of Commerce was giving its namesake a gala send off.

In the harbor, the battleship *U.S. Connecticut* saluted with three blasts of her siren.

"My cue," Gladys said. "Come with me?" She was to take her place on the lower deck to be introduced by the mayor.

"No, we'll stay here, if you don't mind," Craig said. "I hope they make long speeches."

She hurried down to her spot on starboard side. Other passengers gathered along the rail, watching the festivities. Two hundred and sixty-four passengers were making the trip. In seven days they'd stop in Hilo where thousands of islanders were expected to greet them, then Maui and Oahu, thousands more.

Below, spectators lined the dock. A platform was set up with open arches decorated in red, white and blue ribbons and balloons. The mayor started his speech, which, thankfully, she couldn't hear. He had asked her to join them on the platform, but she politely declined. She was on vacation.

Gladys felt a lightness in her chest. As if she were a little girl again. She felt like pinching herself, dancing a jig right here. A splendid ship, German built for tropical service, the brochure said, a war prize overhauled and painted white with black stacks, refitted with a gymnasium and pool. All accommodations first class. Members of the Chamber and their families had priority, but Uncle Carl pulled strings and got them a stateroom with private bath. Gorgeous, all that brass and polished wood.

Laemmle had turned this into a publicity event, of course, yet he didn't offer to cover the $635 round trip fare.

Craig insisted on paying for Mabel, and Gladys didn't argue. His business was going well. You could see it in his step. He would give his girl a Hawaiian vacation.

They'd bought new dresses, sassy open-toed shoes and big floppy hats, all in promenade pastels, lightweight cottons and linen, a few silks for evening. They would dine with the captain, and a royal luau was planned in Honolulu.

New swim outfits too, sleeveless and snug, bloomers only mid-thigh. On the islands they might even go without those God-awful swim stockings. Mostly, they would relax, long hours talking and dozing on deck chairs, lying on warm sand. Mabel had been having headaches lately. She looked a

149

little pale, but a month of sunshine and sea air and lush islands, what could be better?

A woman tapped her arm. "Miss Walton..." she nodded to the dock.

"Oh! Thank you."

The mayor was pointing up at her, repeating his introduction, "Gladys Walton! Star of *Pink Tights, The Man Tamer, Second Hand Rose* and a dozen more films for Universal..."

Gladys waved and curtsied. Then, on an impulse, she took off her hat, gave it a good fling. The breeze caught it, and it sailed across, landing on the dock. The crowd cheered. Those closest scrambled, and a lady grabbed up her hat and waved back.

Gladys didn't care. Six hats were packed in her trunk, and she'd buy more in Hawaii.

Yachts fired their cannons, and on a nearby tug, the Los Angeles Police Band struck up John Philip Sousa's *Anchor and Star*.

She did a last bow and walked back, greeting passengers, shaking hands, autographing programs.

The music stopped, and the ship's horn made two short blasts signaling, all ashore who's going ashore.

When Gladys reached the open deck to the prow, she stopped. Tears filled her eyes. In her whole life she would never forget. So beautiful, Mabel in her sleeveless white dress and yellow sash. Her hat behind her on the deck where it had fallen. Craig holding her in his arms, kissing her under an endless blue sky, the sea sparkling behind them.

She waited, and minutes later they walked with Craig to the lower level.

"Take care of her," Craig said, hugging Gladys, "and you two try not to get in too much trouble."

He kissed Mabel again, turned and sprinted down the gangplank just as the crew began to swing it away.

They stood arm-in-arm watching him, confetti and streamers showering from the upper deck, engines churning, the band playing between deep throated blasts of the ship's horn.

Mabel whispered, "Craig asked me to marry him."

"Again?" Gladys laughed.

"I said yes."

Chapter 30

Hawaii was a dream. Bright flowers of every color against a hundred shades of green, waterfalls at every turn. Black sand beaches, volcanoes, Lahaina with its whaling ships. The sails of smaller boats sprinkled across the harbor, clouds piled white in a blue sky, working themselves up for the afternoon shower. And everywhere the sea!

It reminded Gladys of when she was a girl, and they'd drive up the Oregon coast and picnic on the dunes, only it was always cold. Hawaii was warm even when it rained.

On the trip over and between islands, they lounged on deck talking, planning the wedding.

"Nothin' fancy," Mabel said, "maybe a garden somewhere."

"How about Palm Springs," Gladys said. "Everyone's going out there now. Or one of the missions, Capistrano or San Gabriel. Wouldn't that be beautiful?"

"If they allow Baptists." Mabel laughed. "But, oh, Gladys, I do love that man. Feel like I'm 'bout to pop a seam! Didn't come clear 'til I was fixin' to say good-bye. Ain't that the way? For the life o' me I can't think why I held him off so long." She closed her eyes. "I wish this here ship would just turn itself around and head back lickety split."

Gladys nodded. Mabel had spent a good part of the trip sleeping in the shade, but she needed it. The sun made her headaches worse. She knew Mabel sometimes hid the pain not to ruin the trip for her. The ship's doctor had given Mabel some of these new Aspirin tablets, and she'd brought a small pillowcase full of pumpkin seeds for her nightly milkshakes.

"It won't be long now," Gladys said. "One more island, then the crossing. He'll be there waiting." She touched Mabel's cheek. They always pushed their deck chairs close so they could talk. "I'm so happy for you, Mabel. Craig adores you, and he's solid. You couldn't do better."

How true, Gladys thought, and partly because Craig saw through the constant Hollywood struggle for bigger and better parts and just walked away. She wondered how it would be if she hadn't stepped right into star billing. And how long it would last. Could she have had a life with Craig?

She corrected the thought, someone *like* Craig. She never allowed herself to remember those early days at Sunshine Comedy, those kisses. In some odd way she felt... dangerous. She did not trust herself to stay with one man, could not imagine falling so deeply in love as to give up all she had built. The idea of years rolling on *'til death do us part* made her insides freeze up, like having the breath wrung out of her. Craig deserved better.

She was happy for them, yet a little sad. Marriage always changed things. No more forays to small town speakeasies or Wednesday night dances at the Sunset Inn, Craig walking in with a princess on each arm.

"Mabel," she said, "you will stay in California, won't you?" She could not imagine her life without Mabel and Craig.

"I reckon," Mabel said. "Craig's folks live over in Whittier, but he's gonna build us a little place on one o' them lots he bought. Huntington's nice, 'ceptin' I wish it weren't so far."

"Well, new roads are going in all the time, and I bet they'll extend the trolley line out that way soon." Gladys gazed into the distance. In all their wedding talks, Mabel never mentioned Nathan Andrew or her parents and brothers in Georgia.

Gladys sat up quickly. "Look. Look, Mabel. Diamond Head! Come on. Let's go watch from the top deck."

"Y'all go on." Mabel smiled, her eyes still closed. "I'm doin' me some serious restin' here. Don't wanna miss Honolulu."

On Waikiki beach Mabel sat in a canvas beach chair while Gladys waded out and climbed between muscled, dark men in their outrigger canoe. How handsome these Polynesians, nothing but loincloths, arms and chests tattooed in intricate black patterns. Some had tattoos all the way down their legs. Arms bulging, they paddled out beyond the breakers. A half dozen canoes raced to shore on eight foot waves. Gladys squealed, hands out, catching the spray. She went three times.

"Oh, Mabel, they hardly speak English," she said, dropping onto the blanket. "How do you say, meet me tonight under the banyan tree in Hawaiian?"

Mabel laughed. "I think y'all could get that across. Probably have a pack of 'em. It's a big tree."

A dozen or so bathers were clustered at the shoreline.

"What are they watching?"

Mabel looked. "Duke Ka...hana something. That big lady said he's an Olympic champion. Never heard 'a him myself."

"Duke Kahanamoku?" Gladys stood. "Oh, my God! He's the fastest swimmer in the world." She shaded her eyes, watched him balance on his huge board, riding the wave. She held her breath as he threaded through the pilings of Moana pier.

"They should try that in California," Mabel said, squinting into the sun. "What's it called?"

154

"Surfing, and I bet they will. I'd do it. In fact..." Gladys took a step, then hesitated. "Are you okay, Mabel? You want to go back to the ship?"

"No, I'm fine. Baskin' like an ol' turtle. But I might better move to the shade. Them hammocks look mighty nice."

Gladys helped move their things back to the line of coco palms. Then she walked across to a group of beach boys. They were cute, her age and younger, and they swam like fish, diving for dimes tourists tossed from the ships, or climbing palm trees to bring down coconuts. She'd been flirting with them for two days. What fun to be no one famous, just a girl in a swim outfit, but they laughed when she stepped into their circle of sixteen-foot boards and asked who would teach her.

"Much danger. Not for haole girl."

But finally one said she could lie in front. "But no stand up. Make sure."

On the second ride, she couldn't help it. She crouched on the board, did a perfect dive into the crest and let the wave carry her all the way to shore. Piece of cake for the West Coast Diving Champion of 1918. She laughed, flexing her muscles as she walked past the beach boys, their mouths gaping.

Their last day Mabel was full of energy. "One last adventure," she said, tying on a big hat. They hired a car and motored to the foot of Diamond Head. They rode horses around the point to Hanauma Bay, waded out, splashing and chasing schools of fish in the shallow water. An immense aquarium. Their guide was an older man with a big brown belly and laughing eyes. Hank.

"I know you from cinema," he said, grinning, "the girl with the lions. Very brave. Come, I show you something special." He took them out to the rocky point where the lava shelf formed a hole ten feet wide. They watched the surge enter at the bottom filling it to the brim then drain back out.

"We call it the 'toilet bowl,'" Hank said, "Jump in. Sea take you up and down. Much fun."

"I don't know." Mabel stood back from the rim.

"We'll hold hands," Gladys said. "Don't worry, I won't let go no matter what. And Hank will fish us out." Mabel set her hat on a rock, and they jumped, floating with the surge as the tide filled and flushed the bowl.

That night at the royal luau, they wore matching sarongs, hibiscus blossoms in their hair. They sat between the captain and a real Hawaiian prince. Smooth bare chest, dark eyes, perfect teeth. His tattoos were symbols reserved for royalty, but Gladys couldn't tell the difference. He had a degree from Yale and had seen her movies. He played a mean ukulele. Probably started the ukulele craze sweeping American campuses.

They talked easily, but mostly Gladys could feel the heat from his skin. He took her hand, Mabel's too, taught them the hula, and, oh, the drums! Like no dance she'd ever done, made the Texas Tommy seem tame. Faster and faster, torches blurring against the sultry night sky.

The prince had a six syllable name Gladys could not pronounce, much less remember. Especially with all that rum. No Prohibition in the territories, apparently. In Hawaii they mixed rum with everything, coffee, coconut milk, every fruit juice imaginable, chunks of papaya and mango.

She hardly remembered getting back to the ship.

When she woke *The City of Los Angeles* was already out to sea. Seven days to lounge on deck. Thank goodness.

"So tell me," Mabel said when they were settled side by side on the mahogany deck chairs. "What happened with your prince? I saw y'all walkin' off together."

"Mmm," Gladys groaned from under the damp cloth covering her face. Mabel's Aspirin wasn't working. She'd thought the sea air might do the trick. Hadn't even changed from her sarong, and now she squirmed, adjusting the folds.

"Not much of a prince, I'm afraid. I still have sand in my bottom."

"Oh, why don't they hurry up! How many dern ropes do they have to tie?"

Craig was there on the dock, bouquet of flowers in his hand. Mabel about to burst.

They were the first ones down the gangplank, and Mabel ran to his arms. He swung her around. "Look at you, all tan and beautiful."

Gladys waited, and finally he hugged her too, and they walked to the Packard where the chauffeur stood waiting. It took two porters to push the cart with their trunks and souvenir boxes.

"Wow! Mabel, look at that!" A speedster was parked next to the Packard, and Gladys walked around it while the men loaded the trunks. "Did you ever see such a car?"

Mabel shook her head, but didn't take her eyes off Craig.

A two-seater convertible, shiny red with black fenders, a chrome running board and spoke wheels. The engine compartment was half the length of the car. Big round head lamps. The driver's seat more like the cockpit of a aeroplane.

Craig walked to her, grinning. "Stutz Bearcat," he said, "1923. Do you like it?"

"Like it!" She looked back toward the ship. "I wonder where the owner is."

"Right here." Craig pulled a key from his pocket. "It's yours, Gladys. Mr. Laemmle sent it. I guess he missed you."

Chapter 31

Gladys stared. A 1923 Stutz Bearcat. She could not believe!

Craig smiled. "Don't you want to drive it? Sixteen valve T-head, three-hundred-sixty-five cubes. This baby'll fly, Gladys."

When she still didn't move, he took her hand, put the key in it. He opened the little half-door. "Or you can ride with Freddy. Mabel and I'll take her. Won't we, sweetheart?"

"You bet!" Mabel grinned.

That snapped Gladys out. "Not on your life!"

She got in, ran her hand over the leather, touched the dashboard, the wood all swirled and polished a dark gold, and all these gauges. She turned the key, pushed the starter pedal on the floorboard. The engine shuddered like a race car.

"Y'all look perfect," Mabel said, "like it was made for you. Get ya some goggles and a scarf..."

"Gloves," Craig added.

Gladys splayed her hands on the wheel. "The kind with no fingers, don't you think?"

"Absolutely!"

She thought of Rudy. Oh, when he sees this car!

In the side mirror she could see Mabel and Craig kissing by the Packard, Freddy wedged in back with the baggage.

Gladys called out, "You two go on. I'll take the beach road." She grinned. "Don't wait up." Let them have time alone in the bungalow. They nodded and waved.

She edged onto the road. Gripping the wheel, she eased the accelerator down. The power pushed her back against the seat. My God, it was a race car! A thousand times better than a raise. Uncle Carl. Bless his heart. So much for all her fuming about evil studio executives.

She drove up the coast, past oil derricks and open fields, wind in her hair. Seventy miles an hour, eighty, ninety.

Stutz Bearcat

A gift from Universal Studios, Gladys loved her Stutz Bearcat.

She drove it "Pedal to the Metal" everywhere she went.

Convertibles were always her favorite.

Probably go over a hundred. What a car! When she passed the occasional flivver or touring sedan, heads turned. In the little beach towns of Redondo and El Segundo and Venice people pointed and waved.

She found the cliff overlooking the beach of Malibu where she and Rudy had danced a waltz and watched the sunset in the Hispano Suiza. She shut off the engine, looked out at the clouds hanging over the sea, a fine mist rolling in. She shivered. Mid October, cold after Hawaii. She'd have Craig show her how to put the top up.

Rudy was in the east with Natacha, probably wouldn't return until the divorce was final. She'd heard he was miserable these past months without Natacha, staying to finish his latest film, *The Young Rajah,* which he hated. Miss Rambova's ridiculous costume designs draping his mostly naked body in strings of pearls, silly curved helmet made of satin. Reviewers would have a heyday. The Ice Queen would ruin Rudy's career if he wasn't careful. Why did love make people lose their senses?

Not Craig and Mabel, though.

She got out, walked to the edge of the cliff, not too close to the edge, the wind billowing her skirt. She hugged her arms and looked back at her car. A Stutz Bearcat! The realization caught her. She was a star, a Hollywood star. She'd never felt it so clearly. In less than three months she would turn twenty, and she'd already done that many films.

She twirled, arms stretched high, around and around, never mind the cold. She danced a jig, there on the cliff, holding her skirt above her knees, no one watching but the seagulls. She ran back to the Bearcat, stood on the running board and leaned over the rounded hood, hugging her car. Crazy, but she didn't care. It was warm from the engine.

How lucky she was. She would not trade places with anyone. And when Rudy came back, she would kidnap him in her Bearcat and bring him here, Ice Queen or no Ice Queen.

Hawaii was wonderful, and she would have more vacations. Europe, maybe. London, Paris. She'd take Mabel and Craig next year if they didn't have a baby by then.

For now, she was ready to work. Yes! Six movies scheduled for 1923, and they'd probably found more while she was gone. Monday they'd start prelims for *The Untameable*. Silly film, like *Dr. Jekyll and Mr. Hyde* only no classic. She'd play Joy Fielding, all sweetness and light until the maniacal Dr. Copin uses hypnosis to change her personality. Then she turns cruel and man-hungry, of course, but in the end the doctor is eaten by dogs and Joy's evil shadow slips into what's left of his dead body to be buried with him. And the good Joy lives happily ever after with the run-of-the-mill hero. Gladys laughed. A film with a message.

What the hell, five hundred a week and a Bearcat.

Next they'd shoot *The Near Lady*. Near. That was as close as she'd get to being a lady. She walked around to the driver's side and got in, leaned back, stretched her hands on the wheel. She'd swam naked with a Hawaiian prince. He made love to her on the beach. How many *ladies* could say that? She closed her eyes, remembered lying beneath him, looking up at a starry tropical sky fringed with coco palms, the low waves washing up and back, rocking them to the rhythm of his love making.

She opened her eyes. All right, it wasn't love making. It was sex. Blurred with rum, gritty and slightly painful, wet sand between her legs, his thrusts not nearly as gentle as the waves. The only time she'd had sex and wanted it over as soon as it began.

The wind and cold were making her eyes tear. She turned the key, pushed the starter pedal, the engine chugged to

161

life. She shivered, wiped her eyes. She'd come with only her purse, nothing warm in her luggage anyway. She checked for vents by her feet in case the Stutz had one of those manifold heaters. It did. But she was parked on dirt and grass, couldn't open the vent here. She let the engine warm up, then headed for the paved road.

Some prince. Now she'd have to worry again and count days until her next monthly. Still, it was fun, a memory, a souvenir. She smiled. Better than a palm frond hat or a carved Tiki god.

Chapter 32

Gladys stood at the door to the set waiting for Mr. Baggot to call on his megaphone for her entrance. King Baggot had been an actor for Universal practically from the beginning, big and beefy and overly serious, as if he couldn't get past those early melodramas. He played the original *Dr. Jekyll and Mr. Hyde*. Gladys remembered seeing him in *Ivanhoe* when she was ten, and now she couldn't look at him without picturing that chain mail hood. Everything about him seemed coated in chain mail. A dozen different directors, and now she was stuck with thick-necked Baggot. He was okay for *The Untameable*, she supposed. They were in their fourth week of filming.

She adjusted the bouquet of flowers in her arm, set her face with the appropriate look. In the plush guest room on the other side of the wall, Chester Arnold lay in bed, his head bandaged. Chester had been busy finishing another movie, so they'd filmed the middle first, the parts where Dr. Copin hypnotizes her and she goes demented, beating her maid. Stupid plot. Now they were filling in the beginning.

"Ready, Miss Walton?" Baggot's deep voice. "Remember, your face should show grave concern, then a touch of sweet seduction. Chester wrecked his car. He's badly injured and you're nursing him back to health. He's also a good catch."

Yes, Mr. Baggot. As if she hadn't read the script. She reset her face. Concern, sweet seduction. Right.

"Okay, action."

As she opened the door, she heard Baggot's voice without the megaphone.

"What the... How'd he get in here? Where the hell's security?"

Confused, she slipped out of character, lost the look, but was already through the door. Chester Arnold was sitting up in bed, watching whatever was happening behind the lights.

"Look, buddy..." Baggot again. A scuffle, something knocked over. She turned, blinded by the lights.

Then a familiar voice spoke her name. Craig. But the sound made her freeze. Something was very wrong.

Craig stepped in front of the lights where she could see. He was out of breath, near panic.

Gladys dropped the bouquet and rushed to him.

"Craig, what is it? What happened?"

She could see Mr. Baggot picking himself up off the floor, rubbing his jaw. "I don't know who this guy is, Gladys, but it better be important."

Craig's eyes filled with tears, he was shaking. "God, dear God." His voice a whisper.

Gladys felt her whole body tense. "Where is she? The infirmary?" She took hands. "Craig..."

He breathed in, nodded. "They called Good Samaritan. They're trying to get an ambulance. I had to come. She would want you..."

"Would. What do you mean?"

She took his arm, pulled him across to the studio door, the crew and Mr. Baggot moving out of the way. She got Craig down the steps into her car, ran around to the driver's side, the Packard parked beside it. The tires squealed as she took the corner toward the infirmary. It was way across the lot.

"What happened? Craig, tell me!"

"She didn't have work today. After I finished dispatching, I... I came to take her to breakfast." He spoke in a monotone, his hands in fists. "She was in the bathroom. I... I heard a crash, glass breaking..." He turned to her. "Oh, Gladys. She was on the floor. Her body stiff, her eyes... She was jerking, blood on her mouth... I held her, but it wouldn't stop..." He swallowed.

She glanced at him, then back at the road. His eyes. This wasn't happening.

"I could hardly lift her... the way she kept... jerking. Then she just went limp. I got her to the infirmary. They said... they said it was a seizure. She bit through her tongue."

He put his hands to his face, a low moan came from his throat. "I thought it was gone, Gladys. I thought it was gone. Or maybe it's something else... Something we didn't know about."

They were almost to the infirmary. Parked in front was a paddy wagon used to film cops and robbers scenes. Faster than an ambulance, probably.

Craig pointed. "There. They're bringing her now."

Men were carrying a stretcher out of the infirmary, a nurse holding the door.

Craig was out before the car came to a full stop. Gladys followed. They stood on either side of the stretcher as Mabel was lifted into the back of the paddy wagon. Her head strapped to a board, a rubber wedge between her teeth, a hole so she could breathe. Her eyes half open, only white showing. Flecks of dried blood by her mouth.

Mabel. Please, God...

Gladys wanted to touch her cheek, smooth her hair, find a wet cloth, wipe the blood away, but she could not move. It was as if she had entered a tunnel, everything outside her vision black, no time for thought or feeling, only getting through. That's all, just get through.

Craig. She had to help Craig. She looked up, their eyes met, and she saw that the black surrounded him too.

One of the men climbed into the back, folded down a bench attached to the side opposite the stretcher.

Someone touched her arm. "Miss Walton, we had to make do, couldn't get an ambulance, but you both can ride with her. Plenty of room."

It was the nurse. The one who rubbed salve on her arms that day she slid down the burning roof. First autograph she ever signed. *Pink Tights*. A hundred years ago.

"A Dr. Morris is waiting now," the nurse said. "Don't worry, he's the best."

Gladys nodded. Craig got in, helped her up the step, didn't let go of her hand. They didn't speak. They sat concentrating on the faint rise and fall of Mabel's chest, the odd rasp of air sucking through the hole in the rubber wedge. The sound of hope.

Then the clang of the paddy wagon bell drowned it out.

166

Theater Lobby Card for Rich Girl, Poor Girl

Gladys is seen in the back window on the right. Her dearest friend, Mabel, is seen in the back on the left. Mabel was using the stage name, Alice Andrews.

There was never another friendship as dear to my mother as the one she had with Mabel. Whenever possible, Gladys would get Mabel parts in her movies.

Hey, Daddy Joe, her stepfather, is also here. In the front of the car, second guy from left.

Chapter 33

At The Good Samaritan, men in white coats carried Mabel in on the stretcher and disappeared through double doors.

Gladys and Craig followed as far as the receiving room. They sat on straight backed chairs, waiting. Craig leaned forward, elbows on his knees, staring at the floor. She put her hand on his shoulder. A few others were there waiting, but Gladys avoided their eyes. No fans, please. She was still in costume and make-up, but at least *The Untameable* was contemporary.

The walls and floor were white, sunbeams streaming through tall windows. A nurse sat at a desk a few feet away. Her name tag said Mildred Jones. She wore a stiff white cap, white dress fitted at the waist, white stockings, white shoes. The room *smelled* white, bleach and disinfectant, the smell of sickness.

Gladys had never been in a hospital. When she was born, Dr. Palmer delivered her in the upstairs bedroom. Dr. Palmer always came to the house, tied his horse and buggy to the porch rail. She remembered running to bring carrots from Aunt Minnie's garden. Jasper. What a name for a horse.

Mamma and Aunt Minnie had volunteered to help in the 1918 influenza, the halls of every hospital lined with patients. They wore white masks and each day when they came home they'd close the door to the kitchen and strip down to their "all together," and she'd hear them filling the big kettle, carrying it to the stove. The sound of a sink pump still made her remember. She wasn't allowed near them until they'd boiled their hospital clothes and scrubbed themselves with lye soap.

Why was it taking so long? Seizure. What did they do for a seizure?

She stared at the double doors, willing Mabel to walk through. Smile, say something about feeling a might puny, just needed some rest...

The phone on the nurse's desk rang, and Gladys jumped.

Craig looked up.

"Yes, of course, Doctor. I'll tell them." The nurse replaced the ear piece on its hook, came around the desk. "Dr. Morris will see you now. He has some questions. If you'll come with me, please."

Craig took her arm. They hurried to keep up with the nurse's brisk walk. Down a hallway, past another desk, a nurse pushing an old lady in a wheelchair. A man she assumed was Dr. Morris stood by an open door, stethoscope around his neck. His hair was almost as white as his coat, although he didn't look much past fifty. His eyes seemed kind, not at all like Dr. Eisington.

He smiled, shook her hand. "I've seen your work, Miss Walton. It's nice to meet you. I wish it were under better circumstances."

She nodded. "How is she, Doctor? Can we see her? Will she be all right?"

"Frankly, we don't know yet, Miss Walton. She had a seizure, quite severe, I'm afraid. Does she have a history of epilepsy?"

"No, I don't think so. We're good friends. I've known her three years." She looked up at Craig. They had to tell the doctor. But how could a tapeworm cause something like this? It seemed impossible.

Dr. Morris glanced at Craig's hand still on her elbow. "If we could talk to a family member. You're not by chance Miss Huxley's brother?"

The question surprised Gladys, and suddenly she saw how much Craig and Mabel resembled each other.

"No," Craig said. "Mabel... Miss Huxley and I... we're engaged. Craig Cramer." He shook the doctor's hand, but didn't let go of Gladys's arm. "We'll be married as soon as she's better."

Dr. Morris nodded. "And did she tell you she's pregnant?"

Craig stared. "Pregnant? She said that?"

"No, of course not. She hasn't regained consciousness." Dr. Morris paused. "We don't know yet if it's a coma. Or the extent of the... damage. There may have been hemorrhaging... or a stroke."

His voice was careful, almost tender. It frightened Gladys more. She felt Craig's hand tighten on her arm. He was trembling.

"It's quite normal to sleep after a seizure," Dr. Morris went on. "It would help a great deal if we could contact her family. Epilepsy is one thing, but... if she doesn't regain consciousness in eight or ten hours we will... reassess. Pregnancy would, of course, be another concern. Our gynecologist isn't on staff at the moment, but by the size of her abdomen I'd say she's four or five months pregnant." He lowered his voice. "Seems she was hiding it. She was wearing a corset. We had to cut it..."

Gladys interrupted. "Mabel has a..."

"She is not pregnant! I'd know if she was pregnant!" Craig's voice carried through the quiet corridor. "And I want to see her! Why won't you let us see her?" He pushed past them into the room.

Gladys and the doctor followed.

170

Gladys froze in the doorway.

There on the narrow bed, Mabel looked beautiful and calm, the sheet up to her shoulders, her blond hair on the pillow. They had removed the wedge from her mouth, cleaned away the blood, combed out most of the tangles. Her lips slightly parted, asleep, peaceful. No, not sleep, a coma, he'd said. All these words she knew nothing about. And how pale Mabel was.

She could feel the tunnel closing in. She watched as Craig pulled a chair close. He sat beside Mabel, held her hand. He kissed her forehead, whispering to her, lips close to her cheek. Wiped his eyes.

Gladys felt her own tears starting. She wanted to go to Mabel, and yet...

Dr. Morris touched her arm. "I'm sorry, Miss Walton. I should've brought you in right away. It's just, I need information. A girl her age... Go on, take some time with her. I'll be just outside."

What was he saying? Whatever chance there was, the doctor had to know. Some medicine he could give her, a shot.

"Doctor, I..."

He turned.

She wiped her eyes, started again, her voice low. "Mabel has a tapeworm. She's had it almost three years."

Dr. Morris removed his glasses, looked at her closely.

"I see. Where did she get it, one of those mail order ads?" He did not have to ask why.

"She got it in China Town."

His eyes widened. "China Town. Are you sure? How do you know?"

"Because I took her!" Craig yelled, startling them both. The sound was almost a wail. It seemed to freeze in the air. "I took her!" His voice broke. He held Mabel in his arms, rocking. "She's gone. God help me. I took her."

Dr. Morris dropped his glasses, rushed to the bed. He felt for a pulse, fumbled with his stethoscope.

Craig sat back, sobbing into his hands.

Gladys walked to him. Numb. She watched as the doctor tried and tried to find a pulse. He put his arm under Mabel's back and lifted, arching her body, checked again. Finally he stood back, his eyes helpless, defeated. He ran a hand through his white hair, let it fall.

"I'm sorry," he said. "I am so sorry."

Chapter 34

Craig moved onto the bed. He took Mabel in his arms, held her silently.

Gladys sat in the chair. They stayed that way a long time. No words. What words could there be?

She closed her eyes. Moments before, she'd had to fight the tears. Not now. Now there was nothing. A blank wall. *Gone.* She would not touch Mabel. Or look at her. Did not want the feel of her skin embedded in her mind. You had to be careful what you let in. The slightest glimpse could make a memory to last your whole life. The way the camera catches images on film. Only you couldn't edit memories away. They stayed, even ones you didn't want. Memories were all that lasted. Everything else died.

She put her hands to her face, block out all light, even the faint glow through her eyelids. Remember. Mabel's face behind her in the mirror, the day they met. That smile. That time in the movies, giggling over Valentino. Fannie Ward's party. Hawaii. Mabel and her pumpkin seeds.

Sobs started in her chest. She tightened her hands on her face, bit her lip. Crying would only hurt Craig more. If only Dr. Eisington had sent the pages. If only she'd found another doctor. There had to be medicine.

"I didn't know." The words escaped before she could stop them. "I didn't know."

A hand touched her shoulder. She opened her eyes, expecting Craig.

"You couldn't have known." Dr. Morris crouched in front of her. He spoke softly, barely a whisper. "I'm sorry, Miss Walton, I didn't mean to be gone so long."

She hadn't known he was gone.

"But I wanted to be able to tell you something. I wanted to know for myself. Had to make a dozen calls before I reached someone with... knowledge of this." His voice earnest, yet somehow soothing. Whispering. "I just spoke to a Dr. Reinhart, friend of a colleague. He did missionary work near Shanghai twenty years ago..."

Dr. Morris stopped, tipped his head slightly, indicating the bed behind him. "Shall we go out in the hall?" He stood.

She was tempted to say no. A dozen calls. A thousand, a million. It didn't matter. If she had tried, she could've found out. Mabel could've had her life with Craig. Ten pounds! They were children, living this silly, pointless life, chasing hollow dreams, calling it glamour. Craig had seen through it. Too late.

She could hear his gentle keening on the bed, did not look.

She kept her eyes on the doctor. As a man of medicine he needed to understand and now to tell her. Well, she was through being a child, through hiding from the ugliness. She stood, and they walked quietly out into the glaring white hallway.

She tried to listen. Something about this Dr. Reinhart. After Shanghai he studied in London. Parasitology. Ugly word. She looked at Dr. Morris, tried to concentrate, but in her mind she saw a wide, shallow bay, crystal blue, the two of them splashing, Mabel squealing when a purple sea flower disappeared at her touch, a pair of orange clown fish brushed her hands.

"It isn't found here," the doctor's words broke in, "but in Asia and other areas..."

They stood on a lava shelf watching the sea, in their new sleeveless swim outfits, even in the spray from the waves, the air was warm.

"... a species that forms large cysts... attacks vital organs... the nervous system... causes seizures... brain damage... irreversible."

They held hands and jumped, floating up and down with the surge, laughing. *I won't let go no matter what*, she had told Mabel.

Tears. Her whole body shuddering.

Dr. Morris put his arms around her, held her close, and she cried against his chest.

Minutes passed. Finally she felt the awkwardness and stood back, wiping her eyes.

"I... I suppose I need to contact someone... take care of... I've never done this."

"Cunningham and O'Conner," he said. "I had the nurse call them. I hope that's all right. They'll handle everything, but... we need to reach her family, if at all possible. She does have family?"

Gladys nodded. "They're in Georgia."

"I'll talk to them if you'd like."

"No," she said, "thank you. You've been so kind. I think I should do that."

Later she went to the business office at Universal. They had a contact number, George Huxley in Atlanta. She went across to the switchboard.

As soon as she heard the ringing, Gladys wished she had let Dr. Morris handle it. A woman answered, Mabel's mother. Gladys breathed in, started to explain the best she could.

"Listen, honey," the voice cut in, "y'all kin save yerself the trouble. We had us a daughter, Mabel. Disgraced us all, up

175

'n left for California. Left my sister raisin' her bastard child. Far as we're concerned she's been dead nigh on three years. Ain't no good ever come outta dancin' and carryin' on. That's for sure. We told her and told her, and looks as how she went 'n proved it..."

"Mrs. Huxley, I thought you might want... to have her there. I could bring her... on the train..."

"We ain't got no money for a derned burial. Not when she shamed us, run off 'n..."

"I'd be happy to pay for everything, Mrs. Huxley."

There was a pause. Gladys wanted to tell how Mabel was her best friend, like a sister, how much she loved her.

"And who all d' ya s'pose would come to her buryin'?" Mrs. Huxley said, "'ceptin' to see you. How'd that be? Burials 're fer showin' respects." She laughed. "Respect. Oh, I know who y'all are. The Glad Girl." She spat the words. "Mabel sent letters. I even read some till I couldn't no more. No, y'all 're exactly what she set out to be. Hollywood trash..." Her voice rose, shrill. "We're God fearin' folks here. We don't need yer kind struttin' around all gussied up..."

Gladys reached and pulled the cord out of the switchboard. She sat trembling. The switchboard girl patted her arm. "Georgia," she said, "it's like a whole different country." In a moment she added, "Is there another number you'd like me to try, Miss Walton?"

"Yes, yes there is." She called mamma.

176

Chapter 35

\\ "The Lord is my shepherd, I shall not want..."

They stood on the lawn, a small gathering. Gladys had done her best to contact people. Mr. Steiner had come and Gertrude and Mr. Biggs, The Sunshine Comedy contingent, standing with Craig. A few chorus line girls from the musical reviews, the Dexter sisters who worked in make-up, Alice and Faye. Mr. Cunningham from the funeral home. It surprised her when Mr. Laemmle walked up. But then no one understood the ties of family better than Uncle Carl. To him everyone who worked at Universal was family.

She nodded to him. That's how you get through these things, Gladys thought, greeting the people, being cordial. Just their presence helped. Mamma with her arm around her waist. Aunt Minnie and Uncle Tommy, Joe Mayer.

Standing on the other side of Joe, was Howard. The last time she saw Howard... She wanted to take his hand now.

It made her angry, this being cordial, getting through, as if she could just go on. Mabel buried in a grave far from home, attended by a bare handful, mostly strangers.

"Yea, though I walk through the valley of the shadow of death, I will fear no evil..."

She'd managed to find a Baptist preacher, anyway. Rev. Pringle from Alabama. His voice had the same Southern lilt. She wiped her eyes.

Mamma's hand tightened on her waist. "I know, princess. I know," she whispered.

Gladys looked around. Hollywood Memorial Park, trees and gardens, manicured lawns. Beautiful. She could see the section where Skeets Elliot and Ormer Locklear were buried. She noticed a man standing off to the side. Dr. Morris. How kind of him to be here. If she had found him sooner...

She stopped the thoughts. Let it go. Get through this.

Rev. Pringle finished. He walked forward, pulled some white roses from the spray covering the casket. Roses and magnolia blossoms, shipped in special, already turning brown in the California sun. The scent filled the canopy. The preacher came and handed a rose to her, to mamma and Aunt Minnie. Gladys thanked him, greeted the others, smiled her empty smile.

Howard hugged her. She would not walk to the grave, would not toss a handful of dirt. She looked for Dr. Morris to introduce him to her family, but he was gone.

She left mamma talking to the preacher, walked across to Craig. He had dark circles under his eyes, a stillness about him. His whole future pulled out of his hands.

Gladys hugged him, and they started toward the line of cars.

"She had a child," he said, "a little boy."

Gladys stopped, lifted her veil. "You knew?" She had tried not to think of Nathan Andrew. How his life would be. *Bastard.* His own grandmother used that word. Probably written on his birth certificate. The law in some states.

Craig nodded. "Mabel told me that day on the ship. She showed me his picture. He was part of her. I would've loved him like my own. We planned to go get him after..." He stopped, closed his eyes a moment, rubbed the back of his neck. "I should've gone with you to Hawaii. We could've gotten married there."

"I know," she said.

That night mamma came to her room, got in bed with her. "How are you doing, honey?"

Gladys had been hugging the pillow to her chest, crying into it. She turned, nestled against her mother, breathed the familiar scent of Evening in Paris and her skin.

"I want to go home, mamma. I just want to be in my old room. I want to sit in the swing. I want to be a little girl again. I don't know if I can do this anymore. How can I smile and play the part?"

Mamma didn't speak for several moments. She rubbed Gladys's shoulder, patting.

"I know, princess, but you can. You will. Work is the best healing. And I'll be here. I'm staying. Joe and I are getting married."

"You are?" Gladys looked up. In the lamp light mamma looked happy and young. "Mm hmm. We'll be right over in Pasadena. You can come for Sunday dinner, like a real family. And eventually you'll meet a nice man. You'll get married and have children."

A step-father, Gladys thought. A father who wasn't a gypsy. She liked Joe Mayer, liked listening to his stories of strolling the streets of Montmarte and Pigalle on leave during the war. Paris nightlife, The Moulin Rouge. She filled in the blanks. Joe was thirty-five when he enlisted, not a kid. Think of the moments you would grab if you were facing going back to the trenches.

Marriage. Children. Maybe, but first she would grab moments of her own. Who knew how many were left?

Chapter 36

The next morning Gladys felt the weight settle on her chest before she even opened her eyes. She wanted to curl into a ball.

Then she heard her two mammas bustling in the kitchen, rattling pans, baking Aunt Minnie's famous blackberry scones probably. If she didn't get up they'd bring her breakfast in bed and hover over her, and whatever she might've said, she did not want to feel like a child again.

She got up and sat with them at the kitchen table listening to their talk. A luxury, in a way. Hours drifting by. Gladys listened to mamma's wedding plans, trying not to think of the wedding that should've been.

Aunt Minnie clamored for Hollywood stories, the inside scoop to take home to friends. Of course, having lived right here in Universal City, mamma was too sophisticated to clamor, mostly because she knew Minnie would.

Gladys didn't mind. It filled the space a little longer. She had sent the occasional letter home, more often talked on the phone, and they'd seen every one of her movies several times, but still they loved to hear it all again. She told about the premieres and the time Rudy walked up to her table in the New York Biltmore.

"Imagine," Aunt Minnie said, "our little girl on first name basis with the great Valentino!"

They tsk tsked when she described Natacha Rambova.

Gladys nodded. "The Ice Queen." She leaned forward, warming to the part; she was an actress, after all. "And you know what her real name is? A girl in Wardrobe told me. She had all kinds of stories." Gladys dipped a scone in her coffee, took a slow bite, savoring. "Mmm. Aunt Minnie, how I've missed your scones."

"Oh, posh! Tell us!"

Gladys laughed. "Her name was Winifred Shaughnessy. Struts around like a czarina, and she was born in Salt Lake City, Utah!" It felt good to gossip and laugh.

"No! How in the world did she come up with Natacha Ram... whatever?"

"Ran off to New York with her Russian ballet teacher when she was seventeen. I don't remember his name, but when De Mille hired him as a designer he brought her with him. Had a harem of girls living in his house." She shuddered. "He used Natacha's designs and put his name on them. They say Natacha is..." Gladys lowered her voice. Uncle Tommy was in the living room reading the paper. "... bisexual."

"No!" Mamma and Aunt Minnie looked at each other.

"What about Rudy?" mamma asked. "We've heard he might be... you know."

"I don't think so..."

"Well, I do."

They looked up. Uncle Tommy stood in the doorway.

"Any man who'd wear a wristwatch and let himself get draped in those silly sheik robes. Downright disgusting, the way you females carry on when the guy ain't got the slightest interest in your gender." But he was smiling.

"Oh, you're just jealous." Aunt Minnie laughed.

"Jealous! How can I be jealous when I got the most beautiful girl in the world?" He walked to her, kissed her cheek.

"And now, ladies. I'd like to remind you that the sun is shining and a Stutz Bearcat is right outside begging me to drive my girls to the beach. Let's go to Venice. How 'bout that? Take a ride in a gondola."

Gladys laughed. "Uncle Tommy, I don't think we can all fit in the Bearcat."

"Sure we can. None of you is bigger than a minute. Where's the key, I'll warm her up." He made a shooing motion with his hands.

"We're leaving in ten, ladies. Let's get a move on."

Chapter 37

After three days, Gladys called Uncle Laemmle and told him she was ready to go back to work.

She needed to be Gladys Walton, the star, again, not the pampered daughter and niece. She needed to escape into a character, become someone else entirely. And what better than Joy Fielding in *The Untameable?* Under the hypnotic power of the evil Doctor, Joy Fielding offered the added challenge of two personalities, sweet and good one scene, cruel and demented the next.

Mamma was right about work being the best healing. The lull of routine. More like commotion, crews scurrying about doing a dozen different jobs, all for her entrance. She did fine, managed to get through the final week. Whole hours passed without the ache of remembering, but she did not expect what washed over her the moment King Baggot called, "That's a wrap. Monday we'll do call backs, but it looks good."

Friday night. Aunt Minnie and Uncle Tommy had left for Oregon. Mamma was with Joe Mayer. The bungalow empty.

Gladys hurried to her dressing room, closed the door, leaned against it. Damn tears! She closed her eyes, thought of her Friday night safaris with Mabel and Craig, the three of them in the Packard, laughing, peering past the headlamps to spot a dimly lit sign in some remote corner of the city, or a turn down a country road, a dance hall or speakeasy, homegrown jazz. Craig checking it first, then escorting them in, one on each arm.

She walked to her dressing table, sat with her face in her hands. In losing Mabel, she had lost Craig too. They would only remind each other...

The sound was so low it took a moment to register.

A knock on the door.

She looked up at the mirror. A change in schedule? Mr. Baggot wanting to retake a scene? Nothing that couldn't wait until Monday.

She reached tissue, wiped her eyes carefully, dabbing cold cream to fix the smeared mascara.

The knock again, almost tentative. Not Baggot, that's sure.

She walked across, opened the door and looked into the eyes of a complete stranger. How did he get past security? And why this vague feeling she had met him before?

Immaculately groomed, custom tailored gray suit, shirt pale yellow, silk tie and handkerchief a light plum. The man had a feel for color. She could smell his cologne. Reminded her of Valentino, maybe? Olive skin, but lighter. Same height, almost six foot, but stocky, the body of a wrestler.

Not nearly as handsome as Valentino, of course.

Except the eyes. Power. Like looking into the eyes of a tiger.

He was holding a pearl gray fedora and a bouquet of red roses.

Roses? She looked up at his eyes.

The building was quiet, people left quickly on a Friday night.

He stood taking her in, as if reading her, his head tilted. Kid-in-a-candy-store smile, yet something more. If he could tell she'd been crying, he didn't let it show.

She'd never seen eyes that shade. Gray as fog. Not pearl gray like the fedora, darker.

Roses. She smiled.

184

"Miss Walton," he said finally, "I was afraid you might be gone. Took me awhile to track these down, then talk my way back in. Told the guard we had a date."

He held out the bouquet. "Long stem," he said.

"Thank you." She took the roses, breathed the fragrance, didn't say more. She wanted him to speak. She'd been wrong. They could not have met before. She would remember those eyes, that voice. No accent, or maybe a hint of Brooklyn. The tone one might use reading to a child. Or standing at the edge of a meadow, not to frighten away a doe. In Oregon they set apples out and the deer came right to the porch. Uncle Tommy held one once for her to pet, its heart pounding.

The way hers was pounding now. Only not from fear.

"I watched you for hours today," he said. "Came out from Chicago on the train, just for a few days. Thought I'd see how they put a film together, maybe open a theater back home. Wanted to see the girl that jumped off that airplane. Mazie, Queen of the Air. What a scene!" He shook his head. "Planned to visit some other sets, but couldn't pull myself away. Something about you, Miss Walton. You got spunk, I can see it. Minute you came through that door, the way you looked straight into the camera. Did it all with your eyes. Like you got the world by the... tail." He nodded. "Spunk, that's it. I knew I wasn't gonna leave this town without spending time with you. Or trying."

He smiled, playful. A delicious sort of playful.

Soft baritone. Well modulated, her old speech coach would say. Quiet. Unassuming. Yet she could imagine a room full of people falling silent to hear him speak.

"I'd like to take you to dinner, Miss Walton. We'll put on the dog, maybe some dancing. I'm a good dancer, you know, but... I need to ask you something personal."

185

"You do? And what might that be?" A dinner date! With a stranger, an immaculately groomed stranger.

"Well, you see, my trip is on the quiet side. My... associates needed the vehicle tonight for some business. And the street car, well, I don't do street cars. So... exposed, you know what I mean?"

She nodded, just listening to his voice.

"Do you own a car, Miss Walton?"

She smiled. That was personal?

"I do." Wait till he sees, she thought. A night out.

"I'd have to change," she said, "find a vase for these. They're beautiful."

Dancing! She held the roses to her face, partly to hide her grin.

"We can go by my bungalow, but... I don't even know your name," she added. Not that it mattered.

"It's Al..."

He hesitated as if deciding which name to give. Not unusual in Hollywood.

"Al Capone," he said.

He offered his arm, and she took it.

The name meant nothing to her.

"And what business are you in, Mr. Capone?"

"Ah, yes... I'll tell you over dinner.

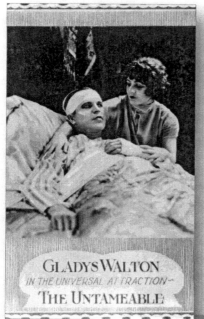

By 1922, Gladys had already starred in more than 26 films.

Al Capone first started dating Gladys while she was shooting this film.

Dapper, and dynamic Al Capone.

In photographs, he always tried to make sure his scar was hidden from view.

187

Chapter 38

She wore a silk chemise, knee length and tight at the hips, fringe all the way down. She rolled her stockings and rouged her knees, just enough. A single long strand of beads, headpiece to match, all a shade lighter than his gray suit. The fringe shivered when she walked. She felt like mercury in this dress. A flapper.

When he saw, he gave a low whistle. She felt his eyes scan up, heat rising to her cheeks.

He drove the Bearcat.

"Some car," he'd said when she led him to it parked by the studio door. "I'm used to more metal around me. You didn't say it was a breezer. Better put the top up, case it rains."

She laughed. "This is L.A., Mr. Capone, not Chicago."

November, already dark, but the sky was clear. She brought her fur jacket, a scarf woven with silver threads. It'd be chilly before the night was over.

She would not think of this night being over.

They drove through the Cahuenga Pass and west on Santa Monica, her speedster eating the miles, scarf blowing.

"So, Miss Walton," he said, and she leaned closer to hear above the wind and the engine, "Hollywood star, I probably don't have to ask if you're wet?"

She knew what he meant, but kept a straight face. "Now, that *is* a personal question, Mr. Capone. If you're going to talk like that, you'd better call me Gladys."

He looked at her and laughed, a big open laugh. He pulled a silver flask from his pocket, held it out. "Canadian, best there is."

188

The cap was gold, tiny diamonds forming the letters A.C. She took a swallow, felt the sweet burn all the way down. Took another.

"Hey, you know a good Italian grocery?"

Grocery? What did he want with a grocery? "There's some over on Main Street, but we're closer to Venice. I think we can find one there." They were headed toward Culver City, the speakeasies on Washington Boulevard, but it was too early for dancing.

"Why?" she teased, "Mr. Capone, you're not expecting me to cook, are you?"

"Heck, no." He laughed. "I'd never do that! It's for tomorrow. Told the boys I'd make my famous spaghetti and meatballs. Or if I can find some good sausage... Venice, hmm. I'd like to see that. Heard they have canals and gondolas just like Italy."

"Well, not *just* like." She laughed. "I don't think there's a roller coaster in Venice, Italy. But it's fun. We could walk on the pier, maybe eat at the Ship Cafe. I'm starved."

He nodded, kept his eyes on the road, quiet. He had that same look as when he saw her "breezer," like he was worried about something.

She waited, turning the flask in her hands. Diamonds. Had she said something wrong? It was going so well. Beyond the open fields were the lights of downtown L.A.

"There," she said, "we can take Pico, circle back. I'm sure you'll find everything you need on Main."

But he didn't turn.

"Miss Walton... Gladys," he said, "people must recognize you when you're out, crowd around? Reporters wanting interviews?"

"Sometimes. Hotel lobbies, especially. Mainly at premieres and publicity events. Anyway, what's an autograph or two, but I don't think they'll bother me when they see I'm

189

on a date." She smiled. "With a very impressive man, I might add."

He looked at her, those tiger eyes. "You think so?"

She nodded, offered him the flask, but he waved his hand.

"I'll wait." He looked out at the road, his grin turning sheepish. "Had a run in with a taxi few months back. Drunk, made a complete ass of myself. Lucky they dropped the charges. But I sure as heck don't wanta ruin this night. Bang up your Bearcat, you'd never forgive me."

They laughed, went quiet again.

"How close is Long Beach to Venice?" he asked in a moment.

"Not close. Twenty miles, at least." What did Long Beach have to do with anything?

"Ah, hell!" He slapped the wheel. "Venice, it is. Just tell me where to turn. Might be as close as I ever get to Italy. Or strolling with a beautiful actress on my arm." He glanced over. "I saw *The Man Tamer, Second Hand Rose*, and... what's that one where you're a mountain girl, big brute has you in his cabin, you get his gun...?"

"The Girl Who Ran Wild."

"Boy, I laughed at that, holding that gun like it was a kitten or something, but damn, even barefoot in rags you were gorgeous. What are you, nineteen?"

"Twenty in January."

"I'll be twenty-four."

He shook his head. "All those movies. Jumping off a plane, working with lions, now that's impressive. Me, I'm just... Come here, you." He pulled her to him, kissed her hard and quick, glanced back at the road. "Mazie, Queen of the Air. I'd make you my queen if I could. You're queen material, that's for sure."

He sounded almost wistful. Who was he? *If he could.* What did that mean? She didn't care, his scent, that cologne, the way he'd reached for her, his hand on the back of her neck, his lips. She took another swallow from the flask, leaned against his chest. She had learned how fragile it all was, how pointless to question. Better to just live.

They turned down Venice, a wide avenue straight to the sea. They were past Lincoln Boulevard when he screeched the brakes, did a U turn, swerving between two sedans. She yelped, braced on the dashboard, and they jerked to a stop in front of a little shop.

Giovanni's Grocery & Sundries.

He didn't even use the door, hoisted himself up and swung over. He came around, reached his big hands under her arms and lifted her out onto the sidewalk.

"Come on, Pixie, we got shoppin' to do."

Some boys were playing marbles by the door. They crowded around the Bearcat, and he handed the smallest one a fiver.

"Here ya go, kid, watch the car, will ya?" He tousled his hair.

Inside, he greeted the Mama and Papa owners as if they'd been neighbors in the old country, strolled the plaza together. Tins of pasta were on the counter, canned goods and boxes stacked on shelves all the way to the ceiling. Wheels of cheese in a glass case, strings of garlic and sausages, spices in burlap bags. The aromas made her stomach growl.

Gladys watched. Mr. Capone seemed in his element, smiling, speaking Italian in that Sunday afternoon voice. He breathed energy, as if the lights flickered brighter the minute he walked in, yet at the same time he seemed to make everyone calm. Like this was the man to know. In the flurry of Italian, Gladys heard him say her name.

The couple turned to her, their eyes wide with recognition. Or maybe it was the dress. Who knew what Al was saying? They came around the counter, wiping their hands on their aprons, chattering too fast to translate, and next the man was tearing off a stretch of butcher paper, handing her his grease pencil to sign.

"Big," he said, spreading his arms, "grandisimo!"

Al stood back and watched, grinning.

Ten minutes later a boy carried out their bundles tied with string, pasta, loaves of crusty bread, ingredients for antipasto, Greek olives, oil, onions, garlic, big orange peppers, chestnuts from Lombardy and sausage, three kinds, cans of tomato paste. Stowed in the compartment by the spare. The register rang $4.72, and Al peeled off three crisp sawbucks from a roll of bills as big as his fist.

As they pulled away, Giovanni was taping her butcher paper autograph in the window.

At the stop sign, Al leaned and kissed her, slow this time.

"Thanks." He put his hand on her stomach, kissed her again, opening her mouth with his tongue. His splayed fingers moving down, just a little.

She gasped, thought she would melt into the leather.

"Now," he whispered, "let's get some food in this pretty belly. What d'ya say, kid?"

Chapter 39

They could see the glow a mile away, but when they turned past Ince Field where the barnstormers parked their planes, the sight was still a surprise. The whole pier trimmed in lights. From the Lagoon Bath House to the huge dance hall, the Race Thru The Clouds roller coaster, Ferris wheel and fun house and carousel, the tall masts of the Cabrillo Ship Cafe; everything sparkled, lights haloed in the ocean mist.

"Oh, it's a dream!" Gladys sat forward, slipping off her scarf. She adjusted the headpiece, licked her fingers to fix the curls on her forehead. "I've never been here at night. Aren't you glad we came?"

He smiled, watching her. "More than you know."

They parked as close as they could to the Grand Canal, hundreds of cars lined the packed dirt. Automobiles weren't allowed on Trolley Way which ran adjacent to the beach a block from Ocean Front.

Al donned his fedora, tipped it just so, straightened his tie in the mirror. He took a swig from the flask, pocketed it inside his suit coat. He used the door this time, came and opened hers with a sweeping bow. "My lady."

She laughed, took his arm. They joined others strolling along the canal, the path lit by wrought iron lamps. On an arched bridge they stood looking out at the red-roofed houses on both sides, a few empty lots, some under construction. The smell of the sea in the chill air, distant rattle of the roller coaster, ladies' screams, calliope music, the whistle of the miniature railroad. More like a toot.

"What a place!" Al put his arm around her. "How'd you like to live here," he nodded, "one of them houses? Have a boat, go fishing in the ocean. You like to fish, Gladys?"

"I do. My uncle used to take me in Oregon. When I was ten I caught a ling cod. He thought my line was snagged on the bottom, but when I pulled it up, it was a fifteen pound cod! The meat was bright turquoise. We made a fire and cooked it there on the beach."

She smiled. The houses were large, two stories, probably five or six bedrooms. A long drive to work, but she had the car for it. Crazy thoughts. They'd just met. She wondered if men were like that, trying on different lives the way women try on clothes.

God, she was hungry!

They walked around the lagoon, past the boat house with its fleet of gondolas, hundreds of tourists on every block, hundreds more disembarking from trolleys. Some stared at Gladys, whispering to friends, but didn't approach. If it was up to her, she'd have gone straight to the pier, food! But, of course, they had to browse the colonnade on Windward, the heart of Venice. Ornate buildings with their tiered Venetian arches and scrollwork, marble entries. And what fun, watching Mr. Capone.

Al stopped, gazing up at St. Marks Hotel. "'Hot Salt Water Bath In Every Room,'" he read the sign, looked at the crowds, shook his head. "Man, talk about a place to do business. If I'd known, I could'a come to Los Angeles instead of Chicago." His eyes wistful again. "A whole different life. Maybe... They got speakeasies here?"

Gladys nodded. "I heard there's one in the basement of the Antler Hotel and Menotti's Buffet. We could eat there instead, if you want?"

"Eat. Damn, I forgot. What's the matter with me? Let's go."

The Ship Cafe was crowded, but Mr. Capone quietly took out his roll of bills, and whatever he handed the maitre d' got them a table by the center window in minutes. A white moon shimmered the waves, the row of piers to Santa Monica, a barnstormer doing loops over Venice Beach.

"The Pacific," Al said, "if that ain't a sight."

They watched the biplane for several minutes, until it flew straight for the pier, swerving up over their heads the last second, the roar rattling the windows. The restaurant crowd gasped and applauded.

The waiter brought fruit drinks which Al "doctored" from his flask.

Gladys pointed out the window. "Those lights are Culver City. The Ince Studios are there and Hal Roach and Metro, a bunch of smaller ones. More studios in Culver City than Hollywood. Speakeasies too, and I heard they put in a horse track..."

"Horse track! Now we're talking."

"So is that your business, Mr. Capone," she said, "race horses?"

He laughed. "More like a liability. I'm a rotten gambler, always drop more on the ponies than I win."

Gladys waited for him to go on. What business allowed you to carry fistfuls of cash? There were hundred dollar bills in that roll.

He studied her a moment, then reached to the inside pocket of his coat, handed her a card. *ALPHONSE CAPONE - Second Hand Furniture Dealer - 2220 South Wabash Avenue.*

She looked up at him, managed not to laugh.

"Yes, of course, I see," she said. Formal, her tea and crumpets voice.

"I thought you would." He matched her tone, his eyes laughing.

"And I imagine most of your... furniture is imported from Canada. The best there is, am I correct?"

"Absolutely. The very best."

"Well," she said, "I hear there's a huge demand for... Canadian furniture."

"That there is, can't bring it in fast enough. Someone's gotta do it. I owe a great deal to those WCTU ladies and their hatchets, bless their crusading hearts." He laughed.

Rascal eyes, turned his whole face handsome. Second hand furniture. She sipped her fruit drink, laughing.

They were still chuckling when the waiter brought a platter piled with lobster and fat shrimp, salads and thick bread. She devoured the succulent meat, breaking the shells, fingers dripping. When she looked up, he was watching her again, grinning.

"Gal with an appetite," he said. "Can't beat that." He reached across, wiped her chin with a napkin, his hand lingering.

She blushed. "Well, I haven't felt much like eating lately, but tonight... You make me... happy." She almost said hungry.

"Good. I want to make you happy, Gladys. As much as I can." His gray eyes soft in the candlelight.

A man approached from behind his right shoulder then, and Al jumped, knocking over a glass as he stood, reaching into his pocket. His eyes flashed dark, the color of steel.

"Sorry, sir. I didn't mean to..." The maitre d' grabbed the glass. "We'll get this cleaned up right away." He motioned to a waiter.

Gladys saw Al breathe in, calm himself.

"No problem, don't worry about it." He sat back down, his hand still in his pocket, watched the waiter wipe the spill.

"Can we get you anything else, sir?" the maitre d' said. He stepped back to make room for the waiter. "Dessert tray, perhaps? We have lovely desserts."

Al turned to look up at him.

It was then she saw the scars, straight lines on his left cheek and jaw, another below his ear, disappearing under his collar. Chalk white against his olive skin. He must've been keeping his good side toward her all evening. She would've noticed scars like that.

"Sure," Al said to the maitre d', "bring a few desserts. You choose. And your best coffee. Then... leave us alone, okay?" He slid him another bill. "We're trying to have us a romantic dinner here. Know what I mean?"

"Of course, sir. Absolutely." He shooed the waiter away. "We won't bother you again, sir."

Al turned, saw her eyes, and his hand went to his cheek. He shrugged, like a kid caught with in mother's purse. "Little scrape in a bar," he said, "Coney Island. Guy pulled a knife. He had a right. I said something stupid to his girl." He laughed. "Didn't know it was his sister. I was eighteen. Guy don't know crap at eighteen." He went silent, turned toward the window, hiding the scars again.

What could she say? She leaned across, touched his cheek, turned him back to her. "I think they're sexy, in a rugged kind of way."

"Go on!"

"They are." She drew her fingers over the scars and down his neck. Could almost feel his skin respond to her touch. "Like your eyes, Mr. Furniture Dealer," she said. "Very sexy."

He looked at her a moment, then lifted her hand, kissed her palm.

Shivers all the way to her toes, she had to force herself not to close her eyes and sigh. People at other tables glancing at them. She could see the headline, *GLADYS WALTON SWOONS OVER MYSTERY MAN IN SHIP CAFE.*

He stood, came and pulled out her chair, spoke close to her ear. That bedroom voice.

197

"Come on. Never mind dessert. I want you close to me. Hell, I want to ravish you." He grinned. "I want to eat you all up! But first let's go find one of them gondolas."

The Ship Cafe on Abbot Kinney Pier, Venice, CA, was built as a replica of Juan Cabrillo's galleon.

It was part of an enormous entertainment complex. Dance houses, bath houses, thrill rides, and romantic gondola rides through Venice's canals.

The Ship Cafe was a renowned restaurant frequented by stars from the Silent Film Industry, and it was reported that just prior to prohibition going into effect, they were charging $300.00 a table.

Chapter 40

Nestled against cushions at one end of the narrow boat, they circled the lagoon, then glided under a bridge down a smaller canal. The sounds from the pier faded until there was only the dip of the gondolier's pole, water lapping the hull. It was dark away from the pier. A fog had drifted in from the sea, and she could taste the salt air. It felt enclosed yet not enclosed, like looking through gauze. Houses loomed one by one, their few lighted windows like eyes glowing. Stars blinked where the mist parted. The lamp posts on the paths had disappeared leaving fuzzy haloes suspended in the mist.

For a long time they didn't speak. They kissed. Long, silent kisses, savoring each other. She arched against him, head back, searching the gauze sky for stars. He kissed her throat, his hand doing its own quiet search. Sliding a strap from her shoulder, then the other, he kissed the softness above her breasts.

She closed her eyes, her questions all but forgotten. How long would he stay? When would he return?

The gondolier dressed all in black like a specter, guarding, rowing them to another world. A world without lights and cameras and flimsy plots and her friend dying. Without... whatever filled Mr. Capone's days and nights in Chicago.

Finally Al let out a long breath. "Whew, baby!" He squirmed, adjusted his trousers. "We got the mast. All we need is a sail, we can head for China."

She glanced down, giggling. A mast, all right. Maybe they should skip dancing.

"So," Al said to the gondolier, "I thought you guys were supposed to sing. Give us a *O Sole Mio* or something." When Al got no answer, he repeated it in Italian.

"Si, si," the gondolier said and started a medley of tourist songs. Al joined in, a smooth baritone blending with the young man's tenor. Gladys listened. The gondolier was about her age, maybe a year or two younger, his skin darker than Mr. Capone's.

When they finished, Al asked him something in Italian.

The gondolier shrugged. "Roma," he said simply.

Al waited, but that was all.

"It's okay, no problema." Al sat back, laughing.

"What was that about?" Gladys said.

"I asked if he could sing opera, maybe some Verdi." He gestured to the sky, the water. "Only thing 'd make this night more perfect's an aria from Traviata." He let his arm fall. "Guy drew a blank. So I asked where he was from. Rome." Al chuckled. "More like Tijuana. Ain't a Italian alive don't know Verdi. I'll take you sometime when you come to Chicago."

Come to Chicago, Gladys thought. So matter of fact.

He reached inside his jacket, pulled out the flask, shook it a little. "Gettin' low," he said, handing it to her. "Time to hit the speakeasies."

He looked at the gondolier. "Señor Poncho, vamos, por favor." He nodded toward the lagoon. "Take us back, okay?"

She gave Al a look. Calling him Poncho.

He shrugged, grinning. "Hey, he knows what I mean. Lady Liberty ain't as welcoming as she seems. Ain't that right, buddy?"

Al repeated it in Italian, and the young man nodded.

Minutes later when they stepped from the gondola, Al took out his roll of bills, shook the young man's hand, thanked him.

"That was quite a ride." He glanced at Gladys. "One I won't forget."

"Da nada." The gondolier smiled. His eyes widened as Al slipped three one hundred dollar bills into the pocket of his black shirt.

"Go to school, kid. Learn English, never mind Italian. This was your land once, you know." Al patted his shoulder, laughing. "Oh yeah, and name all your kids Alfonso."

Eyes still wide, the young man pumped Al's hand.

"Si, señor, seguro que si, the girls too."

It was a short drive to Culver City. They started at The Hot Spot Cafe, then The Hoosegow, but the best was The Green Mill, three dance floors and full orchestras. Hottest jazz west of the Mississippi. Al had the flask filled for later. They drank beer in tall glasses and danced a new dance called the Charleston. What a dance! Her dress was perfect, a blur of silver fringe, except a bit tight for that thing you did with your knees. It surprised her how good Al was. Who would think he could move like that? Doing the kick steps easy, then circling her waist with his big hands, lifting her over his head, then down between his legs, laughing.

The orchestra took a break, and as they walked to their table Gladys nodded to people she knew, or had been introduced to one time or another, the Talmadge sisters, tiny Gloria Swanson in one of her outrageous outfits, all beads and feathers, her face flawless and cold as a diamond. In the doorway Charlie Chaplin stood with Pola Negri on his arm. What was Charlie doing with Pola Negri? Not at all his type. Publicity, maybe.

"Shall I introduce you?" Gladys asked Al.

"Nah," he said, "it's okay. Or if you have to, I'm Al Brown."

She laughed. "Don't worry. They're too drunk to remember anyway."

"Listen," he said, looking up.

Through the wall came the clear, smooth strains of a solo coronet. "I know that horn. Come on." They hurried to the next room and sat listening to Louis Armstrong. "When you come to Chicago, I'll take you to the Lincoln Gardens," Al said. "Right after I teach you to shoot."

Her eyes widened, and he laughed. "I'm joking."

Mr. Armstrong lifted his coronet in greeting, but didn't come to their table.

They danced more, then Al took out a pocket watch, gold, initialed with diamonds, of course.

"Almost one o'clock," he said. "I was supposed to meet the boys in front of Universal. Told 'em to go on if I didn't show. If we leave now we might make it."

Outside in the parking lot, he pulled her to him, kissed her, his hands on her back. "Damn, I don't want to let you go."

He kissed her again, gripping her bottom, lifting her.

She felt him hard against her and smiled, remembering his "mast." Her head light from the whiskey and beer, skin burning. Long, wet kisses, little shocks down her sides. She wanted him. Nipping his lip, his ear, would've wrapped her legs around him except for this dress. She could hike it up. Or find the nearest open field and take it off. If only they had the Packard.

She held his face in her hands, kissed him harder, used her tongue. He tasted of lobster and whiskey.

"That's it. That's it!" He grabbed her up, carried her toward the car. "You're mine. I'm taking you with me."

"Where? To China or Chicago?"

He laughed. "To paradise. You'll see."

Chapter 41

Gladys woke when a jolt lifted her, bouncing her head against his shoulder, her body landing hard on the seat.

"Sorry," Al said, "I'm trying to find the road. Can't slow much or we'll get stuck."

She blinked up at him. It took a moment to clear the sleep away.

"What time is it?"

He kept his eyes straight ahead. "Three, maybe three thirty. We made good time. This baby hums, Gladys. Had her up to eighty, ninety. Only a few more miles."

Three thirty. She'd thought they might stop at one of the road houses between Santa Monica and L.A., but he drove through the city, then the road east following the train tracks. She remembered kidding him, "I never thought San Bernardino was paradise."

She sat up now and gasped. They were on the moon, but it was there shining down on them, the same three-quarter moon they had seen over Venice Beach. No, not the same. Bigger and brighter. In her whole life she had never seen such a sky. Billions of stars, an immense canopy of stars. How could the sky be bigger in one place than another? Yet it was. A vast, endless sky over a sweep of desert up to the low mountains. She gazed around. Nothing but sand and rocks and desert brush. To their left in the distance, tall mountains capped with snow. The same mountains she could see from her bungalow, only now they were in the west.

Road? There was no road, more like a dry wash they were bumping along. The only hints of water were shallow furrows cut in the packed sand along the sides, which could've been here a hundred years.

She shivered, pulling her fur around her neck. She had to pee. All that beer. "Do you think we could stop a minute?" she asked, squirming.

He nodded, hunched over the wheel, concentrating, avoiding rocks the size of melons. "Up ahead where the ground's harder," he said. "It's a long walk if we get stuck."

Where was he taking her anyway? She wished he would kiss her, remind her why she had come with him, to the middle of nowhere, as it turned out. A man she hardly knew. Where was Palm Springs? As far as she could see not a single building or light from a window. Not even a tree, except those wispy things like overgrown bushes. Still, she would not have missed seeing this. Such majesty. She remembered how Rudy spoke of the desert. Strange beauty and emptiness. A little scary, she saw now; the place could swallow you up. It was cold, mid-November, but imagine in summer.   Al stopped the car where there were more dry rivulets and the sand formed a hard crust. He turned the key, the engine did a last shudder.

What struck her then was the silence. A sea of silence.

"Oh my," she said, her voice tiny, engulfed by the expanse.

He drew her close, kissed her. "I guess you'd better go now. It's a few more miles. There." He pointed up ahead, but all she could see were dark clumps in the distance.

"I think I see the road too, though it ain't much better." He came around, opened her door. "Can you manage?" he asked as she stepped out.

"I think so." Her heels sank in the sand.

He steadied her, pulled the handkerchief from his breast pocket, handed it to her. She looked up, questioning. His plum colored silk handkerchief?

"It's okay." He grinned. "Leave it on a bush. Indians will think it's a treasure."

"Indians?" She looked around.

"Sure, the Indians showed me the place." He nodded to the distant clumps up ahead. "They're helping build it. We passed the Garnet train station few miles back. Well, more like a watering stop. Always an Indian or two hanging around when the train comes." He laughed. "You should 'a seen me and the boys riding mules up here our first time."

She smiled, picturing men in tailored suits and fedoras bouncing along on mules.

She turned, looked behind them for the train, but could see only the vast slope of desert, shadowy mountains rising far across, a valley ringed with mountains.

"Want me to come with you, Gladys? I promise to turn my back."

"No thanks. I've been on plenty of picnics." She slipped off her shoes, handed them to him, and set out for the nearest large bush some fifty feet away, the sand cool through her silk stockings.

When she'd gone maybe ten paces Al called out, "Don't worry, rattlesnakes don't come out at night."

"Oh, you!"

But she scanned the ground with each step, avoiding sage brush and piles of rocks. She stopped once to pull a sticker from her foot, how bright it was, the sand almost glowed in the moonlight. The air crisp and dry and silent. A pungent fragrance rose from the larger bushes. When she touched the tiny leaves they were slightly sticky and the scent stayed on her fingers. Something skittered in front of her. A lizard. It stopped, did a few push-ups, eyelids blinking.

"Hello, handsome," she whispered, and it disappeared beneath a rock. Another sound startled her and she looked up. Far off, a yipping echoed over the hills and gullies. More yips took up the chorus miles away. She smiled. The place was magic.

Minutes later she slid in beside Al.

"You should see how that dress looks in the moonlight," he said. "Man!" He kissed her once, and they started again, found the road. It went straight up the gradual slope, then curved east a mile or so, and she watched as the dark clumps became shaggy palm trees, a desert oasis.

"They call it Two Bunch Palms," Al said, "see? Two bunches. Indians have another name, but I can't pronounce it."

They turned onto a dirt path hardly wider than the car. In the headlights she could see ruts from wagon wheels. Some filled with water. The air smelled of moisture and the musk of plant life, the stars and moon twinkling through thick trees. A shadow world, shapes looming on all sides, clear only in front where the headlights shone. An oasis. What a mystery, water bubbling up from deep in the ground. The palm trees not like the ones in Hawaii or the kind brought in to decorate gardens in L.A. These were fat with wide fronds all the way down. Long beards, Valentino had said. The ground was strewn with curved fronds, like tusks in an elephant graveyard. Tall grass and reeds grew between the trees and beside the path, here and there a dead palm, its trunk bent double, bowing.

The road ended at a low wall made of gray stones like they'd seen in the wash and piled across the desert, but these looked handpicked, round and all about the same size, melon rocks. She was surprised when they pulled up beside a big black touring car. It seemed so out of place, as if they'd left the world of machines and automobiles far behind, except the Stutz, of course. Her magic carpet.

"They're not back," Al said. "Gotta be close to four o'clock. What the hell?" He cut the engine, then flashed the headlights three times and left them on.

She wanted to ask what he meant. If *they* weren't back, who did the touring car belong to? But he sounded irritated. She stayed quiet, realizing for the first time she had only the dress and shoes she was wearing, no makeup or toiletries, not even a hairbrush. Where would they sleep, on the ground? All kinds of critters must live in these bearded trees. What had she gotten herself into? The place was so desolate, completely isolated. There couldn't be a telephone, not even electricity.

A small light appeared to their right, twenty feet up, as if someone were sitting in a tree holding a lantern.

"That you, boss?" a voice called. Deep and scratchy like a man with a damaged throat. More like a croak.

She looked at Al.

"That's One Arm," he said, "takes care of the place." Al grinned. "He's my right hand man, only he ain't got no right hand."

He turned and called out toward the light. "Yeah, it's me. And a lady too. A very special lady. We're going for a dip in the grotto. Bring a couple towels and robes, okay? And the Eveready. And we got some stuff to unload."

"Sure thing, boss," the voice croaked. "Boys ain't back yet."

"I see that."

Al got out, came around, lifted her into his arms. He kissed her, soft, slow kisses. He smiled. "Now, we got us some unfinished business, huh, baby?"

She nestled against him, shivering. "But how can we swim, Al? It's too cold, don't you think?"

He laughed. "Don't you worry, I'll keep you warm," and carried her around the wall. In the light from the car she could see a thick lawn on either side of a path that sloped gently down. He stepped across a small, rock-lined stream. To their left another stone wall. Then she saw what must be the grotto. The moon peeked through the trees, reflecting off an oval pool some fifteen feet across, a waterfall tumbling over rocks at one end. The pool was sunken several feet below ground level, and Al moved carefully down the stone steps to a wide ledge.

He set her on her feet, and she stared. Like a picture postcard. Lush grass and ferns around the edge, shaggy palm trees above, moonlight shimmering the water. As still as a church, except the sound of the waterfall. Wisps of steam rose from the surface of the pool.

"I never dreamed..."

"Natural hot springs." Al nodded, slipped off her fur, set it on the top step. "Sacred waters, the Indians say. Cures anything." He unfastened the back of her dress, slid it down, steadied her while she slipped off her high heels. "You won't need those either." He nodded to her step-in underwear, taking off his jacket, loosening his tie.

She looked at his shoulders and chest in that pale yellow shirt, thought of their kisses in the gondola, his hands...

"Hurry," he said, "you're shaking. I'd take more time, but you need to get warm."

He helped her with the snaps, held her arm as she lowered herself into the pool.

Naked.

"Oh, my God!"

It felt glorious, blood warm, silky. Another step and it was up to her shoulders. She moved her hands through the water. The bottom was lined with the same melon rocks, the water so clear in the moonlight she could see her toes. She did a slow dog paddle, felt the warmth on her belly, between her legs, delicious. She held her breath, did a dive, arms to her sides, legs moving like a mermaid tail. She circled the pool twice, and when she came up, Al was there, catching her into his arms, laughing.

"Look at you," he said, "a water nymph. I knew it. You were made for this place."

He lifted her above his head, and she gasped at the cold air.

"I crown you princess, no queen. Queen of Two Bunch Palms. How's that?"

He planted kisses on her belly, then her breasts as she inched down his bare chest. He held her, lapping water from her skin, one nipple, then the other. He ducked them under, his legs twined around hers, did a slow alligator spin and came up, laughing and gasping. He kissed her mouth, her neck, her shoulders, devouring, as he'd said he would. His hand between her legs. So smooth, her arms around his neck, there where her feet didn't touch bottom, and in another minute he slid inside, easy, each slow thrust lifting her out of the water.

Head back, she kept her eyes open, holding every sensation, the night sky, the bearded trees, his kisses warm as the water. Hot. Nice and slow. No hurry. His hands holding her waist, moving her on him.

"Paradise, you weren't kidding," she breathed close to his ear, and her laugh became quick gasps, then a cry, as she clung to him, tears falling on his wet face.

He held her against his chest, and at first she thought the sound was the beating of his heart until he whispered, "Look, look, Gladys. Quick."

She opened her eyes, followed his nod and got a glimpse of wings crossing the moon.

"White owl," he said. "They live here. Indians say they're good luck." He laughed. "Not good luck for the mouse he had in his beak. Did you see it? Man, talk about fast!"

He touched her cheek. "You okay, kid?"

She didn't answer, didn't need to.

"Come on, I'll show you the stone cabin." He stretched an arm out. "Nice big bed would feel pretty darn good about now, wouldn't you say?
"

The miles and miles of arid, desert-like terrain surrounding these two majestic palm groves created an almost magical impression. Above the valley, it was as if an Arabian Nights mirage had been transplanted to the Southern California desert. Warm bubbling, refreshing, restorative are only some of the words used to describe those abundant and clear hot springs.

An ideal hideaway for Capone, this is where he built his "fortress". His plans included expanding into a speakeasy, possibly a casino to serve the newly rich Hollywood crowd just discovering the quiet and solitude of the desert.

Two Bunch Palms is now a renowned resort.

Chapter 42

She was dreaming. Voices in the next room, a party, the clink of glasses. A door opened, the glare of lights, cameras rolling. That scene in the Untameable. She was late. Mr. Baggot on his megaphone. Where was her bouquet of roses? She stepped forward, but the room disappeared. Mabel lying in a hammock between palm trees. She sat up, smiling that blue-eyed smile. "Oh, Gladys, y'all can take me to the water now. Indians say it cures anything."

Gladys woke trembling. So real. Mabel's voice exactly. That surge of joy, then... remembering. Too late for any cure. Tears stung her eyes, her chest ached.

She wanted to go back to the dream, see her again, talk to her, so much to tell...

She curled under the satin quilt, a cascade of pillows in the high bed. The room was dark, no light from the window. Good, the night wasn't over. She remembered the grotto pool, and Al bringing her here to this bed. He rolled her onto him, their skin still warm from the water. The first time she'd actually slept with a man. Well, hardly slept, no more than an hour.

She wanted to be in his arms now, make love again, forget everything else. She turned to nestle against him, but the sheet was cold where he had been. She could smell his cologne. And their sex.

Voices. Outside on the patio, but real. Men talking. Al.

She wiped her eyes, pulled back the covers, slipped to the floor. She found the robe on the chair. Plush rugs on polished hardwood floors, heavy oak furniture. She made her way across to the mirrored vanity, felt for the small lamp, switched it on. Shaped like a candle in a holder, only it worked with a battery like a flashlight. She'd been right about no electricity. The low light made rainbows in the mirror's beveled trim. A silver tray held an ivory handled brush and comb, jars of powder and creams, perfumes in fluted bottles. Guerlain, Chanel No. 5.

And she'd thought they might have to sleep on the ground! Should've known. Everything about the man was luxury. She smiled. Like that king whose touch turned things to gold. She fluffed her hair in the mirror, still damp. Her cheeks pink, no need for makeup.

Holding the lamp, she walked into the next room. She'd had only glimpses on the way to the bed. Several candle lamps were spaced here and there, and now she went and switched each one on. Cabin. More like a small castle, overstuffed velvet sofas and chairs in front of a stone fireplace, kerosene lamps with Tiffany shades. To her left was a bar made of dark wood, stained glass along the top, mirror in back. Bottles lined the shelves, catching the dim light.

The room was maybe thirty feet long, one end curved like the stern of a ship, three tall windows draped in velvet, ruby red to match the furniture, tasseled gold cords. In front of the windows was a game table and two easy chairs, dark blue. Velvet, of course.

She had to admit it looked a bit like a very expensive brothel.

The drapes were closed. She walked across, peeked out, the sky just starting to lighten. She listened. Nothing. Maybe they'd gone out to the cars.

She turned and noticed the table was leather on top, in a corner brass studs formed the letters A.C. The man put his mark on things. On her too, no denying. At least she'd managed to tell him she mustn't get pregnant. He'd reached to a drawer beside the bed, laughing at her word. *Precautions.*

She tied the robe closed, picked up the lamp and went out. To her right was a flagstone patio. To her left, a narrow corridor ran between the two sections of the "cabin." The corridor was dark, but she could see it opened on the other end. Odd to build it this way, his part of the compound separated from the two rooms in front.

She walked onto the patio. My God, the voices seemed to be coming from beneath her feet!

She pulled the robe higher on her neck, walked around to the front, her feet cold on the stone. The stars were starting to fade. Across the lawn, she could see the stream tumbling from the grotto pool. It passed within yards of the cabin, disappearing down the hill to her right, steam rising from the surface. Amazing. The water must flow continually, an endless source.

She turned back toward the cabin. Between the entrances to the two rooms she noticed a door made of rough planks, like the door to a storm cellar. It was swung back. She walked to the opening, shined the light. Steps descended into blackness. Did this explain the underground voices?

She hesitated. What was down there? Should she find out, or... What, go back to bed? Lie awake, waiting?

Gripping the lamp, she edged down the narrow steps. At the bottom she moved the light around, hand trembling. A square chamber, tunnels in two directions. Tunnels? The smell of damp earth, the air heavy and close. Cigarette smoke. Men's voices again, muffled.

She took the tunnel to the left toward the sounds. Slowly, like entering a mine shaft, a catacomb. Barefoot. She held the lamp low not to step on something squirmy, snakes, spiders. She lifted it, scanning for webs, the dirt ceiling only inches above, support beams every few feet. Eerie, roots

213

poking through like hairy fingers, the dark closing behind her, dirt crumbling where her sleeve brushed the wall.

Her heart pounded. Breathe in, calm, like before an entrance. That's it, think of it as a scene in a movie. Not easy without crew and cameras.

What if it wasn't Al? What if he had left her here with...?

Don't be silly.

Light up ahead. The faint smell of kerosene. She walked another few feet and stopped. She was shaking, the light from her lamp moving crazy on the wall. She was only yards from the room, must be directly under the patio.

She switched off the lamp, listened, hardly breathing.

"Shoulda seen it, boss. On our way back to the harbor we seen another boat. Surprised 'em good, just loaded up their crates with ours."

"All that fit. Why it took longer. Had to make a couple more trips."

"Yeah, left me there guarding 'em. Damn near an hour."

Three different voices.

Then a croaky laugh she recognized from last night. One Arm. "Woulda liked to been there myself."

Silence, several long moments.

"That was not the plan." Al spoke low, the words drawn out, more unsaid than said.

She breathed in, relieved.

"Always better to stick to the plan," Al said. Another pause. "But no harm, I guess. Long as it's good Canadian. I don't deal rot gut."

She took a step, hesitated. His tone flat, almost ominous, unless she was imagining. Would he be angry with her too? No. He'd brought her here, after all, and what the heck, act like she hadn't heard anything. Besides, it was only bootlegging. Gladys straightened her shoulders, took a deep breath, stepped into the light.

"So, here you ar..." But her words ended in a squeal as four men jumped up, drawing guns, three pistols and a sawed off shot gun which One Arm swung up with his one arm. His other was solid wood, like a club, his face hidden in the shadows. A hulk of a man.

She gasped, raised her hands above her head, felt her robe open, and reached just as fast to close it. "Oops," she said, grinning. The men stared, a girl hardly more than five feet tall, flash of white skin. Then the one closest turned to the others, gestured with his pistol.

"Hey, ain't that the Glad Girl from the movies? What the hell!"

Al didn't budge. He just sat there in his robe on a stool beside stacks of crates, whiskey on one side, beer on the other, his grin widening. Then he laughed, slapping his knee.

"Miss Walton," he said, "meet the boys."

Chapter 43

Introductions were brief, to the say the least. Hardened faces, names that could not be real. Grits and The Mole and a skinny Indian they called Hawk. "First name's Tommy," Al said, smiling at the joke, but it was clear the way Al stood and walked to her, he did not want her to linger, did not want the men shaking her hand or getting chummy.

They just nodded. One Arm stayed in the shadows.

"Get some sleep," Al said to the boys, "I'm cookin' later. Remember, you got a night of deliveries ahead."

He took the candle lamp, turned her down the tunnel, his hand on her back.

A current seemed to run through his fingers, a kind of restrained power, and she saw how vast his organization must be. Every town from New York to L.A. had a few speakeasies, hundreds in the big cities.

Al chuckled. "Sorry, Gladys. This business don't always attract the most savory individuals. Some of 'em are missing a few tacks."

"What do you expect, dealing second hand furniture?"

They laughed, then she heard footsteps behind them. She turned and saw only a dark silhouette.

"Just One Arm," Al whispered, "don't worry. He's a good man. Toad ugly, hit by a freight train or something, but one of the best." They started again. Al spoke louder, over his shoulder. "Keep trying to get him to come east with me, but he won't leave Two Bunch. Thinks the water's gonna turn him into a prince. Right, Arm?"

"Right, boss. Pretty soon I'll be as handsome as you."
That gravelly voice.

"Yeah, yeah, mug like mine, regular dream boat. A
sheik." Al laughed.

They reached the square chamber. The opening at the
top of the steps showed a patch of sky streaked pink orange
with the sunrise.

Al looked at her in the light. "Something else, Gladys.
I gave One Arm a new assignment. To keep you safe. Your
own private body guard whenever you need. You can come
out here anytime, relax, enjoy the water. Bring friends. Hell,
throw a party. One Arm'll take care of everything." He
touched her cheek. "You're my queen, aren't you? The place
is yours. After I'm gone."

Gone. She did not realize how close the tears were to
the surface, but the way he was looking at her, and that word.
The word Craig had said in the hospital when... She
remembered her dream. She blinked, but couldn't stop the
tears. She looked down.

"What is it, Gladys? Did I say something wrong?" He
tipped her face up, searching, but she looked away.

"No, of course not. It's just..." She wiped at her eyes.
Her hand shook. "Oh, I'm not usually like this." She tried to
smile. "But I... I lost someone... close to me..." Her throat
tightened on the words.

"A lover? Did he leave you?"

His voice didn't change.

She met his eyes. "No, not that. A friend... she... died.
Not quite two weeks..."

"She was your age?"

"A year older."

"Mmm." He nodded. "So that's what I saw when you
opened your dressing room door. I'm sorry, Gladys."

His eyes glistened. Those gray tiger eyes. He drew her into his arms, held her while she cried. "It's okay," he whispered. "This life ain't easy, is it? But we'll grab what we can, huh, sweetheart? You and me, whenever we can."

His voice. She would take that voice with her.

"I'm not leaving till the end of the week," he said, rubbing her back. "Stay with me. You can tell me all about it. I want to know everything. I'll have the boys go into Palm Springs, telegraph the studio. Get you some clothes too. Sun dresses, anything you need. You can make a list. Grits should be able to handle that."

He turned her head up, kissed her lightly. "You finished the film, didn't you?"

She nodded. "But... I need to telegraph my mother too."

"Sure, no problem."

"And what about a bathing outfit?"

He smiled. "If you want, but no need. Boys wouldn't come within fifty feet of the grotto pool if their lives depended on it." He took her hand. "Then it's settled. A week in these waters you'll be like new. Right, Arm?"

"Right, boss. Absolutely." A voice from the tunnel.

She smiled. To spend a week here with him. Swim naked in the grotto pool. In broad daylight! Where could she ever do that? Frolicking like otters. The way he'd lapped water from her skin. Queen of Two Bunch Palms. He was so funny, clowning with One Arm like big kids. And the nights, that room. The things he knew. She had enough experience with men to know how rare that was. The thought sent chills up her sides.

"So, what we need now is breakfast. One Arm makes a killer omelet." Al laughed. "And coffee that'll curl your toes." He started her up the steps, then called back. "Oh, and grill us

218

up some of that Italian sausage, okay? And tell Grits to bring plenty of ice. Tonight we send the boys off with a feast."

Gladys blinked as they surfaced into a clear, bright morning. Palm oasis, lush and wild, desert hills rising beyond the trees.

"Looks like we missed the sunrise," Al said. "Sunset's better anyway. We'll watch from the turret. No, this way, over here," he said when she turned toward the patio, back the way she'd come.

He led her across and down some steps to a walled passage that opened onto the corridor she'd seen before. They'd made a circle all the way around the "cabin." She could see the front door at the other end of the corridor.

He stopped by another door she hadn't seen. "I wanted to show you the back entrance. Just in case. Anything happens, you go out here and around to the tunnels. The one on the right comes out behind the hill. We keep a car there. Key's in it." He saw her look. "Oh, nothin'll happen. Not with One Arm around. I just wanted you to know."

Getaway car, Gladys thought, turret, back entrance. Tunnels! She felt her blood rush, Gypsy blood, like standing on the wing of that Spads XIII, wind in her face, watching for Skeets Elliot to give a thumbs up. Now. That's all you ever have, the now.

Chapter 44

Not twenty minutes later there was a knock on the front door, and they went out to the patio to find breakfast set on a wrought iron table. Plates of omelets, sausage and toast on a white tablecloth. Coffee in a silver decanter, orange juice, champagne, a vase of flowers.

No sign of One Arm.

Al held out a chair for her. "Shall we?"

In the daylight Gladys could see that the cabin was perched on a hill looking out at the wide valley. No trees on this side, nothing but view, desert sloping gently down then rising to mountains and a cloudless blue sky. A light breeze, the air just crisp enough for robes.

Al pointed across. "See that patch on the tallest mountain, about half way up, forms a kind of V? Locals call it the Angel of the Mountain."

"Where? I don't see it."

He came around, his head close. "There. Look right up my arm. The rocks are lighter, almost white."

She breathed his scent, felt the warmth of his skin, tried to concentrate.

"Indians say it's a god. Tahquitz, the rascal god. See the wings? They say he swoops down and steals chickens... and women sometimes." Al grinned. "My kind of god. Stole the chief's wife. Warriors went and got her, she'd just run off again." He made his voice deep. "Tahquitz have heap big... medicine."

He nibbled her ear, and his hand found an opening in her robe. His cheek on hers. When had he found time to shave?

"See it now, baby?"

She smiled. "Oh, yes."

An odd clacking sound. She jumped as a large skinny bird hopped up onto the patio wall. It bobbed its long neck as if surprised to see them. Then hopped down and sprinted across the lawn, its head low.

"What in the world?" Gladys laughed.

"Roadrunner. They're all over the place. Rabbits too. Whole villages of rabbits. We'll take a walk later. There's a pond down the hill."

After breakfast they went back to bed, made love, slept, and when they woke again, Al pulled her onto his chest.

"Tell me about your friend, Gladys. What was her name? Was it an accident?"

She thought a moment. "I suppose it was, in a way."

And she told it all, or tried. Just words. How could she ever make him know Mabel? She did not cry, but had to stop and breathe in before she told about Nathan Andrew, how Craig would've been a father to him. And that phone call to Mabel's mother.

"Disowning her daughter," she said, "wouldn't even let me bring her home to be buried. I'm worried about Mabel's little boy. How could a woman call her own grandson a bastard?"

Al shook his head. He stayed quiet a long time, holding her. Then he sat up.

"Get your robe. I want to show you something."

He took her hand, led her out past the grotto pool and up some steps. A path on their right led to a low structure built into the hillside. He opened the door, and they stepped onto a small landing. To their right, a tall stained glass window cast a glow, an art deco pattern of rectangles and squares, amber and red, indigo blue. To their left was a staircase down. In the mottled light she could see between the planks to the cement foundation below.

"We've got a ways to go on this part," he said. "Gonna be a speakeasy. Palm Springs is growing. Few years it'll be a playground. Folks need a place to let down their hair."

He took her arm. "Watch your step."

At the bottom was the bare bones of a room, walls were up, but not much else. It was as big as the cabin only not made of stone. Bags of plaster, boards stacked along the unfinished walls, sawdust, carpenter tools. The smell of cut wood and drying cement. There were tall rectangular holes for windows, and beams of light shone through, catching dust motes in the air.

"The windows will be stained glass like the one on the landing," Al said. "Found a helluva craftsman down in Tijuana. Hey, maybe we'll drive down this week, do a little gambling. They got some crazy clubs in Tijuana, mariachi music, jazz too. We could take one the touring cars, bring back a supply of tequila and rum. Kill two birds, you know? You ever been to Mexico, Gladys?"

"No," she said, "but I've heard about it. Everybody's going now. I'd love to."

He led her across the room, watching for stray nails on the rough floor, both barefoot.

"Gotta get you some shoes too," Al said, "remind me to tell Grits."

In the far corner was a large shipping crate. The front panel had been pried off and lay on the cement slab. Stamped in big red letters were the words, *Hall's Safe & Lock Company, Cincinnati, Ohio*, and inside the crate was the biggest safe Gladys had ever seen, nearly as tall as she was, black with gold scrollwork around the edges.

Al worked the huge combination lock.

"Wasn't easy getting this here from the train. Had to bring a heavy wagon from over in Indio, six mules, took most of a day." He chuckled. "Got it this far and just built the walls around it. This'll be the office."

There was a click. He turned the handle, swung one side back, then the other. The doors were six inches thick.

She gasped. Beneath a row of small wooden drawers were three shelves, full of money, stacks and stacks of bills with paper bands.

She looked up at him, and the words were out before she thought better. "Why, Mr. Capone, you're not a bank robber, are you?" The thought made her skin tingle. Jesse James.

"Hell, no!" He put his hand to his chest, offended, but his eyes twinkled. He puffed up, and his voice rose a notch. "Truth is, I've reformed my share of bank robbers and other... malefactors. Haven't seen all their resumes, but we have hundreds of men on payroll. Thousands, indirectly. Men who'd be out on the streets disturbing the peace, pulling jobs... Take The Mole." He nodded over his shoulder. "Guy burrowed into vaults. Get caught, then burrow out of prison. Now he's our tunnel man. Regular salary does a lot for a guy..."

"Al." She smiled. "If you're running for office, you've already got my vote."

He looked away, a sheepish grin. "Yeah, listen to me." His voice low again. "Like we're running a damned rehabilitation program." He chuckled, but his eyes clouded. "Guess it gets to me sometimes. I mean, if it weren't for this prohibition joke, I'd be a regular businessman. Wouldn't have to watch my back, associate with goons. Hell, I'd incorporate. Maybe I would run for office, president! Better than that fool Harding. Talk about a crook." He shrugged. "But without prohibition there'd be a lot more competition. Prices would drop. So there you go. Caught in the middle. Ain't that the way?"

He was silent for several moments. He met her eyes. "I started as a bookkeeper, you know, construction company in Baltimore."

"Baltimore. Mmm hmm." She nodded. "This is another second hand furniture story, isn't it? Because I cannot see you going over ledgers all day." Kidding, trying to pull him out of his mood. She wanted the playful Al back.

"It's no story. That's what I did. You can check. Aiello Construction." He gestured to the unfinished walls. "That's how I know something about building and especially accounting. Coulda worked my way up in the company. Thing I do best is balance sheets."

She laughed, touched his cheek. "No, Al, that's definitely not what you do best. Unless you're talking about a different kind of sheets." She ran her finger over his lips, kissed him. "Besides if you stayed with that company, you wouldn't be here now. You wouldn't have met me." She smiled. "Movie stars don't usually date accountants, you know."

She lowered her robe off one shoulder, gave him her best vamp look, her voice husky. "Race you to the pool, big guy."

He looked at her a moment, then grabbed her up, swung her over his shoulder, laughing.

"I like you, Gladys. You're an imp, you got spunk."

He swatted her behind, carrying her like a sack of potatoes.

She squealed, kicking her legs, giggling.

They were almost to the steps when she looked behind them.

"Ah, maybe you'd better close the safe?"

"Oh, shit!" He stopped. "You made me forget why I brought you here." He walked back, set her down.

"Now, behave yourself, okay? No shenanigans." He pulled her collar up around her neck. "There."

She couldn't help it. "My, Mr. Capone, what a big safe you have." But she wasn't looking at the safe.

"Gladys!" He fixed his robe. "Be good. I'm about to make a speech."

"Well, you got my attention."

He crossed his arms, gave her a look.

"All right," she said, still giggling, "I'll be good. Haven't I been good?" She batted her eyes.

He waited.

She put her hand over her mouth, made her face serious, sort of.

"Are you ready?" he said.

She nodded. Serious.

"Now then... where was I?" He cleared his throat.

He reached into the safe and took out two stacks. Hundred dollar bills, a fortune.

"Gladys, I... there's something I decided." His tone was completely different, his eyes...

Her giggles vanished. What was he doing?

"I hate things like what happened to Mabel. Nothin' I hate more. Bum deal all the way around, and I know how it is when the cards come from the bottom of the deck, believe me." He spoke so low she had to lean in to hear. "Reason I quit Mr. Aiello... my father died, heart attack." He shook his head. "Ma still had four kids at home. My brother Ralph was already married and James, the oldest, took off long before that. Broke Ma's heart."

He paused, looked up. And in his eyes she saw something she hadn't realized before, in all her teasing. He admired her, maybe even envied, wanted her to know he could've had a regular life. Not that her life was so regular. But part of him still clung to that, like the way he looked at those houses along the canals in Venice.

"What did your father do?" she said.

"He was a barber, little shop, managed to move the family to a better neighborhood." He gave a laugh. "Couldn't get much worse than where we started, Brooklyn docks. Papa made more money in Italy, probably wouldn't 'a come if he knew." He shrugged. "Anyway, when Pa died I moved back home, looked up my friend, Johnny Torrio. Had my own... responsibilities, but no way could Ma manage taking in piecework."

He stopped, looked at the stack of bills in his hands, then at her.

"So I'm gonna take this to the woman who's raising Mabel's boy. Or send someone I trust. You have the address?"

She nodded, too stunned to speak.

"We'll make it clear, it's for the boy. Check up now and then..."

"Oh, Al..." she whispered, "it's too much." But she hoped somehow Mabel knew.

"Naw," he said, "it ain't too much. Can't ever put it right, but it's something."

Al's safe at Fortress West is currently on display in the lobby of Two Bunch Palms Resort and Spa in Desert Hot Springs.

A black and white photo falls far short when it comes to showing the gorgeous gilt and glitter of the gold embellishments typical to the large and expensive safes in those days.

Chapter 45

Al in an apron, stirring his famous spaghetti sauce. Now, there was a sight to remember.

Hours before he had set it to simmering, a delicate process on a wood burning stove. Then they went up and watched the sunset from the turret, a wood shack on the flat part of the cabin's roof, open windows all the way around, steel prongs for aiming. Two chairs and a low table. A rifle leaned in one corner by an oblong box, which held more guns, probably. They sipped champagne, the sky over the mountains ablaze with color, the air shimmering pink.

Now Gladys sat on a stool by the stove, watching Al fork pasta onto plates. She was wearing men's khaki trousers and a flannel shirt, too chilly for one of the sun dresses Grits had brought from Palm Springs.

The kitchen was in One Arm's room, across the corridor from Al's suite. Cast iron stove, kerosene lamps, tall ice box, a sink with a pump like the house in Oregon. Grits and The Mole and Hawk sat drinking cold beer at a square table with a checkered cloth, a paper in front of them. The list of the night's deliveries, Gladys supposed.

"Where's One Arm?" she said when Al set the plates out, handed her one.

"In the turret. He'll eat later."

The shadow man, Gladys thought, always listening for their footsteps, disappearing around corners. It didn't seem right.

"Why don't I take a tray? I'll eat with him. That way you men can talk business. If I'm going to come here later, I should get to know One Arm, don't you think?"

Al hesitated. "I suppose. And the boys and me do have a few things to go over. But don't surprise him."

Together they made up a tray, plates of pasta, steaming sauce with chunks of Italian sausage, garlic bread and beer, two big bottles already opened. He set a candle lamp on the tray, held the door. "Can you manage? I'll carry it, if you want." He kissed her cheek, but seemed a little distracted.

"No, I'll be fine. Smells delicious!" She started out, then turned. "What's his real name, anyway?"

He shrugged. "Hell if I know. That's something we never ask, sweetheart."

The moon was almost full, the path bathed in cool light, easy to see her way. The steps were just past the back entrance.

At the bottom, she called out, "One Arm... it's Gladys. I'm bringing dinner."

No answer.

She thought of the sawed off shotgun, tried again, louder. "I'm coming up."

In front of the turret was a flat sun deck, and she walked across, half expecting to hear him scramble down the other side. Poor man. Quasimoto. She stopped by the doorway, braced the tray on her hip, switched off the candle lamp.

"It's Gladys. Don't shoot, okay?"

A raspy chuckle. "If you insist, though I ain't shot me a movie star... yet."

She laughed and went in. He was sitting in the chair, facing away. She set the tray on the table. A good thing, because she might've dropped it when he turned toward her. She managed not to react, not so much as a gasp. She'd

228

worked with lions, after all. In the moonlight she could see enough to know the sight would've made her scream had she met him in any other dark place. His face was crooked, one side drawn down, caved in was more like it, and deeply pocked, or scarred, she couldn't tell. His left ear was a gnarled stub, not even a cauliflower. The smoothest thing about him was that club of an arm.

And yet his eyes, out of kilter as they were, smiled. And half of his mouth. As if his face was a test, and she had passed.

She sat in the other chair, held out her right hand, then changed to her left. "Nice to meet you." She spoke quickly to cover the awkwardness. "I just thought, if you're to be my body guard, we might have dinner, talk a little. So you'll know if I'm worth guarding or not," she grinned, "although I can't see why I'd need a body guard. I've done pretty well without one so far."

She went on talking as she emptied the tray, set out steaming plates, silverware and napkins, the bottles of beer. "Darn, afraid I forgot glasses. Well, I can't go back. Don't want to barge in on their meeting. But I do plan to come out here on my own. Who wouldn't? I see why you don't want to leave." She laughed. "Queen of Two Bunch Palms, Al says. Never thought I'd be queen of anything. Not even in a movie. Not the ones I get."

She stopped her chattering, but still he didn't speak. She put the tray on the floor, handed him a beer.

"Cheers," she said, lifting her bottle.

"Cheers," he croaked.

The silence fell around them. She downed half the bottle. Sat there. Nothing. Complete silence. Not even a breeze rustling the palm trees. At Universal there was always some sound, voices, music, even late at night.

They ate, leaning over the low table. She tried not to watch how he braced the plate with his wooden arm, twirling spaghetti on his fork with his left hand, shoveling it in. Hard to tell how old he was, mid-forties, maybe fifty.

Finally she said, "So, Mr... One Arm, may I ask you a question?"

"Grizzly," he said, chewing.

"What? Your name is Mr. Grizzly?"

He laughed loud, grabbing the napkin to catch the spray. "Sorry." He kept laughing.

She waited. What was so funny? The Mole, Tommy Hawk, why not Mr. Grizzly? It certainly fit.

"I meant my face," he said when he could speak, "and this here." He lifted his wooden arm. "Boss always jokes about a freight train, but it happened in the Klondike, back in '96. Came around a rock by the river, next I know son of a bitch's chompin' my head. Eight feet tall, swingin' me like a damn rag doll. Lucky he didn't snap my neck."

"Good Lord!"

He chuckled. "Guess he decided my arm tasted better. Seen him carry it off, my hand flapping from his jaw, like it's waving me good-bye."

She stared at him, and her hand went to her mouth, stifling a laugh. It *was* funny, but, oh my God!

"My panning arm. Was the worst part." He shrugged one shoulder. "So much for the gold rush."

They looked at each other, and she laughed, couldn't help it. They both did. And drank more beer.

"Waving good-bye... You really saw that?"

"Yep. Never told anyone, not around here. Bear ate my arm. But then no one ever took the trouble to bring me my dinner." He paused. "'Course there's more to it. Managed to tie it off with my belt 'fore I passed out. Miner found me, rode me on his mule twenty miles to Whitehorse. Woke up the local sawbones middle of the night."

Gladys wiped her eyes. She was feeling an edge, tipsy, spifficated. She set down the beer. What had she wanted to ask? His real name. Didn't matter.

A sound in the desert below. She looked up, listening. That yipping again, only close, like it was coming from just down the hill.

"Coyotes," One Arm said.

"Do they ever come up here?"

"Sure, all the time, for the rabbits, but I never heard of a pack attacking a full grown human. 'Course you ain't much bigger than a rabbit." He did something like a wink. "Don't worry. Boss gives me a job, I do it, and by the look in his eyes, it's a damn important job."

"Really?" She grinned, sat forward, her head suddenly clear. She wanted to know more, everything. What had Al said?

But One Arm stood. "Better get you back 'fore he comes looking. And by the way," he said, glancing at her khaki pants, "I like your outfit. Better 'n them fancy dresses."

Al preferred dresses, and later she modeled her new clothes for him. He chose a simple one, straight with a square neck, a soft cotton so thin it needed a slip, but of course Grits wouldn't know that.

"Might have to give that boy a raise," Al laughed.

They spent the evening in the room, logs crackling in the stone fireplace, ragtime and jazz on the Victrola, a stack of those new gramophone records beside it in the corner. They played gin rummy at the game table, whoever lost had to go crank the Victrola every few minutes. Mostly Al. When she kept winning he went to the bar and brought a wooden case with poker chips, taught her five card draw.

"Opera," he said when his chips were almost gone, "maybe that'll change my luck. What kind a gambler can't beat a girl who just learned?"

I'll loan you some, she was about to say, but thought better.

Al seemed far away again, something else on his mind, but he came back when he put on Verdi.

"Forget poker," he said, and danced her around, singing arias in Italian, but when the music boomed with a dark, violent passion, he stopped, closed his eyes. "Vespri Siciliani," he said, his tone almost reverent, then he swept her back, fierce kisses, her mouth, her neck, she didn't care, voices and trumpets and drums crashing as he took her on the bed.

It happened so fast. A sound jolted her awake, a shotgun blast out by the cars. She rolled out of bed, felt her body knock against something, a man standing by the bed. A gun went off as he stumbled.

She huddled on the floor, covered her ears.

"What the hell!" Al moved on the bed.

Another shot. The man was flung against the wall then fell beside her on the floor.

In the dim light she could see his face, or what was left of his face, a bloody hole where his eye and part of his head had been.

She screamed, pushed the body away.

Al knelt, lifted her onto the bed, held her. She was shaking.

"It's okay, baby. It's okay. I'm not hit. His shot went wild."

A light in the doorway. "Boss, you alright?" One Arm, that familiar croak.

"Yeah, I'm alright. Who the fuck screwed up?"

Al moved from the bed, switched on the lamp. He stood there naked, his face bright red, his gray eyes almost black. She'd never seen such rage. A pistol still in his hand, he started emptying the bullets from the chamber. Why?

"Sorry," One Arm said. "I got one of 'em out by the cars. I hurried, but... There might be more. We better go look.

A grunt, then a dragging sound.

She saw only feet and legs being pulled into the next room. Blood spatters on the wall and the satin quilt.

She sat frozen, staring.

Then One Arm was back in the doorway. "Boys musta been followed."

He glanced at her, relief in his eyes.

"Lock's broke, boss."

"God damn fucking morons!" Al set down the gun long enough to pull on his pants. "Followed! Miles of empty space... I told 'em specifically not to drink. Stick to the fucking plan!"

One Arm nodded over his shoulder. "Might've come around the backside of the hill, boss. We gotta hurry."

"Go. Tell the boys get their asses up, check the grounds. Hawk can find 'em. I'll come soon as I get Gladys set."

He was leaving her alone?

In the doorway she could see the bottoms of the dead man's shoes.

Al moved onto the bed, took her hand, put the pistol in it. "You ever shot one of these?" His voice quiet again, firm.

She shook her head. "The county fair, shooting gallery."

"Hold it with both hands. There. Straight out, steady. The most important thing is to stay steady. Now pull the trigger."

She looked up at him.

233

"It ain't loaded. I took out the bullets." He touched her cheek. "I have to know you can pull the trigger."

She breathed in, tried to stop shaking. She saw the face again, half of it gone.

"Don't close your eyes. Never close your eyes. Deep breath. Pull, Gladys."

She squeezed the trigger. It clicked.

"Good. Remember that." He took the gun, moved to the night stand, reloaded it. He came around, got her robe from the chair, helped her put it on, took her arm.

"Come with me."

As they passed the vanity, he paused. "So that's where the bullet went. Wonder it didn't shatter the whole thing."

There was a hole toward the bottom of the mirror.

She glanced the other way. Blood. A pool of blood. A path smeared to the doorway. Her hand went to her throat.

"Sorry about this, Gladys."

He turned her toward the living room, led her behind the bar, pulled her down, crouched beside her.

"Stay here. Don't come out till you hear my voice. Or One Arm's. Hold the gun like I showed you. If someone comes, shoot. I'll be back."

Chapter 46

She sat huddled in the dark, elbows on her knees, the gun gripped in both hands.

Listening.

Trying not to think.

Amazing the sounds walls make when you really listen. The house in Oregon held whole conversations at night, especially the attic, creaks and groans, like an old man mumbling to himself. "Just telling its mullygrubbles," mamma said, holding her when she cried out.

Apparently the cabin had nothing to say. Stone silent. Too new.

You'd think it might complain about a dead body in the back bedroom.

Maybe it would later, the guy's spirit seeping into the walls even now. Not likely a happy ghost.

She shuddered.

Might have to rethink coming here alone. Might have to rethink everything.

No, not everything.

She knew what her mind was doing, better to hear her own chatter than those sounds again, the sight of that bloody face, half gone.

How could so much blood pour out in seconds?

At least she didn't have to wonder if he was dead.

Still, she kept her eyes open, hardly blinking. Nothing but black, as if she'd gone deaf *and* blind.

Impossible to tell how much time had passed, seconds, minutes? Her shoulders and arms ached, her butt gone numb on the hard floor, legs cramping. She was tempted to stretch, lean against the bar, but didn't budge.

The sun would come up eventually. Then what?

A shot rang out and she jumped, bumping her head and shoulder against a shelf, the sound of bottles knocking against each other.

More shots, four, five...

Not close, beyond the trees, maybe.

Silence.

Gunshots. She saw the blood on the bedroom floor again, pooled black in the dim light, shiny, the smeared trail, the bottoms of the dead man's shoes. Her whole body trembling.

Steady, Al had said. *The most important thing.* Concern in his voice, more than concern. She took long, slow breaths, shifted the gun, shook the crimps from one hand, then the other, gripped it again. How the hell could she listen with her heart pounding in her ears?

Breathe. Okay. If the worst happened, wouldn't they, whoever it was, just leave? No. They'd come here and take the booze, the money. And whatever else they wanted.

Her finger moved lightly on the trigger. Almost caressing. She thought of the men lifting her into that car when she was seven, forcing her mouth open, taking turns.

Her jaw tightened. Oh, yes, she could shoot. She could definitely shoot.

More long minutes.

Faint sounds, real or in her mind?

Footsteps, yes, a low knock on the front door. She scrambled out, made her way in the darkness.

"It's me, Gladys, it's all right." A key turned in the lock.

Noises at the back entrance too.

The door opened. Al. The sky behind him. She blinked. Starlight, after nothing but black dark.

He took the gun still trailing in her hand, set it on a chair, held her against his bare chest. His skin was cold.

"You okay, baby?"

She nodded. Tears of relief and a tangle of feelings.

"Colder than crap out there!" he said, his arms tightening around her. He was shaking.

"Let's get in the water, warm up," he said. "I want to hold you."

Sounds from the bedroom, grunts, feet shuffling with a heavy weight.

She stared. "One Arm... is he okay?"

"Fine," Al said. "Everything's fine now."

He turned her to the door out to the patio. "Except my feet." He grimaced, limping, leaning on her slightly. He was barefoot. "Got scratched up. Feels like needles. Maybe you can pull 'em out after we soak."

"Of course."

That was all. And somehow she knew he'd say nothing more about what happened that night, and she would not ask.

Chapter 47

They spent the day doing "nothing at all," as Al put it. They soaked, holding each other, let the healing water do its job.

At the door he had called instructions to One Arm, and when they got out of the water, towels and a blanket were stacked neatly on the ledge. And tweezers. A tray of coffee, biscuits and honey, but they had no appetite.

They spread the blanket on a secluded patch of lawn behind the grotto, and Al lay on his belly while she knelt and plucked tiny spines from the soles of his feet.

"Jumping cholla," he said, "meanest cactus in the desert. Little suckers hide and wait. Ouch!"

She repositioned herself, cradled his feet in her lap, working carefully. It was a long time before her fingers found only smooth skin, speckled red from the barbs, but smooth. She massaged his feet and ankles, his muscled calves. He had nice legs, strong. She hadn't noticed before. Smiling, she looked up to tell him, but he was asleep, his head turned to one side, only a towel covering his backside.

She edged from under his feet, lay beside him, pulling her robe around her. She watched the gentle rise and fall of his shoulders. His face calm again. Young. Eyes moving under their lids. What dreams did such a man have?

Lying on his left side, hiding the scars even when he slept. How she loved being with him. Love. What was happening to her? She didn't even know what day it was. Sunday. Sunday morning. They'd met Friday. She'd known him less than forty-eight hours.

Gladys *and* Capone, *the Untold Story*

Impossible.

She couldn't sleep, hardly close her eyes. The bearded palms stood sentinel not twenty feet away, a clearing sheltered on three sides, only she no longer trusted these trees with their piles of dead fronds. Dark splotches on the ground where the water oozed up, the smell of dust and decay thickening as the sun warmed the moist air. Rustling and shifting with the slightest breeze. Sometimes a frond would snap and land with a low thud.

Still, she didn't want to be in that room. Not yet.

A new sound startled her, an odd warbling, and she looked up. Chubby birds, some kind of partridge, coming across the grass, two bigger ones in front, their half grown babies following in a line. She smiled. The leader had a curled plume like a flapper's headpiece, his eyes outlined in black too. The daddy. She raised on one elbow, watching the mottled brown heads bob, pecking the grass, not the least bothered by two large creatures lying on a blanket. When she broke a biscuit and tossed crumbs, they skittered within reach. She stayed still. And noticed more movement. Rabbits, six, eight. There all along, hunkered down, almost hidden in the tall grass, noses twitching as they chewed.

Great, she thought, next there'll be coyotes.

Then she saw the man. He was sitting on a fallen trunk not twenty feet away in the shadows of the palms. A scream died in her throat as she realized it was One Arm. Sawed off shotgun resting on his club. Their eyes held for long seconds. Just doing his job.

She returned his nod and settled back, watching the critters until her eyes would no longer stay open.

"Pack your bag, baby. We're gonna do some sightseeing, find what's kicking south of the border. I've had

239

enough quiet, gotta fire the pistons. Maybe drum up some business while we're at it."

She laughed. "What bag?" And he pulled a leather valise from the armoire, set it on the bed. Never had she traveled with only one bag. Might be fun.

The blood spattered quilt had been replaced, the wall scrubbed clean. The only evidence of last night was a three foot square of new boards in the wood floor.

They left early the next morning in the big touring car, their suitcases in the far back next to crates of Canadian whiskey, covered with blankets. A case full of money stowed under the front seat along with the pistol.

She wore one of the dresses Grits brought from Palm Springs, Al a different tailored suit, robin's egg blue shirt, mauve tie and handkerchief, and of course the fedora. She thought of her wardrobe at home, wished they could stop at her bungalow, but when they turned east past the Garnet watering stop, she forgot everything but the view. Desert, mountains, sky, not another car on the two lane road until they got close to Indio and had to pass trucks full of produce from surrounding farms.

They stopped for gasoline across from the huge Southern Pacific switching yard, freight trains lined up. They bought sodas at the A & P then walked to the Western Union office in the train station. She sent mamma another telegram. ALL IS FINE DESERT PARADISE—STOP—NEVER BEEN SO HAPPY—STOP—TELL YOU EVERYTHING NEXT WEEK.

Well, not everything.

They headed southeast past date groves that looked more like Arabia than California. Then, in the distance, she thought it was a mirage at first, amazing, an inland sea. For miles and miles they followed the shore, marshy with tall reeds, thousands of birds, ducks and geese and cranes.

Pelicans! On one stretch they could see the tops of submerged telegraph poles a hundred yards out.

"I saw this from the train," Al said, pointing. "Tracks are under there too. Fifteen years ago this was all dry land, The Salton Sink. Couple guys got rich mining salt. Salt." He shook his head. "Helluva lot easier than bootlegging."

She leaned across, staring out his window. "All that water?" She couldn't even see across.

Al kissed her, looking up just in time to miss the side of a bridge where the road narrowed over a dry wash.

"Sorry." She sat back, his arm around her. How good it felt, out on the road, taking a trip together.

"Colorado River broke through," he went on. "Porter said the railroad had to move a twenty mile section. Whole valley woulda been under water way it was pouring in, regular Niagara." He laughed. "Damn smart, those S & P boys. That's who we're leasing Two Bunch from. If the water reached the foothills on both sides they'd be shit out of business. Cut the lifeline to L.A. So they made a deal with Teddy Roosevelt, built a trestle across the gap, used trains to haul rocks and fill." He chuckled. "Last trainloads they tossed in, cars and all!" He slapped the steering wheel. "If that ain't good business. See what's coming and take drastic measures."

He screeched the brakes and backed up to a sign she hadn't even seen. Hand painted on a wood plank: *Mullet Island. Boats & Tackle. Dine & Dance.*

They looked at each other, and without a word Al turned down the dirt road. It ended at a sandy shore. Fifty yards out, a rugged butte rose from the water, a ramshackle building smack in the center, three boats tied to a dock.

They parked by a one word sign, *HONK.* Another said, *Capt. Davis' Alfalfa-fed Mullet.* They could smell the sea.

Al tooted the horn and got out. "We'll need fishing clothes. You pack your khakis?"

She nodded.

And twenty minutes later a man in Levis, flannel shirt and a rumpled hat was rowing them across, chatting as if he hadn't seen human beings in weeks.

"Sea captain with an Atlantic fishing fleet. Got itchy." The man grinned, tilted his hat, revealing more of his sun weathered face, a square jaw, blue eyes. Handsome enough for a sea captain, sinewed arms. Not old, forty at the most.

"Came west in '98," he said, "camped on this dry butte. Dead volcano, what it is, two hundred feet below sea level. Geysers and mud pots further south. Where I get my paint. You folks should stop and see 'em. Nothin' but a wasteland back then, white with salt." He let off the oars and the boat nudged the dock. "And damned if the sea didn't come to me!"

He stepped across, tied up the boat, gave Gladys a hand. "Should've seen me fighting the snakes crawling up here to escape the water. Hundreds of 'em."

Her eyes widened.

"Oh, they're gone now. Fileted and fried up, or rattlesnake stew. Ate like a king for weeks. Normally I have to go all the way to Calipatria for meat."

His blue eyes lingered a little too long, as if maybe he recognized her, although it was a hundred miles to the nearest movie house. A pelican took off from a post at the end of the dock.

Captain Davis turned suddenly, extended his hand to Al who was standing there holding their clothes and the case full of money. "Sorry, sir, forget my manners sometimes." He eyed Al's impeccable suit. "Pleased to meet you, Mr..."

"Brown," Al said, freeing an arm, "Al Brown from Chicago. He shook the Captain's hand, nodded to Gladys. "And my better half, Mrs. Brown... Gladys."

She met Al's eyes, little shocks went up her sides. Better half.

"Well, you and the Mrs. come on up. Place's humble, but I'll make some lunch, or you can catch your own. Nothing like fresh mullet raised on alfalfa." He lead the way.

She took Al's arm.

"Seemed less complicated," he whispered, "hope you don't mind."

"Not at all, Mr. Brown." Mind? Her insides doing cartwheels.

Alfalfa bails were stacked beside the "cafe," the front decorated with driftwood, anchors and floats, thick ropes. Another hand painted sign leaned against the porch.

"Hell's Kitchen." Al chuckled. "Has a ring to it."

"Come in August, you'll see." Captain Davis held the screen door.

"We'll take a boat and tackle," Al said, "little woman's a fishing fool. Everywhere we go she's gotta drop a line." He winked at her.

The Captain laughed. "Well, you'll get no sympathy from me on that one!" His eyes lingering again.

Inside was a bar draped with fish net and life preservers, diver's helmet at the end, a brass porthole in one wall. Shells and sponges, nautical flags, as if this were Cape Cod instead of the middle of the desert. Fishing gear behind another counter. Two tables, straight backed chairs, a piano, the floor in the middle clear for dancing.

Al set the case and their clothes on a table, walked around, nodding.

"I like it. I like it. Yeah."

Gladys could see his wheels turning. Place has potential. A fishing and boating resort, tours to the geysers. It was fun watching him work. The bottles behind the bar were all tequila and rum from Mexico.

He stopped at the piano. "You play, Captain?"

"Sure. Sing too. Sea chanties, mostly." He glanced her way. "Some not fit for mixed company. Lately I been trying a little stride. J.P. Johnson stuff."

"No kidding. How much business you do here?"

"You'd be surprised. Some Saturdays are packed. No place else for fifty miles. 'Course, packed ain't much by Chicago standards."

Al put a big hand on his shoulder. "Why don't we row back to my car while the little woman changes to her fishing duds. I got somethin' might interest you. Regular deliveries too." They started toward the door. "Don't suppose you get many feds out this way."

Charles Davis, born in Massachusetts, son of wealthy parents, was expected to follow a gentlemanly career. He shocked his family by signing on as an ordinary seaman, and by age 18 had won the rating of captain, using that title for the rest of his life.

He wandered west in search of adventure. Alaska, Texas, throughout the southwest, then heard of the Salton Sea. Intrigued with the idea of living on a dead volcano 200 feet below sea level, even before the wild water had been brought under control, he acquired the butte, now become an island, and had begun construction of his cabin. A hand-painted sign propped against the building proclaimed that this was He3ll's Kitchen.

In 1908 he built the boat landing, cafe and dance hall, which were to flourish for nearly a quarter century, selling his alfalfa-fed mullet.

Chapter 48

As it turned out, they stayed the night, sleeping in a small room off the back of Hell's Kitchen and didn't cross the border into Mexico until noon the next day.

They'd had way too much fun rowing to the next butte where the Captain said fishing was best, Al pulling the oars while she basked in the sun and breeze off the clear water. Then reeled in silver blue fish one after another, could've filled the boat if the Captain had a bigger icebox. Instead they found a sheltered cove, stripped down to their skin and swam, laughing when mullet schooled around them, expecting their hand-fed alfalfa, probably.

"Hey, that ain't bait!" Al yelled, when one got too friendly, and Gladys laughed so hard only the extra buoyancy kept her afloat.

Later they washed off the salt in the makeshift outdoor shower, famished. They feasted on fried mullet and corn bread and tomatoes from the garden, evening by then, and could hardly refuse sharing the Captain's new supply of good Canadian whiskey. Or a turn on the dance floor to his honky-tonk version of stride piano. Not to mention those nasty sea chanties, Al joining in on the chorus, two strong baritones. Gladys wore her silver fringed flapper dress at Al's request, and did a sailor's jig, whiskey glass balanced on each palm. Captain Davis stopped singing and stared. "Damned if she don't shimmer like a mullet out of water." They laughed, and Al clapped rhythm while the Captain danced with her, but moments later Al said his polite good nights and whisked her off to their room.

Now they drove through the village of Tecate, around the sleepy plaza, past yards of red brick and tile baking in the sun, squat adobe houses surrounded by the dry stalks of harvested corn fields, skinny dogs asleep in the shade. They turned west to Tijuana, little more than a village itself, *Habitantes 1109* a sign said, but growing fast with a dozen new casinos and clubs on the outskirts, born overnight with prohibition.

They took a room in a hotel with a flowering courtyard and headed for the The Tijuana Jockey Club near the border. According to the sign by the gate, the stadium, bar and restaurant, even the barns were destroyed by flood, then fire the first year and rebuilt. Third time's a charm, but not for them. No matter what system they tried or how loud they cheered, by the last race they'd gone through more than half of Al's money.

"Damn, never can win with the ponies!" He laughed, donning his fedora, "but at least you ain't any better. Come on, girl, let's shop while we still got dinero. I wanta see you in one of those bright dresses with embroidery," he grinned, "and nothing underneath." He pulled her to him, kissing her there in the middle of the crowd. Mostly Americans, too happy to notice. Not only was betting on the horses legal, they didn't have to hide their flasks."

An hour later they were following a boy carrying their packages of souvenirs, except the sombreros they both wore, and her new peasant dress, yellow with blue and red embroidery. Al stopped suddenly, called out, "Momentito, muchacho, aqui," and hurried her across to a shop he'd spotted, the boy running to keep up.

Gladys smiled. She was getting used to Al and his sudden detours.

The shop, hardly more than a cubicle, was full of handmade instruments, displayed on shelves floor to ceiling. Guitars, all sizes, from those big bellied ones they saw in strolling mariachi bands to ukuleles and violins. A dozen shades of polished wood.

"You ever play an instrument, Gladys?" Al gazed up, his neck craned.

"Piano for awhile when I was six, one thing I didn't take to. Mamma decided to concentrate on dance and voice. It'd be nice, though."

"Sure would." He walked back and forth, ran his hand over a guitar the color of honey, his fingers following the swirls. "Feel how smooth." He plucked the strings. "If I had the time..."

She felt where his hand had been, nodded. The look he got when he listened to opera.

At the back of the shop was a work bench. A man with black hair flecked gray at the temples and a huge mustache sat polishing a neckpiece, parts laid out in front of him, cans of stain on a shelf to one side. Al sat on a stool, and in moments the two were talking easily in Italian - Spanish, rephrasing when the words were too different. They went on for ten minutes or more.

Gladys browsed until she heard the word "cinema" and her name and Al motioned her over. The man stood, excited, and she came and shook his hand, smiling.

"Señor Dosamantes," Al said, "Miss Walton, the Glad Girl." She felt an odd disappointment, preferring Mrs. Brown to being a Hollywood star? Both would be nice.

Moments later Señor Dosamantes went back to a room that must be even tinier, a closet, and came out with a case. Nestled against dark green velvet was a mandolin, the wood burnished red-brown, exquisite. It had six paired strings, and he tuned each, then strummed out a song. The notes filled the room. Gypsy music, only gentle. A lovely sound, the mandolin, an instrument for serenading.

"It is the best. One, no mas," Señor Dosamantes said, handing it to Al. Then he disappeared again and returned with three chilled bottles, Mexican beer. "Salud, dinero, amor, y tiempo para gastarlos," he said, and they clicked bottles and drank.

And for the first time Al paid exactly what was asked, not a centavo more. A different kind of respect, Gladys thought, and he carried the case in the crook of his arm as if it were a baby.

Late that night they returned from the clubs and casinos, the Norteños still carousing on Avenida Revolucion, and made love on the bed, its rustic frame carved with flowers and birds painted in bright colors, and afterwards she heard him on the balcony, plucking out a simple tune, over and over, finally with no mistakes, humming softly.

She stretched on the coarse sheets. She could move to Chicago. Why not? Plenty of things she could do besides movies. There was theater in Chicago, stage plays, musical reviews. She could even sing and dance in a nightclub, although the idea didn't have much appeal. Better than being half way across the country from him.

What was he playing? A parlor song. Just the refrain, but so familiar.

She listened. Ah, yes. *Apple Blossom Time*.

Chapter 49

"I leave tomorrow, Gladys. I have to get back."

They had pulled up beside the Bearcat, which was covered now with a tarp. Al turned the key, the engine took a moment to shudder off, but he made no move to get out.

"I know," she said and swallowed. The bearded trees, the clipped lawn sloping to the pool, the stone cabin. They'd stayed an extra night in Mexico, drove the coast road down to Ensenada for some real fishing, Todos Santos Islands, huge waves pounding the rocks, beautiful.

Tomorrow was Friday. It might've been better just to stay here, she thought. Here time might've gone slower, drawn out by the quiet, no hurry, only the desert and sun and stars moving hardly at all.

And yet... Difficult to say which she would remember more, their trip or this silent oasis with its magic water. This, definitely. That first night. Every night.

"Gladys, I..." he paused, as if choosing words, "there's something I... have to tell you... something..." He touched her cheek, his tone shifted. "You are so beautiful! Those eyes..." He smiled. "We had a time, didn't we?"

She nodded, breathed in. No tears. There were still some hours left... don't ruin it.

He shook his head. "What a sight, you landing that sea bass."

"Not without help."

"Weighed damn near as much as you."

They went silent then, their eyes locked. Moments passed. He looked down. Like a little boy about to confess some mischief.

"I'm gonna miss you. When can you come to Chicago?"

"Well, I was thinking... soon, as soon as possible." She'd almost said, *thinking of moving there.* But men did not like being backed into corners. Why was talk suddenly so difficult with time running out? Everything too important. Better to keep it light, flirt and laugh.

She leaned close, played with his tie. "So is that all you wanted to tell me, Mr. Brown, that I'm beautiful? That you like how I catch a *big*... fish?" She ran a finger over his lip, her other hand undoing his tie. "Hmm, Mr. Brown? Is that it, after all our years together?"

She expected a laugh, to be whisked off to the cabin, but instead his eyes clouded. Then he looked past her.

"Welcome back, boss, Miss Walton." The voice startled her, One Arm leaning in the passenger window. "Sorry, don't mean to interrupt, but can I have a word with you, boss?"

One Arm opened her door and she scooted out. "Did you have fun?" he said.

"Oodles," she hugged him, "but we missed you. We brought you a sombrero."

Al came around. "Yeah, green, to match your eyes."

One Arm laughed.

"Got some tequila and rum to unload too," Al said.

She walked slowly up the path, did not want to wait in the room alone.

"Handled it, boss." One Arm's voice carried, even in a whisper. "No bodies, like you said. Broken bones, smashed ribs..." The smack of wood against his palm. "They won't be working the harbor no more."

Gladys walked faster, went and sat on the patio. She closed her eyes, leaned back, taking in the afternoon sun, trying not to think at all.

They fell asleep early, exhausted from their trip and from scurrying around packing. She woke in the middle of the night, Al's hand on her waist, pulling her across the bed in one quick sweep, kissing her. The whole time he moved inside her, rocking, easy, smooth, he never stopped kissing her. Except to whisper once, "I love you."

Or did she dream it?

A knock on the door. "Boss. It's almost seven. Train leaves at eight. Car's loaded. Bearcat too."

"Oh, shit!"

In minutes they were up and dressed and bumping along the road that was hardly a road, One Arm and Grits following in the touring car. They could see the train snaking through the pass.

"Hold on."

But they couldn't go much faster without breaking an axle. Less than a mile. They watched the train pull into the Garnet station, let off steam. Not a single passenger waiting on the platform. The conductor leaned out. A workman swung the metal arm from the water tank.

"They'll see us. They'll wait."

I hope not, Gladys thought. One more day. Just one.

But the train was still there when they parked by the platform. One Arm and Grits stopped farther back by a baggage car, unloading the trunks.

Al put on his fedora, got out and came around. He lifted his valise and the mandolin case from behind the seat, took her arm.

252

At the step, the conductor checked his ticket, set his luggage inside, and Al turned to her.

"Gladys..." He reached into his breast pocket, pulled out a slip of paper, put it in her hand. He spoke quickly, his voice strained. He kept his head down, didn't look in her eyes.

"The address in Chicago. You can telegram when you're coming. A phone number too. And... I wrote the combination to the safe. Take whatever you need. Anytime. I mean that." He looked at her a moment, then away.

She had money. She didn't need money, but she couldn't say that. Her chest tight, eyes filling with tears.

"Al..."

"Wait. There's something else. I tried to tell you yesterday..." The train was getting up steam, he had to talk loud over the noise. He took a breath, met her eyes.

"Gladys, I should've told you from the beginning, but God, I wanted to be with you! You're so... alive. Everything I could want. But the worst was that Mrs. Brown stuff that day on the island. I never should've said that," he shook his head, "but I hated the way the guy was looking at you." His voice lowered. "Handsome son of a bitch."

The train started to roll.

She couldn't speak. Tears in his eyes. Her heart pounding in her ears, as if she were about to step off a cliff. What was he saying?

Cars chugging by, faces in the windows.

He pulled her to his chest, spoke into her hair, the words spilling out.

"I'm married. My little boy turns four next week. I can't change any of it, don't think so. Besides, you have a good life, better than it'd be with me. It ain't any way to live, not really. But we'll see each other when we can, if you want. Or you can tell me to get the hell out."

Heat from the steam. A whistle blast.

He held her at arm's length, looked into her eyes, kissed her hard.

"I love you, Gladys. Damn it, but I love you!" Then he ran and jumped onto the last car, his fedora sailing off onto the tracks.

Chapter 50

She stood watching the train recede into the distance, her mind blank. She felt hollow, her body a stiff shell, legs trembling. She needed to sit down. The platform was empty, not even a bench. The yard man had disappeared into the tiny shed by the water tower.

She walked across, sank onto the steps.

Silence, the train too far away to hear now, not even a hum from the tracks. How quickly the desert swallows sound.

Married.

It was like a stain, spreading. Everything changed, ruined. Even those words, I love you. What good was that now? He had a wife and child. Not telling her until the last minute. Why? But she knew why. The oldest reason in the world. She hugged her arms.

"I'm sorry."

She looked up, thinking for a crazy instant, he didn't go after all.

But of course she knew that voice. One Arm, the sun glaring behind him, his face a dark splotch. She shaded her eyes, half blinded.

"Here. You'll probably see him before I do," he said.

He was holding Al's stupid hat.

She turned away, eyes blurring with sun spots and tears.

He sat beside her, placed something soft in her hand. A handkerchief, plain white cotton, nothing fancy. A real handkerchief, not plum colored silk useless for anything but decoration.

"I'll drive you home, if you want," One Arm said, "catch the train back. No problem."

She shook her head, crying into the handkerchief.

"He didn't mean to hurt you, Miss Walton."

Her cheeks flushed. Oh, yes. *Mrs. Brown.* Calling her the little woman, his better half. Paradise. What a fool she was! He had a child. Four years old. Al must've been nineteen when...

"I have to go." She stood, hurried to her car, got in.

One Arm followed. "Let me know when you plan to come back," he said. "There's a Western Union in Palms Springs. I check every few days. Make it to Joseph MacKenzie."

She met his eyes. "That's your real name?" Her voice teary.

He nodded.

"It's a nice name."

"Ain't bad." He smiled.

"Where's Grits?"

"He went with Al."

They were quiet some moments. She wiped her eyes, started the engine. How good it felt to sit behind the wheel. Stutz Bearcat. She'd almost forgotten.

He held out the fedora. "You want this?"

"No... Yes." She snatched it up, set it on the floor board, half-wedged under the passenger seat so it wouldn't blow out. Tears again, her chest aching. She found a dry spot on the handkerchief, blew her nose.

"Gladys..."

She looked up.

"Listen, it ain't my business," he paused, collecting his thoughts, "but I seen how you were together, and I doubt it'd be any different if he'd told you from the beginning. You

256

would 'a come with him. I'd bet my arm on that," he grinned, "the good one."

She couldn't help but smile. His face so damaged, grotesque, and yet his eyes... When she concentrated on his eyes, the rest seemed to disappear, reshaping into how he'd been before. Almost. She thought of the conversation she'd overheard yesterday when they got back, something about breaking bones and ribs, taking over L.A. harbor. Kind as he was to her, still a thug. But she liked him. Not to mention he had saved Al's life and hers too, maybe.

He was right, she would've come.

"Anyway," One Arm said, "it was an honor to meet you, Miss Walton." He stepped back, swung his club up in a salute. "You could take the train next time, if you want, bring friends. I'll pick you up, show you Palm Springs, the Indian canyons. We'll ride horses." He laughed. "Hey, maybe I'll get discovered, one of them horror films. Wouldn't need no makeup."

She looked at him. My God, what was she thinking? About to just drive away. She got out, walked to him, took his face in her hands, a face no woman was likely to get past.

She kissed his cheek. "Thank you, Joseph. I had the time of my life."

He laughed, blushing. "Heck, I ain't the reason."

"But you kept him alive." She did her best Glad Girl wink. "And I know I'll never have a better... omelet."

Chapter 51

Nothing like a fast car to sharpen the edges. She hadn't even topped the pass through the mountains when she felt a lifting in her chest. Her life handed back to her. The Bearcat took the grade as if it were flat ground, wind in her hair, the surge of power when she eased down on the accelerator. Her getaway car. What had she escaped? Being a wife.

The speedometer crept past seventy, eighty. She didn't let off.

What the hell! She was nineteen.

The next months would be more than busy. There were eight films on her 1923 list, and they always found more. She'd spend weekends in the desert now and then. Between films, she would go to Chicago. As soon as she got home she'd check the schedule.

When she pulled up at her bungalow, Joe Mayer's car was in the driveway. She looked at her face in the mirror, fluffed her hair. She could do this. But when the front door opened, she could tell mamma had news of her own, Joe smiling beside her. Daddy Joe, Gladys called him now, partly in fun, but she liked the sound of it.

"We've set the date, honey," mamma said, hugging her. "We're getting married Christmas day. In Portland, the prettiest little chapel. Come see my dress. It's perfect! Then you must tell us all about your new gentleman friend. Maybe we'll have another wedding before long."

They finished filming *The Near Lady* in time for the Christmas break. She was glad they were making the trip home. She might've been tempted to try to see Al, even one night, but of course holidays were for family.

Al sent weekly telegrams. Short phrases, "I WANT YOU IN MY ARMS. —STOP" or "LAST NIGHT I HEARD YOUR LAUGH. —STOP.—THOUGHT OF THAT HUNGRY MULLETT.STOP.
Once he sent just a word, "HURRY."
Always ending with "LOVE AL."
Sometimes he'd call late at night, ask how she was doing, tell her how much he missed her, thought of her. There'd be loud music and laughter in the background, women's voices, and in minutes he'd be pulled away to "handle some business." He ran clubs in Chicago. What did she expect? The Four Deuces. That was the address he gave her.

Just as they were leaving for Portland a package arrived. Daddy Joe was pulling out of the drive when the delivery boy sprinted up and handed it to her in the back seat. The size of a shoe box, but beneath the layers of packing was a velvet case that seemed too large for jewelry. Inside was a single long strand of pearls, flesh colored, a platinum clasp with large diamonds.

Mamma gasped. "Real pearls! Oh, my! What does your Mr. Brown do?"

"He sells second hand furniture." Gladys smiled. "Well, imports it. Large shipments."

"I'll say!" Daddy Joe whistled as she passed the pearls to mamma in the front seat. "Must be five foot long. Clasp alone's worth a fortune. Better hang onto this one, Princess."

So they didn't mind making a quick detour down to Venice Beach. Gladys remembered seeing a music box, handmade in the real Venice and shaped like a gondola, lacquered shiny black with gold trim. It played *O Sole Mio*. She sent it off in the same box.

In January they started filming *The Love Letter.* King Baggot directing again, a plot Gladys actually liked. Mary Ann McKee works in an overall factory and starts slipping mash notes into the pockets. The usual Mr. Right answers, but not before Mary Ann's crook boyfriend, Red Mike, has her pull a job with him and she nearly gets caught.

They were shooting the scene where Red Mike gets out of prison and comes after her when Gladys heard noises behind the cameras, gasps turning to angry murmurs, and she remembered Craig barging onto the set that awful day. Her hands went to her mouth, eyes filled with dread. Perfect look for the scene, it turned out.

"Impossible," someone said. "I don't believe it."

Then Mr. Baggot called, "Cut. That's it for today."

Baggot held the newspaper that had been circulating around the set. Gladys walked to him, read the headlines:

"WALLACE REID DEAD AT 31"
"Morphine Addiction Takes Final Toll
On America's Favorite Film Hero"

Nowhere did it say the studio had kept him on morphine so they could stay on schedule. "Damn fools," Baggot shook his head, "Wally was a good man. Would've made them money for decades."

The next night Gladys took out her funeral dress, her shoes, her veiled hat. She sat on the bed, shivering, the room cold, but she didn't reach to turn up the radiator. At Mabel's funeral she had meant not to look, had stood back while the others filed by, but at the last moment... A glimpse only. Beautiful against the white satin before they closed the casket. It had been three months.

Tired from work, she usually fell asleep instantly, but the room felt so empty. Her bed empty. What luxury, those few nights with Al. Seven nights. To hear him breathing next to her, to reach and touch him, the way he pulled her across...

Her throat closed, and she lay back on the bed. She could try to call, but hearing his voice was almost worse, those noises in the background, imagining a woman on his arm. She wanted to be held. She wanted him inside her, devouring her with kisses like that night he'd played the opera music. What was wrong with her to fall in love with a man she couldn't be with?

She followed the line of cars and limos from Forest Lawn Memorial Park to the Reid home in Beverly Hills. Wallace Reid's wife, Dorothy Davenport, stood in the entry with his parents, their faces like stone. A family of actors, Hal Reid had been in movies with his son. Wallace and Dorothy had been married ten years. They had a boy and a girl, if Gladys remembered right. She hugged Dorothy, managed to say something. A widow in her twenties.

Gladys edged among the sea of black suits and dresses, veils lifted now. Heads shaking, "Such a shame. Terrible shame."

"The way the papers made it sound."

"To even mention Wally Reid in the same sentence with Arbuckle or Desmond!"

Half of Hollywood had worked with Wallace Reid, and even those who hadn't were there.

She stood talking with the Talmadge sisters and Marion Davies. Hearst was in the East. So was Valentino, Rudy and Natacha touring the country, dancing the tango from *The Four Horseman* to pay off debts. They lived like royalty on Rudy's less than royal salary, and recently he'd lost a suit to end his contract with Lasky and wasn't making any films.

"Poor man," Constance Talmadge said when the subject came up, "Lasky was rotten to him from the beginning, and I don't think it's just Natacha."

"Thank God I don't have to deal with that," Marion said.

Marion did all her movies for Hearst. Expensive productions, but he chose every role, preferring her in classic dramas with elegant costumes when everyone knew Marion was best at comedy. She adored him, or seemed to. No explaining love, Gladys thought. She liked Marion, always so friendly, and they had more in common now, both seeing married men.

Constance nodded to the milling guests. "I see none of the Lasky bigwigs showed up."

"They wouldn't dare," Norma said.

They moved out to a courtyard by the pool, the overflow of funeral sprays everywhere. A waiter brought a tray of cocktails, and as they sipped Gladys told about her oasis in the desert, the sunsets and starry nights, the magic water. "I swear it's the fountain of youth," she said, "makes your skin like silk. I made tea with it one night. Comes out of the ground that hot."

She paused to return Charlie Chaplin's nod.

"A bootlegger from Chicago owns it," she went on. Why was she whispering? It didn't matter, no one cared. "He's building a speakeasy, said I can invite anyone. I'm dating him."

"Really!" Marion's eyes lit up. "So what can you get us?" With Hearst gone she could drink more.

"Canadian whiskey and beer, the best. Rum and tequila, but that's easy."

"I hear Palm Springs is *the* place," Constance said.

They moved onto the grass, their backs to the crowd.

"We should do it, just us girls," Marion laughed. "Leave the men home. I have friends who'd love that. How many rooms are there?"

"Four," Gladys said. One Arm would give up his room. Would he ever! Imagine his reaction when they pulled up. Better yet, imagine their reaction.

Marion grinned. "Look at you, Gladys. You're glowing. So what's this guy's name?"

"Al Capone."

"Well, if he's a 'legger he must be rich," she gave Gladys a nudge, "and by your eyes, he must be a regular sheik."

Gladys laughed. "Well, he did kidnap me and carry me off to the desert... among other things."

Later, walking out to her car, she saw Craig. She was not prepared for the jolt. How handsome he was, standing by one of the limos talking to a tall man. My God, it was Howard! She walked to them, hugged one, then the other, her eyes tearing. She'd gotten through the whole funeral without crying. She wiped her eyes.

"You look beautiful, Gladys," they both said, then laughed.

"I was short on drivers," Craig explained, tipping his chauffeur cap.

He took her hand. She would've liked to see either man alone, but this felt awkward.

They talked small talk, the weather perfect as usual. How strong Dorothy was.

Gladys was about to say how horrible that the studio took no blame when she remembered Howard was with Lasky.

Craig didn't let go of her hand.

Finally Howard kissed her cheek. "I have to go," he said. "It's good to see you. Can I call you sometime, Gladys?"

"Sure."

She might be in love, but she wasn't dead. Was she supposed to have nothing at all between the times when she could see Al? She was quite sure Al was not having nothing at all.

They watched Howard walk away.

Craig squeezed her hand. "How are you doing, Gladys?"

"Managing. Staying busy."

"Me too."

Their eyes met.

"You think we could have dinner sometime?"

"I don't know, Craig. I just don't know."

He nodded. "You're probably right."

She thought of telling him about the money Al was sending for Nathan Andrew, but it seemed too complicated.

"I'd better... Take care, Craig." She slipped her hand away, hugged him, walked to her car.

Only when she was driving away did she wonder if she'd made a mistake telling Marion Al's real name, but then why would Hearst be interested in Al Capone?

Chapter 52

She saw Al only twice that year. Her 1923 list of films grew to thirteen. There was just no time.

In March she stopped in Chicago for the openings of *Gossip* and *Wild Party* and *The Town Scandal.* One night, then she had to take the morning train to New York.

Cheeks flushed, she pulled her fur coat around her neck, tried to hurry through the station. The porter was so slow! She took a taxi to the elegant Hotel Sherman, and when she stepped from the lift, two men in gray suits and fedoras stood by the door to the suite, their faces as bleak and icy as the streets outside. She thought it was the wrong floor until she noticed their diamond belt buckles.

"Miss Walton," one said. He nodded, took her bags from the bell hop. The kid pocketed the tip, retreating before the elevator closed.

Then the door to the suite opened, and she saw only Al's eyes and smile.

They fell onto the bed, tugging at each others' clothes, laughing. He rolled her across. "You're here, baby! Finally. And, hey, you're wearing my pearls."

She did not stifle her cries. Who cared if the men outside heard?

She thought Al would escort her to the premiere, but he shook his head.

"Better not. You got a career to think about. I'll wait here." He nuzzled her neck. "Hurry, baby."

She did a brief appearance at the after party then left.

They made love again, slowly like before. She closed her eyes and imagined they were back in the desert, listening for the rustle of palms, water tumbling over rocks.

Later they dressed and went down to a club called The College Inn off the Sherman's lobby and danced a few numbers to the Isham Jones band. Thirty pieces, two grand pianos, horns, clarinets, even a string section.

Al took her elbow. "This ain't jazz. Bunch of white guys, what do they know? Come on, I'll show you jazz. Even better than what we heard at the Green Mill."

He hurried her toward the exit. The suits fell into step behind them. A big Cadillac was parked in front.

They drove to the South Side, The Lincoln Gardens. The place was dingy, walls and columns chipped and peeling, sawdust covering cracks on the cement floor, but it was packed. Tough, swarthy faced men with an air of swagger even sitting down. Women in gaudy flapper dresses, some as bleached blond as their men were dark. Nods at Al as they walked by, cold stares too.

They sat at a scarred table right in front of the dance floor, sandwiched between bodyguards. She felt sparks in the air, could tell patrons from guards by who was smiling, who sat or stood stiff and wary, hands in their pockets. Whiskey and beer bottles on every table. She was quite sure everyone here was packing, like walking onto a battlefield where a flimsy truce has been called just for the music.

Nothing proper here. She loved it!

And the music! All black, King Oliver's Creole Jazz Band, straight from New Orleans. Six men, drums and horns and base fiddle, a woman, Lil Hardin, on the piano. They made Isham Jones' white boys seem like amateurs.

They danced and drank and listened for more than an hour, and then the leader of the band grinned, lifted his coronet to Al. He spoke into the mike, grinning. "Now you'll get a chance to see Papa Joe's red underwear." A big man with a wide chest and belly, he blew chorus after chorus until his stiff shirtfront popped and revealed his red long johns. Then Louis Armstrong stepped from the back, and the two did duet breaks in perfect harmony as if reading each others' mind, and the crowd went wild, standing on chairs and tables, hooting and shouting.

Suddenly Gladys was pushed to the floor, and shocks went up her spine as she realized the pops she'd heard were gun fire, a scuffle in a back corner, bottles shattering, the band playing louder to drown out the racket. Al had been pushed down too, and they looked at each other under the table. He shrugged, took her hand and they scrambled toward a back exit, the guards covering them. As they passed the band, she saw the drummer had pulled a gun, beating rhythm with one hand.

Outside she leaned against a wall, laughing, catching her breath, fear lulled by the whiskey.

"You staged that for me, didn't you, Al?" she said.

"Naw, happens all the time. We just stayed a little too long."

It was May, 1924, when she noticed the changes.

They met at the same suite in the Hotel Sherman, but Al didn't greet her at the door. She had called, left a message. They'd scheduled her in New York first this time, the train was late, she'd be there after the premiere.

She found him sitting in the dark, only a sliver of light where the curtains parted. On the coffee table, a whiskey bottle, an empty glass. A silver tray, streaks of white powder. "Holly dust" some called it. She'd seen it at parties, but it wasn't true that everyone in Hollywood did it.

Al was wearing a silk robe. He stood, took her in his arms. "Gladys." His voice a whisper, a little slurred. "They killed my brother. Ralph and I went to the morgue. Couldn't even count the bullets."

She tried to meet his eyes, but he stared past her.

She breathed in. His brother.

In the bedroom they lay quiet for a long time, her head on his shoulder, hand caressing his chest. She did not ask how or when. She could feel the muscles in his arm twitching. Gradually his breathing calmed.

She thought he was asleep, but when she checked, his eyes were open.

"It's all in my hands now," he said. "Not sure I want it. Frank was the businessman."

"You could quit," she said. "Come to California." If something happened to Al... "We could stay at Two Bunch. Or could go to Mexico. Get a place on the beach." She would give it all up to be with him, but even as she said the words, she knew.

"I got family," he said. "Kiss me, Gladys." He smiled, tapped her nose with his finger. "You get more beautiful every time I see you."

A Laemmle nephew met her train in L.A. She told him her mother was ill. If he'd please take her bags to her bungalow.

"Tell Mr. Baggot I'll be there Wednesday. If mamma is better," she added, and walked out to the Bearcat. Today was Monday. She'd sent a telegram from the Chicago station. Joseph Mackenzie, Palm Springs. She drove east to the desert.

One Arm was sitting on the stone wall when she pulled up. He came and opened her door, hugged her.

"No girls this time?" he said, "or is Miss Davies coming in another..." Then he saw her eyes. "Did something happen? Al...?"

"They killed his brother. I don't even know who. I couldn't ask. I can never ask, but I have to know. I try to be strong, just keep working, but... I miss him so much, Joseph. And now if he takes over the business..." She covered her face with her hands, crying.

"Come on, let's get you inside. I'll make us some tea." They sat at the kitchen table in One Arm's room. He put his hand over hers. "It's tough, I know. Gonna get worse, I'm afraid. I won't lie to you, Gladys. Too many... bootleggers in the same town. Not really, if they'd do like Johnny Torrio and stick to the boundaries, but trouble is, they ain't smart. For Torrio and Al it's just business, but those other goons... " He shook his head, sipped his tea.

The cup like a toy in his big hand, fine china in the middle of the desert. She listened, wondering how that croaky voice could be so soothing.

"But it wasn't goons killed Frank," he said. "It was cops."

She looked up. "Cops?"

He nodded. "It happened last month. Al and his brothers were fixing the election in Cicero." He laughed. "Not like that's a first in those parts. But some reporter got on his high horse and went to the Chicago police. Not even their jurisdiction. Frank walked out to the street just when a line of cars pulled up. Thirty or forty cops opened fire, shot guns, pistols, fucking arsenal. They weren't in uniform. Frank reached a gun from his back pocket as he fell. Never fired. They just kept shooting into his dead body."

She stared at her cup. *Ralph and I went to the morgue.*

"Sorry, Gladys. My language, too."

They sat there. Neither spoke. It was hot in May, close to ninety degrees, the window open. She could hear a faint buzzing outside. Locusts. She sipped her tea, holding the cup with both hands.

"There's somethin' else," One Arm said.

She looked up. He seemed to be searching for words.

"Look, Gladys, I... don't get me wrong, I'm completely loyal to Al. Inside he's a good man, but things are happening, and you... you're special to me." He paused, smiling. "We had us some good times this last year, didn't we?"

She nodded. "We did."

When Marion came with her friends, they drank whiskey, cranked up the Victrola and danced the Charleston in the stone courtyard. They rode horses into the Indian canyons, went shopping in Palm Springs first, bought cowboy outfits. Marion Davies in chaps and a ten gallon hat. And once when Gladys came alone, she went with One Arm on a delivery to Hell's Kitchen, and they caught mullet. Captain Davis not about to make advances with her bodyguard there.

"Truth is," One Arm said, "I... I kind of think of you as a daughter. No offense." He was blushing.

"Hell, I'm old enough. Never had no kids, ain't likely now, but I... don't want you to get hurt." His voice husky, he looked into her eyes. "If I was your father I wouldn't let you near this Al Capone. Lock you up in your room if I had to." He laughed, then this broken face grew serious. "You ain't a kid, but you got a right to know so you can decide for yourself. You can end it, Gladys. He'd understand."

Chapter 53

She drove fast, the sun rising behind her.

One Arm had to hear her go, probably watched from the turret, but she never looked back.

She'd hardly slept, her mind buzzing. What he had said seemed impossible. Could not be true. Just trying to protect her. And yet she did not think One Arm would lie. She would've left last night, but didn't want to risk not finding the road in the dark.

The speedometer hit eighty. Miles passed in a blur, then she'd blink, try to place where she was. She hardly slowed when the highway went through towns, main streets empty, only farmers up this early. Banning, Redlands, acres and acres of citrus groves, San Bernardino, the open fields of Pomona, horses grazing.

She thought of Al sitting there in the dark, traces of white powder on the silver tray. Staring at the ceiling when they lay in bed.

Not just his brother, One Arm had said. Racketeers killing each other. Chicago Beer Wars, the papers call it. Not in California. She'd seen nothing in the papers here about murders in Chicago. She remembered the couples at The Lincoln Gardens, hardened faces, women looking cheap despite their jewels. Some of them prostitutes, she realized now. Gun shots.

It isn't a movie, One Arm said. *We buried two men in the desert that night.*

She reached the city but didn't let off the gas. Bodies decomposing under the sand, or dug up by coyotes. They killed his brother. It could've been Al.

On Santa Monica Boulevard she swerved around traffic. Bells clanged. She kept going. No police car could catch a Stutz Bearcat. Police drove Fords. She passed the turn to Cahuenga, open stretch now, nothing but bean fields. The speedometer edged toward ninety. She glanced in the mirror. Two motorcycle cops had pulled ahead of the first car, still far behind. She'd lose them well before she got to the cliff in Malibu. Sit and think, sort through it. *You can end it. He'd understand.*

A truck pulled out up ahead, a car on the other side coming toward her. She honked and the truck edged to the right. She grasped the wheel, passed between them, saw the terror in the driver's face. Fear shot through her chest. What was she doing? She stepped on the brake, and the Bearcat fishtailed wildly. Tires screeching, she fought for control and came to a stop on the wrong side of the road. She leaned her head on the wheel, shaking, heart pounding.

It could not be true. How could One Arm be sure? She should never have gone to talk to him.

"I'm afraid you're under arrest, Miss..."

She looked up at the officer, managed a smile.

His eyes widened. "Miss Walton!"

He cleared his throat, made his voice serious. "Well, star or no star, you're still under arrest. Speed limit's forty here. You were doing twice that, at least. You'll have to come with me. One of the men will bring your car."

Of course. They'd probably draw straws. The officers crowded around the Bearcat as she got out.

"Morning, boys." She tilted her head the way she did in her movies. "Guess I've been a bit naughty."

They grinned. Something to tell at the family table. We arrested the Glad Girl today.

Two police cars were parked sideways on the road, blocking traffic, although there was only the farm truck, the driver staring. She waved, got in the back seat of the Ford.

At the station they took her information, lead her to a small windowless room while an officer contacted the studio. A table, two chairs, light bulb hanging from the ceiling.

Thirty minutes later Uncle Laemmle himself entered, closing the door behind him. For several moments he just looked at her.

"What's going on, Gladys?" he said finally. "This isn't like you."

She didn't answer. How did he know what was like her? All he saw, all anyone saw, was what was on the screen.

He paced the cubicle. "First you leave the premieres early, then send a message you'll be late, now... this." He gestured to the gray walls. "Baggot called your mother. She isn't sick. Didn't seem concerned either. Mentioned some place out in the desert where you go. Bunches of palms or something."

Gladys smiled. It sounded funny with his accent. Tiny turnip of a man. She watched him. Three steps across, three steps back. Almost as bald as a turnip too. He'd been good to her, but she'd done her job. In four and a half years the only time off she'd had was the trip to Hawaii and... when Mabel died. Oh, and her week with Al. Her eyes burned.

Laemmle stopped pacing, turned to her.

"There's a rumor, Gladys..." He paused, shook his head. "Never mind. That's your business. But you... you are *my* business. I can get you out of this, of course, but it would look bad. Reporters will be here any minute. So..."

He sat in the chair, thinking. "This thing you said to the cops. I like it."

"What?"

"About being naughty."

"They told you?"

"Sure, they're out there laughing about it now." He nodded to the door. "And waiting for autographs." He stood, slapping the table. "So we go with that. I get reporters. You do, let's see, three days in jail. Work in the kitchen." He laughed. "Yeah, Gladys Walton on kitchen duty. Good, good."

He said good like it rhymed with boot.

"Can I go home for some clothes?" She looked down at her silk traveling suit. Three days in jail.

"Sure," Laemmle said, "I'll tell the chief. Just be back in time to do dishes. They'll want photographs."

He stopped at the door. "And Gladys, when you get out, come by my office."

274

Chapter 54

He killed a man.

That's what One Arm told her. The guy was a small time crook, but still...

Gladys lay on the cot in her jail cell, a sink, a toilet, steel bars, her cellmate asleep six feet away.

Murderer.

No, she would not think the word.

She closed her eyes, felt Al's arms around her, lifting her above his head, there in the grotto pool, playing. The way he loved her, treated her like a queen, how they laughed together.

He was kind to people, even strangers, handing out money, telling the gondolier to go to school. The Mama and Papa Italian grocers. Pulling stacks of bills from the safe, making sure it would get to Nathan Andrew.

One Arm and his warnings. So she could decide for herself.

Decide? There was no deciding. She knew him. A man was more than the circumstances of his life. His brother gunned down in cold blood. Al in charge now, a target himself, surrounded by goons. Every nerve frayed. Never without body guards. That Cadillac was solid steel. He'd had it fit with a combination lock on the door so no one could plant a bomb.

Or was she kidding herself? There were plenty of ways to make a living. All he had to do was quit.

Ain't any way to live, he'd said that morning before he ran for the train. She wanted to go back to the night she'd opened her dressing room door and he was there, back before she knew. Stay in that week forever. Bootlegger, that's all.

To pull a gun and shoot, see a face ripped and torn by bullets. It happened the day before they met at the Hotel Sherman. Last Friday. My God! Is that what Al saw when he lay staring at the ceiling?

She remembered the blood on the floor that night in the cabin, the smudged tracks where the body was dragged out.

It frightened her to think how that could change a man.

Gonna get worse, One Arm said.

Dago pimp. That's what the guy called Al. Worst anyone could say to him. He hates it.

Pimp. She'd had a hard time even saying the word. Why pimp?

And One Arm told her. *They run brothels. Ain't unusual for a gambling joint to have a whore house above.*

Whore. Those voices in the background when Al called late at night. Second hand furniture dealer. Women's bodies is what he dealt. Did he also...? Of course he did.

He's complicated, Gladys. Part of him thinks only business, another part hates the ugliness. Gets sucked into it, few men wouldn't. Hates himself for that too, if you go deeper. Then there's a complete other side that loves his... way he loves you.

He'd been about to say, his family.

Mostly he's just trying to stay alive.

To empty a gun into a man's face. Point blank.

She closed her eyes, tried to sleep, the light in the corridor glaring through the bars.

Rumors, Mr. Laemmle had said. *Come by my office.*

"Your contract expires in December," Laemmle said three days later. "You're welcome to stay in the bungalow until then, but, well, seems the times have moved past the characters you play, Gladys. We've... canceled this year's list. I don't like it, but that's the way it is."

What was he saying? Hardly looking at her. She felt sorry to cause him this trouble.

"You're talented," he said. "You'll be fine. There are plenty of companies that aren't bound by the same rules. The Bearcat is yours, of course."

He stood, came around the desk, took her hand, his eyes sad. "I like you, Gladys, always have. If you ever need help, come see me."

She could only nod, surprised she didn't feel more. It made no sense. Thirteen movies last year, all solid at the box office.

Rumors. That she was seeing a bootlegger, a man involved in the Chicago Beer Wars? Will Hays, the country's new "czar of righteousness," his morality clause in every contract now. Apparently she no longer passed the test.

As she walked out her first thought was, Al must not know.

When he called in the next months, she said she was busy filming, would come as soon as she could. Same as before, and it was true. She made three movies with small companies that summer and fall for release early in 1925, but she had top billing in only one and the premieres were all in L.A.

Luckily mamma was caught up in her own life and didn't question when Gladys told her the decision to leave Universal was hers. With a rich boyfriend, she didn't need to work as much. That was true too. Take whatever you need, Al had said. Anytime. Every few weeks she'd drive out to Two Bunch Palms, and she did not hesitate to use the combination to the safe. Better than dipping into her savings. She would not change the way she lived for Will Hays.

In late October Marion called asking if she could bring another group out to Two Bunch. "Charlie wants to come, but not with Pola."

"Of course," Gladys said.

If Marion or one of her friends had let something slip about "her bootlegger," she couldn't blame them. No one in Hollywood took Prohibition seriously. Who knew bootlegging qualified as a breach of their silly morality clause? Cockeyed world, the heartland dictating morals, when what everyone craved on and off screen was scandal and glamour and sex, the more salacious the better.

"And Gladys," Marion said, "we're having a party next month on the yacht. You're invited. We'll sail from San Pedro. A birthday party for Thomas. You know Mr. Ince, don't you?"

"We've met a few times." Once, actually.

"Good. You'll get us some champagne and beer, won't you?" She lowered her voice. "And some whiskey for me?" Marion's laugh could brighten anyone's day. "Have One Arm put it in a champagne bottle. You know how W.R. is."

"Sure. He'll bring it to the yacht when we're out of the harbor."

She'd gone on a few runs with One Arm and Hawk these last months. How fun, racing out in the speed boat. A wood hulled Chris Craft. Tri-cockpit Torpedo, One Arm called it. Twenty-five feet long and fast, like a Bearcat on water. Once they went early and fished off the pier, waiting for the sun to set. She supposed she was an accomplice now. What the heck. Might as well be hung for a sheep as a lamb, Uncle Tommy always said.

"The party's November 15th," Marion went on, "Chaplin coming, and a new columnist W.R. is bringing from the east, Louella something, and a few others. Well, I'll tell you more this weekend."

278

Gladys blinked. Looking over the rail from the deck of the Oneida, she could not believe. Al! My God, he was here! Standing beside One Arm in the boat below, light blue suit, white tie and no hat, there in the dim light from the portholes below.

Roses, he was holding roses. It'd been six months. Longest six months of her life. And even from here she could see his eyes. He hadn't changed. Her heart gone wild, tears. She didn't even try to hide it. If it weren't for the others standing at the rail, she'd slip off her shoes and dive. Easy. She'd done higher dives than this, twice as high.

Al grinned and waved. "Come on, beautiful," he called. "We'll have our own party. I'll bring you back, if you want. But I don't think you'll want."

Chapter 55

"Jump, baby, I got ya."

Al held out his arms. They had pulled the boat around to the loading platform at the yacht's stern, Gladys waiting on the ladder.

She jumped. High heels, new dress, fur jacket and all. Only a few feet.

He caught her, swung her around, almost losing his balance.

Then she was in his arms, there in the middle cockpit, kissing, breathing his cologne, his skin so familiar, only vaguely aware of the applause and laughter from the deck and One Arm tying up the boat for crewmen to lift the crates onto the platform. One Arm was wearing one of those whaler hats that tied under the chin and hid his face. The boat rocked as he made his way back to the driver's seat.

They sank onto the cushions, the engine chugging.

"You're here! I can't believe it." She nestled against him.

Al smiled, retrieving the roses from the floor, kissed her again. "You didn't think I'd miss our anniversary."

"Anniversary?"

"Two years. Well, maybe not the exact day. I ain't that good, but it was November. I remember that. Best week of my life."

"Oh, Al."

The scent of roses and sea air. A clear calm night, music from the Oneida, the lights of L.A. harbor in the distance. She wiped her eyes. Nowhere in the world she'd rather be, and glad to be off the yacht. Hearst wasn't in the best of moods. Pompous old fart, like he expected everyone to bow.

"Where to, boss?"

Al looked at her. "Ever been to Catalina, beautiful?"

She shook her head. "No."

"Me neither. How 'bout it, One Arm, think you can find Santa Catalina?"

They made love between blankets in a cove around the corner from Avalon Bay, no light but the stars. The town itself all but empty, just the pier and a scattering of dark houses. November, not even a bar to welcome them. Not that they needed it.

One Arm had left them off with blankets and cushions and flasks, then motored to the far end of the cove. "Maybe drop a line," he'd said.

Gladys kept her eyes open, clutching Al's back, drinking the night sky with his kisses. Memorize everything.

"This isn't fair." Her words carried in the stillness, and she lowered her voice. "You have to see the stars. Roll me on top."

Al grinned, did his famous roll, hardly a break in rhythm. She shivered, her shoulders bare, goose bumps. He pulled her close, tucked the blanket around them, still moving.

"That good?"

"A little slower, maybe."

He laughed. "I meant if you're warm enough."

"Oh, I'm warm," she gasped, "where it counts."

There was a sound up the slope, like a bellows letting out air, then a loud snort.

"Holy shit!" Al scrambled from under her, grabbed his gun from beneath his coat.

They looked. Black forms were clumped together where the grass met the beach. Huge, as tall as a man and shaggy. Maybe twenty yards away. One lifted its head, and they saw a silhouette of horns, eyes glowing.

"What the fuck is that?"

She laughed. "Buffalo. Paramount did a picture here, some Zane Grey story. Guess they couldn't round them all up." Her voice a whisper.

They watched a minute more, shivering, naked in the night air.

"They ain't gonna stampede, are they?"

"I think they're more interested in the grass."

Al set down his gun, gathered her under the blankets.

"Now where were we?" He lay back. "Maybe you better coax him a little. He chuckled. "For a minute there I thought the Feds 'd come up with new disguises. I've seen goons almost that hairy."

They found the dippers and what they thought was Venus and counted three shooting stars, side by side, the blankets to their chins, heads on boat cushions.

"Four." Al pointed. "See it? Regular shower."

They were quiet, waiting.

Then he said, "I only have tonight, Gladys. Have a meeting in Tijuana at noon."

Her chest caught. She'd thought they'd drive to Two Bunch, at least a few days. She edged closer, her head on his shoulder.

"Can I go?"

"Better not. I'm taking the afternoon train from San Diego. Besides, I've done enough damage to your career. I'm sorry about Universal, baby."

"You knew?"

He nodded, rubbed her arm.

She looked up at the stars. They were quiet for several minutes.

"Five!" they said at the same time and laughed.

"Amazing. I've never seen so many."

She would not talk about wishes.

Gladys raised on one elbow. "Al, I was saving it for a surprise, but... I got another movie. *The Sky Raider*. We start in January." She paused for effect. "They're filming in New York. Then a Broadway show. I auditioned last week. Just a dancing part, but that's better than acting, almost, and it could run for months.

She straddled him, took his face in her hands, kissed him. "Oh, Al, I'll be working in New York most of next year! I'll be a New Yorker. Have to find an apartment, furniture..."

He grinned, turned her onto her back.

"You leave that part to me. Least I can do. Look at your eyes, all happy. God, you're beautiful!"

Chapter 56

The phone rang early Wednesday morning.

"Isn't it awful? That poor man, and you were there. Are you all right, honey? Goodness, I hope they don't call you as a witness."

Gladys sat up in bed. "Witness? Mamma, what are you talking about? What happened?" It couldn't be about Al. She'd never even told mamma his real name.

"It's on the front page. 'MOVIE PRODUCER SHOT ON HEARST YACHT!' Mr. Ince is dead. Unless it's some mistake. I thought you went to the party."

"I did, but..." Dead. How could that be? Who would shoot Ince? Hearst in a jealous rage? But the talk was about Marion and Charlie, not Ince, although Gladys never believed the rumors. Marion was too devoted to her 'old man.' Monster. Hearst was capable of anything. She'd felt it the first time she saw him. Staring at her that day on the set. Probably already seeing Marion.

"But what?" mamma said.

"I didn't stay for the party. Al came in a boat, and... Listen, mamma, tomorrow I'm bringing some boxes to put in your garage. Mostly household things and bedding. Craig is coming with the Packard."

She'd been sorting and packing the past two days, boxes and trunks labeled *New York* or *Storage*. She leaned against the pillows. Dead. His birthday. Mr. Ince was forty-two, a top director. It felt dark and sick. There'd be an investigation, a trial. Unless it was an accident. Having a gun was no accident. Thank God, she hadn't stayed.

"Honey... are you still there?"

"Yes, mamma. We'll talk tomorrow. I have something to tell you. It's about Al."

Mamma's voice perked up. "Mr. Brown is with you? Bring him along, honey. I'll cook up a roast. Joe and I are dying to meet him." She paused, then an excited whisper. "It's a wedding, isn't it? Oh, a wedding! Will it be here or Chicago? Or maybe New York. That big church on Fifth Avenue. Wouldn't that be beautiful! We'll all come out on the train."

There was no trial, no witnesses, not even an inquest. After that first headline, no newspaper ever mentioned a gun shot. Acute indigestion, ulcer, perhaps. Cause of death, heart failure. All kinds of speculations were reported, but apparently no one was on the yacht, in some accounts, not even Ince. Chaplin denied being there. Marion backed up his story. That new columnist, Louella Parsons, wasn't there either. A ghost ship delivering a dying man to a water taxi in San Diego. The body was cremated before anyone could examine it.

Services were Friday. Gladys didn't go.

Instead she packed. It would be so good to leave Hollywood. She'd miss her bungalow, but it felt awkward living here at Universal, doing films for other companies. Sometimes when she'd see a group by the lunch wagon or the door to a set, they'd stop talking, and she could feel their eyes on her as she passed.

It would be different in New York. Al could visit every few weeks.

So many gowns, so many shoes and hats to sort through. She was pulling dresses from the back of the closet when something fell from the top shelf. A flash of gray. She bent to pick it up. His fedora, still smudged from the train tracks. She tried to brush the dirt away, but her hands were

285

suddenly trembling, eyes blurring with tears. She sank to the floor, the hat clutched to her chest, crying.

If only he were here. If mamma met Al in person, she wouldn't have said those things. She shouldn't have told her. Should've stayed here yesterday, sent Craig with the boxes.

At first mamma just stared.

"Capone." Her voice a whisper. "Al Capone."

She'd been checking her pot roast, poking potatoes and carrots with a fork. Mamma closed the oven door, set down the fork, wiped her hands. She turned, her hands still twisted in the apron.

"You've been lying to me, all this time, what, two years? I'm your mother. Making me look like a fool, all my wedding talk."

"Not lying, mamma. Brown is... a name he used. He's just a bootlegger."

Mamma took a step, and the look in her eyes...

"Your Mr. Capone is not *just* a bootlegger, Princess. You must know that, unless you're lying to yourself too. It was in all the papers, the week before Marion's party."

Gladys met her eyes.

"The papers make everything a scandal, mamma. Like what they did to Wally Reid, exaggerate and distort to sell..."

"Gladys!"

She jumped. Mamma had never yelled at her. Not like this.

She lowered her voice. "There was a murder in Chicago. I know, there are always murders in Chicago, but this was different."

It was the tone mamma had used helping her with homework, calm, deliberate.

"Ten thousand people marched in the funeral. There was a photograph on the front page. Photographs do not exaggerate, Gladys. I don't remember the dead man's name,

286

something Irish. He had a florist shop, a front for the rackets, of course. These men are ruthless, and the article said Al Capone was a suspect. I remember that."

"Then why didn't they arrest him?" Defiance in her voice. She was not a little girl. She was almost twenty-one.

Mamma gripped her shoulders, as much fear in her eyes as anger.

"Honey, you must end this. Break it off. You have to. If they don't arrest him for this, it'll be something else eventually. Is that what you want, a boyfriend in prison? Or dead? You're beautiful and talented. You deserve better, and... and why hasn't he asked you to marry him?"

Gladys looked away.

"Look at me. Because he already has a wife, doesn't he? Of course he does. They all have the little wife who stays home while they're out..."

She stopped. Too late.

"Oh, if I had known." Her voice thick with disappointment now. "If you'd told me the truth instead of all that Mr. Brown nonsense. He's the reason your career is finished. Isn't he? How could you let it happen? It isn't worth it. All we worked for..."

Gladys pushed past her.

At the door she turned. "We, mamma? We?"

Papa Joe was in the living room, but she didn't lower her voice.

"I don't care what the papers say! I don't care what anyone says. I know who Al is. How he treats me, how he loves me." She glanced around the cozy kitchen, little house in Pasadena. "You have your life, mamma. Let me have mine."

Her voice wavered, but she forced it back. "And my career is not finished! What do you think I'll be doing in New York," she glanced at the stove, "cooking up pot roast?"

She walked out, slamming the screen door.

She had planned to go to Oregon for the holidays as usual. Not now. She'd go to Two Bunch, spend Christmas with One Arm, as much a father as she'd ever known. But she hadn't cried. She hadn't cried when Laemmle said her films were canceled.

Now, sitting on her closet floor holding Al's crumpled hat, she couldn't stop.

Chapter 57

Gladys stood at the bay window looking out at Central Park, the trees and paths dusted with snow, glistening in the lamplight. January 25th. Al's telegram said he'd arrive by six o'clock.

It was after 7:00. They had box seats, Lucrezia Bori in *Romeo And Juliette* at the Metropolitan Opera. Thirty-ninth and Broadway, easy. She'd bought a new beaded gown, had her hair done, found a silk opera scarf for Al, monogrammed, of course.

A taxi pulled up on the street below, and a man in a dark overcoat got out, broad shoulders, a fedora. Her breath caught. Then a woman followed holding a small dog, and they disappeared beneath the canopy.

His train must be late. Al would not miss the opera. She sat on the window seat, her back straight not to crease her gown.

She could still hardly believe her apartment. Top floor of a six story building on the east side, and twice as big as the bungalow at Universal. High ceilings, floors and wainscoting of white oak. The latest Art Deco furniture from France, sleek and stylish, all ivory and pale blue. The drapes were layers of pale silk, and in her bedroom a dressing table with a huge half-moon mirror, a round bed to match. Simple yet elegant. Nothing like the gaudy furniture in the cabin. Al must've hired a decorator.

New York made L.A. seem like a small town. Buildings fifty stories high, tallest in the world, people bustling, taxis everywhere, even the air felt electric. With the

289

subway you could get from the Village to Harlem in twenty minutes.

And snow! When she had moved in, she found a black mink coat in the closet. She bundled up and went walking, learning the neighborhood, up Madison, down Park Avenue, smiling at the matrons with their muffs. Some recognized her, she thought, too gentrified to stop and chat.

On Sundays she'd meet Claire and Lydia from the cast, go to a matinee or shopping. The signs were true, "All Cars Transfer To Bloomingdale's." It took up an entire block, and mamma thought shopping in L.A. was good!

Mamma. They'd hardly spoken since that day.

The mantel clock said 7:50. Gladys stood, checked the street again.

It wasn't like him to be this late.

At 9:00 she fixed herself a drink, fully stocked bar, of course. She leaned back on the divan, dozed and woke not sure where she was, at first. 11:15. What could've happened? She felt a shudder but pushed it aside, angry. He could've called! She remembered mamma's words, *in prison or... dead.*

No.

More likely his white powder. Or some woman!

In the bedroom, she took off her gown, hung it in the armoire. She hesitated. Change to something less formal? A group from the cast was going up to Harlem tonight, listen to jazz, one of those all black revues, cootch dancing. How she wanted to see cootch dancing, like that new Broadway show, *Chocolate Dandies.* Bring your boyfriend, they'd said.

She could take a taxi. Those places never got started till after midnight, but how would she find them? They'd mentioned *Hot Feet*, a new show at Connie's Inn. Or Princess Vikana or Bessie Smith or Bojangles, whatever club he was playing. There were a dozen clubs where white people went, hundreds more where they didn't. How could she go alone?

290

"Speaks." Gun fire, "pineapples" tossed in, blowing out back walls.

Never mind. She slipped on a robe, walked back to the living room. She poured another drink, her hand trembling. Damn! She threw the glass, and it shattered against the wall.

He didn't call until the following evening. She kept her voice icy. "Where are you? I waited..."

"I'm in the hospital," he said, and her anger vanished.

"The hospital! Are you...?"

"I'm fine. It's Johnny Torrio. I can't talk long, the phone might be... Gladys, I'm sorry, but he got shot up bad. On his fuckin' doorstep. Doctors didn't think he'd make it, but looks like he will. I'm sleeping on a cot in his room, case they try again."

His voice sounded tired, strained. She wanted to hold him.

Then it lifted, and she heard the smile. "Are you in the living room?"

"Yes, why?" Now what was he up to?

"Look out the window. I sent you a surprise. Make things easier. Gotta go, baby. I love you. I'll be there as soon as I can. We'll do the town, opera and all. I'll make it up to you, I promise."

And the line clicked off.

She walked to the window. Below, parked at the curb was a long black car, two men in dark suits standing beside it." She laughed, shook her head.

It was hard to stay mad at Al.

Chapter 58

Al's "as soon as I can" became two weeks, then four. Gladys waited. She tried not to think of what else he'd said. *In case they try again.*

Finally he called and explained.

She understood.

When Johnny Torrio recovered, he handed the entire operation over to Al. Then Torrio left for Italy. A huge operation now, they moved the headquarters to the Metropole Hotel, two whole floors, the series of tunnels connected to the basement, a bonus. Al and his tunnels.

A limousine, complete with her own driver and body guard wasn't a bad consolation, although she sometimes missed exploring the city on her own. The men rarely spoke, disgruntled with the assignment, maybe, away from Chicago and the action, chauffeuring the boss's mistress instead of the boss.

"They got families," Al had said when she asked, "moved them all to Queens."

The few times Al did come to New York that year, he made it up to her, all right. Showering her with gifts and money, an envelope of bills on her dressing table when he left. Hard to say which Al loved more, opera at the Met, the fights at the Gardens, or their Harlem safaris.

Gladys noticed changes in him, though. The way his eyes got when he sniffed his white powder, and he no longer cared about being incognito. Everywhere he played the crowd, tilting his hat, waving. *The* Al Capone, a man to be reckoned with, and they never went anywhere alone. Now and then they'd spend a quiet evening in her apartment, Al cooked spaghetti, then they'd "go for a romp" in her big, round Art Deco bed.

She'd wake in the middle of the night to find him gone. Business. Always he'd sleep till noon, catch a train back to Chicago.

She was busy. *The Skyraider* wrapped the end of April. Rehearsals started for *June Days*. It opened August 6th at the Astor. A hit, eighty-six performances. How she loved dancing again, no morality codes on Broadway, and each night her limo was waiting.

Once Al was there, too, surprising her from behind the stage door. "My show girl!" He grabbed her up and carried her, the first time she saw her body guards crack a smile. They headed for Harlem, and later, she did her own version of a cootch dance just for Al.

In September he didn't come at all.

Or October.

June Days closed. She auditioned for a new show, *Lemonade*, a spoof about bored housewives who set up a stand to sell lemonade, laced with gin, but rehearsals didn't start until January.

In November the weather turned bleak, and Gladys felt a sadness she couldn't explain. Gorgeous apartment on the east side, maid service once a week, what more could she want?

She sat on the window seat looking out at the gray sky. For days she didn't even get out of her robe, reading the trades and these new tabloids cover to cover, especially the *Evening Graphic*. Pornographic people called it, sex scandals and violence and fake photos. Hooked like everyone else. Best thing about having her own driver was the armful of "tabs" he brought each morning. She didn't even have to get dressed.

Bored. Homesick, maybe. For California sunshine, the desert. She missed her Bearcat, parked at the house in Pasadena. She missed mamma. They were talking again, almost every week on the phone. Mamma had finally broken her silence and called.

They avoided the subject of Al.

She'd go home for Christmas. Al could never be with her at Christmas. She should be used to that by now, but couldn't help picturing him with his family, a house full, all those brothers and their wives and children. His mother and younger sister.

His wife and son.

She glanced around her apartment. What point was there in getting a tree, decorating, piling presents around it, no one here to open them. She looked down at the street below, her limo waiting by the curb as usual. Guarding her.

She was tired of being guarded. If a man even asked her to dance at a club, she'd feel those stony eyes on her back. What, reporting to Al? Al didn't mind. A dance, that's all.

Shopping. Get dressed up and go shopping. That always helped. In the bedroom, she sat at her dressing table, did her hair and makeup, chose her best shopping dress, mink coat. Grabbed her umbrella on the way out.

In Bloomingdale's she found gifts for Aunt Minnie and Uncle Tommy, and the perfect hat for mamma. She was waiting for it to be wrapped when the idea came to her. Have her packages delivered. Make a break for it. The guard never followed her to Ladies Wear. She walked all the way through to the Lexington Street exit. Down a block, over to Fifth Avenue. It was starting to rain. She pulled her coat higher around her neck, opened her umbrella.

Free! Walking the streets of New York in the rain! She felt happy again. Hadn't even realized she was a prisoner.

Crossing Fiftieth, she saw the crowd, a swarm of black umbrellas around a touring car stopped in the middle of the intersection. Horns honking. In the back seat, a man and a woman were handing something out the windows. A mounted policeman blew his whistle, waved the car on, but it could only crawl, people clamoring for whatever the couple was giving out.

Then the man in the car turned, looked out the back window.

Gladys squealed, started through the crowd. "Excuse me, please..."

"It's Gladys Walton," someone said, "look, the Glad Girl."

They closed in.

"Oh, I saw all your movies."

"When's your next one? Everyone's waiting!"

"Could I have an autograph, Miss Walton?"

She laughed. "Maybe some place drier." It was pouring rain now, some of the crowd running for cover. She shouldered through, took the coin from his outstretched hand as the car started to move forward.

"Rudy... Rudy!" she called, and he must've recognized her voice.

He leaned out the window. "Gladys! Come, get in. Driver, wait!"

He opened the door, she hurried, fumbling to close her umbrella. He took her hand, practically lifted her in beside him.

"You are drenched," he said, "oh, but it's so good to see you!" He hugged her.

Nervous suddenly, Gladys looked at her hand, then her lap. "I lost my coin. What was it?" She'd thought the woman sitting by the other window was Natacha, but no. Maybe what she'd heard was true, Natacha had left him, filed for divorce.

Rudy smiled. "Plenty more, here." He reached a handful of coins from a burlap sack on the floor. "Rubles." He laughed. "For *The Eagle*, my Cossack movie." He held up a coin. "Only they are made of brass and on the back not the czar, but me."

He turned to the woman. "Miss Livingstone, this is Gladys Walton. Miss Livingstone is my publicist with United Artists. "

"I'm honored, Miss Walton. I've seen your films. They're such fun."

Gladys smiled, leaned across to her shake hand.

"Nice to meet you."

She could smell Rudy's cologne.

Publicist. Made sense, not an ounce of glamour about the woman. So they were not a couple. Good.

She felt a twinge of guilt.

"We're on our way to the opening now," Rudy said. "It's at The Strand. You must come, Gladys. I hear the crowd is already big. For the stage show an orchestra will play. Tchaikovsky and folk dances, the balalaika. After, we'll go down to Little Italy for dinner, a place with spaghetti almost as good as mine. If we can get through the fans, that is."

He touched her cheek. "Come with us, Gladys. You cannot say no. We have much to catch up on, don't we?"

She turned the coin in her hand, surprised the way her heart was beating. What had it been, three years? He was even more handsome.

"We do," she said, "and I'd never say no to you, Rudy."

She blushed, laughing, hadn't meant it the way it sounded.

She touched her dripping hair. "But I'll need to fix up a bit."

296

Chapter 59

The minute she stepped from the train at Christmas and looked up at a clear California sky, Gladys decided she would come west whenever she wanted, best of both worlds. Why not? Five luxurious days on the train. She could even stop in Chicago. If Al couldn't come to her, she'd go to him. Meet at the Hotel Sherman as before.

She was back in New York the first week of January. There were delays. *Lemonade* finally opened on Broadway April 15th. And closed two weeks later. What fun the critics had with that. *Lemonade is a lemon.*

She left the next day. In Philadelphia a newsboy got on and she saw the headline.

"GANGSTERS TURN MACHINE GUN
ON WILLIAM MCSWIGGIN"

"TWO OTHERS SLAIN IN CICERO WITH ASSISTANT
STATE'S ATTORNEY"

"'SCARFACE' AL CAPONE ACCUSED"

Gladys didn't buy a paper. Whatever the details, whatever explanation, it didn't matter. Al wouldn't be at the Sherman. Sometime in the next couple months she would hear from him. A crackly call from up in Michigan or Moose Jaw, Saskatchewan. But he wouldn't be able to see her. He kept her out of all that.

She did not for one minute believe he killed an assistant state's attorney. Not on purpose.

Like those shootings at that club in Brooklyn. Christmas night. Impossible. What would Al be doing in Brooklyn Christmas night?

She stood at the door as the train pulled into the Chicago terminal. She'd get off just long enough to telegraph Joseph MacKenzie to meet her at Garnet.

Then she saw the police.

Officers were spaced along the platform and at each entrance. The porter opened the door, and two officers standing close to the tracks looked up. They recognized her, she could tell.

She managed a smile, then touched the porter's arm. "Goodness, I forgot my hat." She turned, hurried through to her compartment. Heart racing, hands clasped in her lap to keep from shaking. What if they barged in and questioned her? Or took her to the station? What would she say? What would the headlines read then?

At least Al hadn't been arrested. The police wouldn't be there if he'd been arrested.

She thought of mamma.

In St. Louis she sent the telegram.

Chapter 60

A rider was coming toward them up the long slope from Palm Springs.

Even from here you could tell the horse was magnificent, stark white against the carpet of wildflowers, purple and orange and yellow.

One Arm had taught her the names. Verbena, Chuparosa, Desert Primrose, Brittle Bush. In the washes Smoke Trees were dusted lavender with blossoms too tiny to see, and on the craggy hills tall Ocotillo, their spires tipped bright red. It had rained last week, and the air was pungent with creosote and sage. Even the cacti were blooming.

Spring time in the desert.

"Who do ya 'spose that is? Whoa!" One Arm struggled to rein in his horse. The mare knew a stallion when she saw one, or at least the way back to the stables.

"I don't know," Gladys said, which wasn't precisely true. She even remembered the stallion's name, Jadaan. It had to be, that curved neck and tapered head, but to think their paths would cross again, here at the base of Tahquitz Canyon.

Gladys reined in her bay gelding and watched.

How straight he sat in the saddle, yet easy, as if it were the most natural place for him to be. The way he moved in the tango. He leaned forward slightly, and the horse went into a gentle lope. Beautiful, the desert sloping behind.

Then the stallion must've caught the mare's scent because he stopped suddenly and reared, snorting, pawing the air, his shrill whinny breaking the stillness. Maybe forty yards away.

"What the hell, bitch, I said, whoa! Whoa, damn you!"

Gladys turned. One Arm was hanging on, his wooden arm high like a rodeo rider as the mare spun, tossing her head. Then the mare bucked and he hit the ground, luckily still holding tight to the reins.

Gladys swung down, walked to him, leading her horse. "You okay?"

She couldn't help laughing.

"Sure, but I'm fixin' to knock her block off. Fine time to fall in love!"

He looped the reins around his wooden arm, got to his feet. Yelled across at the other rider. "Keep your damned Romeo away, buster!"

Gladys laughed. "That's Rudolph Valentino you're yelling at. He's riding the stallion they're using in his new Sheik movie."

She'd half expected Rudy to be tossed too, the way stallion was acting up. Should've known. He controlled Jadaan, walked him farther away to a Palo Verde tree and stood talking to him, stroking his neck.

"Valentino?" One Arm grumbled. "Well, if that don't make sense. Stud with a stud. Ought'a geld 'em both..."

"We're friends," Gladys said.

He looked at her. "You are?"

She nodded. "We hadn't seen each other for a long time. Then I ran into him in New York last November, the opening to *The Eagle*, that Cossack movie. I had dinner with him. And his publicist," she added quickly.

One Arm was quiet for a moment.

Last night they'd sat in the turret and talked. She'd told him about the headlines, the police at the Chicago station. *It don't look good for Al,* he'd said. *I'm afraid if they don't get him for this, it'll be something else. You gotta do what's best for you, Gladys.*

Now she met his eyes. "It isn't what you're thinking, One Arm."

"What? I ain't thinking nothin'" He tossed the reins over the mare's head, grabbed the saddle horn. "Except getting this filly to the stables 'fore she backs up to Mr. Fancy Ass and he mounts us both."

"You are speaking of my horse, I hope."

They turned. Rudy walked to them, grinning. He did not show the slightest reaction to One Arm's ruined face. How handsome in jodhpurs and tall boots.

"I am very sorry for this trouble," he said, gesturing back toward the stallion. "But Jadaan is tied now. He won't bother your mare again. Mr. MacKenzie, is it?" Rudy held out his left hand to One Arm. "Gladys told me about you. It's nice to meet you."

One Arm let go of the saddle horn, shook his hand, mumbled a greeting. Embarrassed. He looked at Gladys, then back at Rudy. A long moment.

She could see his mind working.

"I hope you aren't leaving because of me," Rudy said.

"No, of course not," One Arm said, "but I think I'll ride on ahead. Got a delivery to make down at the Salton Sea." He paused. "Say, you wouldn't mind driving Miss Walton over to Two Bunch Palms, would you? Or you could ride. Why not? Beautiful day for it. I'll tell them at the stables."

He didn't wait for an answer, swung up onto the saddle.

"S'pect I'll stay the night at Hell's Kitchen, Miss Walton, do some drinkin' with the Captain." He saluted with his wooden arm, grinned. "Adios."

A kick and the mare lurched into a gallop. "That's it, bitch, find the barn! Eee Ahh!"

They watched him bounce along as the mare galloped down the long slope. They looked at each other and laughed.

Quiet settled around them.

"Well," Rudy smiled, "looks like you are stranded, but I have wanted to see this Two Bunch place." He paused. "How long would it take to ride there?"

She shook her head. "Four or five hours. One Arm. It'll be dark by the time we get there." Too late for Rudy to ride back.

"Hmm, a clever man." His eyes twinkled. "There is a room where I could stay? I don't want it to be awkward for you, Gladys. Or if you prefer, I can drive you. I have my Voisin, something like the Suiza, but French. The road is good?"

She laughed. "No, the road is not good. But there is a room. It won't be awkward. Not for me," she added.

It made her sad. Before, she had burned for Valentino, blurting his name that night with Howard, and now she wanted only to be with Al. She missed him so much. For weeks she'd had no idea where he was. And that evening at dinner, Rudy had talked only about Natacha, how he'd win her back, start again.

How cruel life was. To be in love with the wrong person.

"So, we go then?"

Rudy cupped his hands, boosted her onto her horse. He walked beside her across to the Palo Verde tree and Jadaan.

As they rode, he told about filming *The Son of the Sheik* in the sand dunes at Yuma. He hadn't wanted to be a sheik again, but this time he got to play two parts, the handsome, headstrong son and the father, Ahmed Ben Hassan, the role that launched him to stardom. Beyond stardom. Thousands of fans were turned away that night at The Strand. Thousands more clogged the streets in Little Italy just for a glimpse. The man Howard had said wouldn't amount to anything had become the biggest star in America.

"It is strange," Rudy said, holding Jadaan back for her gelding to keep up, "playing the father, seeing myself old." He touched his chin. "Gray beard and wrinkles. I do not think to get old, do you, Gladys?"

She laughed. "What choice is there? And you said you would come and take me for rides in your fancy cars, with our scarves blowing, remember?"

"Ah, yes." He nodded. "For this only will I consent to get old."

They rode in silence, skirting Palm Springs to avoid rumors. "It is enough with Pola Negri telling the papers we are engaged," Rudy said. "She follows me everywhere." He winked. "Sometimes I do not mind. Then she yells at me in Polish." He shook his head. "The great lover, but my luck with women is not good." He laughed. "No, it is terrible."

On the flat stretch north of town, they galloped, Jadaan way ahead. Gladys had never seen such a horse, pure Arabian, muscles taut, nostrils flared, white mane and tail flowing. His tail reached the ground, but when he ran it curved high in a question mark. On loan from the Kellogg ranch in Pomona, Jadaan was the old sheik's horse. For his part as the son, Valentino rode Firefly, his own horse, black as onyx.

She could hardly wait to see the film.

The sun was setting when they turned down the road to the oasis, the tops of the palm trees glowing pink orange. Rudy gasped. "Why didn't you tell me?" His voice hushed. "Like a cathedral. Listen." Only the horses breathing, hooves squishing in the mud. "Oh, if this were mine, I would never leave. I would find a squaw, make lots of babies and let them run naked."

She laughed.

But later, sitting at the table in One Arm's kitchen watching Rudy make spaghetti, she started to cry. On the ride she had told him about Al and the police at the Chicago station.

Rudy knelt beside her. "I'm sorry." He wiped her cheeks with a kitchen towel, handed it to her. "He is Italian, of course." He shook his head. "These Italians. Where was he born, Sicily?"

"Brooklyn." She cried harder, laughing too, wiping her eyes. "His parents are from Naples."

"Ah, yes, the Camorristi. La mala vita. This is not something a man can leave. Especially the padrone. Come, gypsy, you're tired, you need to eat. Even if my spaghetti isn't as good as his. And do we have wine?"

She laughed, wiping her eyes. "Do we have wine? By the case."

Later, while she did the dishes, Rudy unsaddled the horses, rubbed them down, tied them in the tall grass, set out buckets of water.

They sat side by side on the ledge in the grotto pool, the water up to their chests, ribbons of steam rising into the night air. She wore the bathing outfit she'd bought for the trip to Hawaii, left here from when Marion and the girls came. Rudy, his under shorts. It was dark. Who cared?

"Is that what you would want, Rudy?" she asked.

"What?"

"Lots of babies?"

"Oh, a dozen, at least."

She laughed, splashing him. "I'm serious."

He leaned back. "The truth, I cannot think more reason to stay alive," he said. "I had everything, but... What I create... the films they give me are, how do you say, trivial? Only *Four Horseman* I am proud of."

"Mmm. *Blood and Sand* too, and this new movie sounds wonderful, but I know what you mean. None of mine are even close."

They didn't speak for several minutes. The waterfall tumbling, hum of locusts in the trees, the far off yipping of coyotes. Faint click of a beak, the all but silent swoop of wings. She knew the sounds well now. How she loved this place.

He sat forward. "Natacha did not want children. That was our biggest problem, I think. And how she took over my career. I never minded that. She is so talented, a genius, but they banned her from the set. A proud woman. Of course she left me after that." He shrugged. "What could I do? It was in the contract."

He cupped his hands, watched the water slide through his fingers. His voice low. "She was pregnant. More than once, I think. Didn't even tell me. Nita Naldi went with her..." He stopped, dipped his hands again, rubbed his face.

Gladys tried to think what to say.

A flash of white, an owl landed on a palm tree not twenty feet from them. It stared down at them with big, round eyes.

"Rudy," she whispered, "do you remember when you first told me about the desert? I was waiting for the trolley, after our ride in the Suiza."

"I remember."

"You said we would find an oasis and dance the tango for the owls."

"I said that? Not bad."

"Yes, you did." She pointed. "And there's the owl. See?"

He laughed. "Well, then." He stood, took her hand, lifted her to her feet. He led her to the grassy area swathed in moonlight, did a slight bow.

"Miss Walton," he said, "will you dance with me?"

Chapter 61

Early the next morning Gladys walked with Rudy to the road, the horses content from their night in the tall grass. It was a three hour drive to Yuma, he had to get back.

Rudy laughed, "Jadaan came with his own trainer. He will think I kidnapped him."

He kissed her cheek, held her against his chest. "Thank you, Gladys. This place is the desert's soul. I hope to come here again." He was trembling.

A wind had picked up in the night, and she felt a chill.

Then he tipped her chin up and kissed her.

They had never kissed before.

She breathed his scent without the cologne.

"We will see each other more," he said, his hand on her cheek, "when I finish the film, then get back from New York. We should find out, don't you think?"

"Yes." She nodded, shivering.

She would be in New York, too, but she didn't say that. She hadn't told him about her apartment. The thought of him walking past her guards sent different chills. Her gilded cage.

He pulled her robe around her neck, rubbed her back.

"The desert... two hours, it will be hot again. Go, gypsy, get under the covers."

He swung up onto the saddle. When she handed him the gelding's rope, he leaned and kissed her again, a different kiss. It brought tears to her eyes.

In a moment she stood back, her cheeks flushed. She watched him go.

Where the road curved, he turned, shaded his eyes to see her. He stayed that way for several moments, looking at her, as if to remember this for the weeks ahead. Jadaan seemed to sense it too and stood perfectly still. There in the morning sun.

Then Rudy waved and turned down the hill.

She hurried back, climbed the steps to the turret and watched him following the road that was no road, sitting straight and easy on the white stallion, the bay gelding trailing along beside.

We should find out.

She thought of the police swarming the Chicago station. The two officers looking up at her from the platform. She remembered the fear, that they would follow and interrogate her. What would it be like to have a future without bodyguards and bullet proof cars and headlines screaming of one murder or another? To have a lover who didn't disappear for months at a time? A lover without a wife and family somewhere else.

Oh, she would not trade a minute of what she'd had with Al. Yet how long could it go on? What future could there be for them? She thought of what Rudy had said about his luck with women. And her luck? She had traded a career for love. And months of emptiness between.

How would it be to actually build a life together? Hollywood couples didn't exactly lead normal lives, of course, but some came close. Maybe revive her fading career. Maybe even get married, have children of her own. Was that too much to ask? Mrs. Rudolph Valentino. Silly thought. Or perhaps not.

She shivered, pulled the collar of her robe higher, hugged her arms against the chill. She sat in the turret and watched until he was a tiny speck in the distance.

Chapter 62

It was the last she ever saw him.

Gladys sat in the back of her limo, numb. Throngs of people as soon as they crossed Central Park and turned south. Even with the pouring rain, people clogged the streets, clamoring, hysterical. Thousands and thousands, they'd been gathering since dawn, she'd never seen such a crowd and still blocks from Sixty-sixth and Broadway.

The driver looked at her in the rearview mirror.

"Miss Walton, this ain't good. We'd better go back while I can still turn around."

"I'll walk!" she said, angry, but the door wouldn't open. She pushed harder. Someone moved, it gave, and she stumbled out into the crowd. Swept along, just another veiled woman in a sea of umbrellas, rain pelting. She didn't care.

Angry. At herself, mostly. She should've gone to see him in the hospital. Busy with rehearsals. No, it wasn't that. She wanted nothing to do with hospitals. She remembered that day with Mabel, white walls, the nurse in her crisp white dress, white stockings, white cap, even the air bleached white with disinfectant. All to mask the reality. Dr. Morris whispering explanations she did not understand, no longer mattered. Too late.

Drenching rain, the crowd closing tighter, pulling her along. She could see nothing but dark suits and dresses. Women sobbing. Up ahead people were yelling. She could feel the anger and her own. Stupid women. She wanted to scream, You don't know him! All they knew was his gilded image on the screen, concocted for their silly fantasies. But even in her anger she knew part of the Valentino they saw in the movies was real. The grace, the boyish laugh that could turn to longing. The sorrow in his eyes they mistook as passion. Someone shoved against her and she pushed back. A glimpse of a street sign, Sixty-sixth and Broadway, the entire intersection a mass of people, shoulder to shoulder.

All week she'd read the reports in the papers and did not believe. Would not believe. Rudy in the hospital.

He was young and strong. Just four months ago they had galloped together across the desert. He seemed in perfect health. She tried to remember the slightest sign that he was ill. Nothing. Four hours they rode. They ate dinner, they danced beside the grotto pool, her head against his chest. He was sad, talking about Natacha, but not later.

We should find out, he'd said.

They kissed.

That morning, the way he'd stopped where the road curved and looked at her, as if to remember. Or a premonition?

Emergency surgeries. Appendicitis, ulcers. Not things to die of.

At first she'd thought the whole thing must be a publicity stunt. Stupid tabs with their fake photos. Rudy naked on an operating table, only his lower body covered, a nurse smiling. Stupid charade! The *Graphic* reported him dead two days ago, then retracted.

Finally, yesterday, *The New York Times*, August 23, 1926. "VALENTINO PASSES WITH NO KIN AT SIDE"

She should've gone.

A man jostled against her. She held her own. Plenty of men in the crowd. So much for men hating Valentino. Through the rain, she could see the square awning of the funeral home. Mounted police riding into the crowd, herding people into line. A cordon of police. Whistles blowing, men yelling, throwing punches, the shrieks of women. A horse reared and came down. A scream. Someone trampled by the hooves? It was a riot, not a viewing. Impossible for this many people to file by the casket. Were they refusing to let them see the body?

Body. "Oh, God!" She sobbed.

A loud crash, glass breaking. They must've pushed through the huge plate glass window. She had passed Campbell's Funeral Church before. The crowd surged behind her, shards of glass crunching under her feet. She grabbed, a sleeve, anything, not to fall and be trampled. She could no longer see, tears streaming. *We should find out.*

A gun shot behind her. Close. A man's voice calling her name. An elbow knocked the side of her head, her knees buckled, and she fell. Strong hands under her arms, lifting her, passing her to other hands, pushing, making a path through the crowd, carrying her away.

Another gunshot. "Get back, damn it! Move! I'll knock your fuckin' head off!"

Her body guards.

Chapter 63

They carried her to the limo, then up to her room.

The maid came. She bandaged her cuts, put ice packs on her bruises. Helped her into a warm bath, then got her to bed. Her funeral dress was torn and ripped, tossed away.

Al arrived late that night.

Gladys clung to him, crying.

He did not ask. He just held her. "It's all right. I know, I know."

But he didn't know. How a door could open a tiny crack, then slam shut. Rudy was thirty-one years old.

Finally she slept, didn't wake till afternoon the next day. Al was there watching her. Then he piled pillows behind her and brought breakfast on a tray, Italian sausage, omelet and toast, champagne in a flute, a single red rose.

Al sat beside her, nodded to the tray, that twinkle in his eye.

What? She looked again, had to smile. On the stem of the rose was a large diamond, set in platinum.

"It'd be a wedding ring, if I could." He paused, as if thinking what else to say. "They dropped the McSwiggin case. That's quite a shiner you got. I'll get more ice. And coffee."

She ate every bite, then leaned back, closed her eyes.

"I want a baby," she said, and didn't have to look to know he'd spilled his coffee.

The words just came out, some corner of her mind she hadn't even explored.

A baby. Yes.

"Well... if that's what you want," Al said when he recovered. "We'll throw precautions to the wind."

It didn't happen right away, but that was fine too. Time to plan.

She was on a mission now. When Al couldn't come to New York, she went to him. They met at a hotel in Miami where he was buying an estate. "So I can retire from the rackets," he said, "live respectable for a change," but she didn't believe it. They met at that cabin he liked by a lake in Michigan and at the Lexington Hotel, his new headquarters.

That was only once. The place was a fortress. It made her sad. How obsessed Al was with security. Bullet proof chair, always taking the freight elevator, meals brought up from a private kitchen, making the chef test the food in front of him. Even if he kept escaping arrest, he was already in a prison.

Al was putting on weight, and often he fell into dark moods she didn't understand. No, that wasn't true. She understood. She knew about death, more than he did, she thought.

The deaths he knew were mostly enemies, except his brother, almost five years ago. Enemies. As if it were a war. It was. A war they made themselves, over money and territory. Like all wars.

How much money did one need? Some said Al was making a hundred million dollars a year. She'd seen the house where he lived with his wife and family, visited really, when he wasn't at the Lexington. Hardly a palace.

When he fell into his moods, he'd reach for his stash of white powder, and she would simply get up and leave.

She had learned to travel with one bag.

A baby.

312

Gladys remembered Rudy's words. *I cannot think more reason to stay alive.*

She even told mamma her plan. Christmas, at the house in Oregon. They were in her old bedroom.

Mamma stared. "You're pregnant?"

"Not yet, but soon," she said. "I hope. Oh, don't worry, mamma, I'll find someone to marry me."

Gladys walked to the window. "What do you think? White curtains? We'll paint the wainscoting light yellow in case it's a girl. And new wallpaper, something for a nursery."

"Gladys, who would you marry? This is crazy!"

"I don't know yet, but I have an idea. And don't look so shocked, mamma. I don't need a man to raise a baby. Who knows that better than you?"

The idea came to her in October, a party at the Chelsea Hotel. A bohemian crowd. She was doing a movie again, her first since *The Skyraider,* almost three years ago. Hard to believe. This new one, *The Ape*, was a horror film based on a real murder, and the director invited her to a Halloween party.

In Wardrobe she found a slinky, black gown draped in strands of tiny fake pearls, black to look like spider webs. A matching headpiece. She frizzed out her hair, lots of black around her eyes. Spider Woman. She wished Al could come. Dress him up like an F.B.I. agent or a judge, although he might not think it was funny.

At first she didn't recognize Howard. Much too tall and skinny for a toga. Gold wreath on his head.

She made her way across the smoky room. With this crowd, hard to tell who was in costume and who was not.

"Howard? Howard Thomas?" He looked sheepish, like he might turn and hide.

"Gladys, it's... so good to see you. How've you been?"

"Fine. I'm acting again. I didn't know you were in New York."

He nodded. "I'm in distribution now. In charge of the whole east coast. Money's good, but... I'm hoping to get back into directing." He touched her arm. "You look fabulous, Gladys! The pearls are great."

She glanced at the man standing beside him. They were wearing matching togas.

"This is Larry," Howard said. "Larry Van Fleet... Gladys Walton. The Glad Girl. You've seen her films, I'm sure. I knew Gladys when she was just getting started. What were you, sixteen?"

Howard was blushing.

She nodded, shook Larry's hand. "Nice to meet you."

"Larry's the finest makeup artist on Broadway," Howard said, beaming.

That's when she realized Howard might have morality clause issues of his own. It explained a lot.

Two weeks later Al called. "Start packing, baby. We're going to Mexico."

"To stay? Oh, Al!" *The Ape* had just wrapped. Perfect.

"Naw, only a few days. Dempsey's building him a mansion in Ensenada. Needs a partner. Gotta go see what I'm investing in. Do some fishing off Todo Santos while we're at it. What d'ya say, kid?"

Of course, he and Jack Dempsey were pals.

Not every woman can know the exact time and place she conceives, but Gladys knew. A wide bunk below deck on a Mexican deep sea fishing boat. November 3, 1928.

314

The next day they pulled in more than a dozen tuna and sea bass, none under forty pounds, and on the trip back she felt sea sick. That never happened before.

Al laughed, holding her at the rail. "Five foot chop might have something to do with it. Better not celebrate yet."

Then she told him the plan, her arranged marriage. Even with her career waning, it wouldn't do for a star to be pregnant and unwed.

Al laughed more. "I like it. Yeah. I'll send the rings, pay for everything. Nothing but the best."

When she had missed two monthlies, she called.

"Al's in Miami, honey," the voice said.

Gladys did not care. This was her baby. All hers!

She called Howard and explained. He agreed.

It was a simple wedding at a Justice of the Peace. A huge star sapphire ring for Howard. She already had her diamond. Larry Van Fleet was the best man, more ways than one.

The following day she sent a telegram to Joseph MacKenzie, packed two trunks and took the train west. She did not stop in Chicago.

She was lying in a lounge chair, basking in the sun on the flat roof behind the turret, when she heard One Arm on the steps. "Damn! What the fuck were they thinking?" He stood beside her, a newspaper in his hands, reading. "Didn't even get Bugs... Crazy! This ain't like..."

Then he seemed to remember her "condition," as he called it, tried to hide the paper behind his back.

She sat up. "What is it? Al...?"

He saw the fear in her eyes.

"No. Aw, shit." He handed her the paper.

"7 CHICAGO GANGSTERS SLAIN BY
FIRING SQUAD OF RIVALS

315

SOME IN POLICE UNIFORMS
VICTIMS LINED UP IN A ROW"

The date on the paper was February 15, 1929. The Saint Valentine's Day Massacre.

It was over. Gladys knew that as soon as she read the headlines.

She had gotten pregnant just in time.

Chapter 64

Gladys stood with the crowd at Chicago's Dearborn station. The Dixie Flyer, a regularly scheduled Pullman train, was ready to take Al to the federal penitentiary in Atlanta. She held her baby in her arms, a toddler now. John John she called him, her Punkin.

A cool evening in May, she wore a light traveling suit, a hat with a short veil. People still recognized her occasionally, although she hadn't made a movie since *The Ape*, hardly a success. They would not expect Gladys Walton to be holding a child. Gladys Walton would stay forever that spunky, laughing girl, with her "virginal sexuality" and "chaste tease" smile. The Glad Girl.

The twenties were over, even the fashions had changed. Clothes fit for a Depression, as they were calling it now. May, 1932.

In the past few years Gladys knew Al only from what she read in the papers and what One Arm could tell her when she visited, which wasn't often anymore. She and Howard bought a house in Beverly Hills. Sham of a marriage, but at least they were friends, and Howard was directing again. Gladys had a child to raise. She wanted more children too. The most important job she would ever have.

Cars pulled up, people continued to crowd onto the platform. Gladys wasn't surprised. Al had been in the Cook County jail for seven months, a huge cell with all the amenities of a hotel, so they said. He used the jail telegram and phone system and ran his operation just as he had from the Lexington, only now the taxpayers paid his tab. As many visitors as he liked, his wife's home cooking, family feasts for the holidays as usual. The warden, Mr. David Moneypenny, swore Capone was getting no preferential treatment, then reporters broke the story that Moneypenny was found driving Capone's deluxe, sixteen cylinder Cadillac, which happened to break down on his way from Springfield to Chicago.

The people loved it, Al thumbing his nose at the government. A government that had not been able to protect them from the crash. No one forgot that it was Al Capone who opened the first soup kitchens in Chicago, paid department stores to dole out clothing to the poor. Partly to distract attention from the trial, Gladys knew, but tell that to a businessman reduced to selling apples on the street.

John John squirmed to get down.

"No, Punkin, there's too many people." Journalists among all the well-wishers. Eleven years for income tax evasion. The news shocked the country. Bets had been two or three years at most. Never had anyone gotten such a sentence.

"Look, look at the big train, honey. Choo choo, see?" She bounced him, blew against his pudgy neck, and he laughed.

How she loved his laugh.

Her baby. She'd never been so happy. Rudy was right, no better reason to be alive. She thought of Mabel and Nathan Andrew.

Al had never seen John John. When he was born, Al was in prison in Pennsylvania. A year sentence for carrying a concealed weapon. "Practically checked himself in," One Arm said, "called a couple detectives he knew, got himself indicted and sentenced in hours."

It made no sense. He could've just gone to his estate in Florida.

"The other bosses wanted him out," One Arm said. "Valentine's Day Massacre changed everything. Guess he thought the safest place was jail."

John John was eight months old when Al was released from Pennsylvania. The Federal investigation started soon after. No, long before. It took them years to build a case. Then the trial. She'd see the front page photographs, Al in his fancy suits, each day a different color combination, right down to the silk handkerchief, but his eyes were different. Behind the smile he looked worn, almost sick. Afraid. The man who wanted nothing more than to be respected. Redeemed, maybe.

Public Enemy Number One.

Sirens in the distance. Gladys shifted John John to her other hip, walked to the far end of the platform. She did not want to see Al in handcuffs surrounded by police and F.B.I., that Eliot Ness grinning for the cameras as always, making himself the hero.

"Al hardly knows the guy," One Arm said. "Bustin' up a few breweries. Meant nothin' to Al. Those I.R.S. geeks brought him down, that's all."

U.S. marshals stood by the door to the train, his escorts. A caravan of cars pulled up. She could see the excitement shudder through the crowd as police moved the prisoner along, reporters closing in, cameras flashing. Minutes passed as Ness and his "Untouchables" searched the Pullman cars, afraid the syndicate would pull a rescue somewhere along the route.

Then she got a glimpse of Al's broad back. Manacled to another prisoner, they stumbled up the steps into the train. She put her hand to her mouth, fought the tears. No. Don't let him see tears. She adjusted John John in her arms, smoothed his sandy hair.

She lifted her veil.

Al was there in the window, smiling for the crowd. The train started to move.

This way, she thought, look this way.

She held John John higher. "See, see the train. It's rolling. Can you wave, Punkin? It's your Papa. Wave, wave for Papa."

She took his hand, showed him. And he waved on his own, laughing.

When she looked again, Al was directly across. Their eyes met. Stunned, his lips formed her name. He saw the boy and grinned, tears in his eyes. Hand to his chest, he mouthed the question. "He's mine?"

She nodded, smiling.

Then he was gone.

Gladys and "John John"

John favored his mother's looks.

A beauty at any age.

Chapter 65

The next day newspapers reported spectators lined the tracks at every stop all the way from Chicago to Atlanta.

In August of 1934, a "secret" train transferred him to Alcatraz. A prison built mostly for Al Capone and others like him. They were wrong. There were no others like him. They had expected their "Public Enemy Number One" to take over in Atlanta, but he was quiet, a model prisoner. Still, they guarded that "secret" train heavily, and spectators gathered along the route west.

Alcatraz.

Another word for hell. Rumors drifted out. Nine by five cells, cold and damp, weeks, sometimes months in isolation, total darkness. Prisoners not allowed to speak. Attacks by other inmates. Men disappeared. Perhaps worst, the sounds that drifted the short distance from San Francisco, laughter and music, people living ordinary lives. The voices of women.

Gladys called once. No visitors but family, and then only fifteen minutes through a tiny window.

Al was sick. His last year he was confined to the "bug cage." Reports were vague, mental problems, slurred speech, long hours alone in his cell, never an actual diagnosis. Gladys began to suspect the disease everyone knew but never named. It made sense, considering what One Arm had told her - the upstairs part of the business.

Their baby was born healthy. Thank goodness.

Gladys *and* Capone, *the Untold Story*

In January, 1939 she read that Al was being transferred to the Federal Correctional Institution at Terminal Island near Los Angeles. He would serve his last months there. Gladys called for permission.

She had two more babies now, a boy and a girl. She took them to mamma's house, drove down, crossed the harbor in a small prison boat.

She sat in one of the visitor cubicles, waiting behind thick glass, the walls institutional gray. Too sick to stay at Alcatraz, the article had said. Something must be very wrong for Al to give a deposition against Johnny Torrio. Either his mind was slipping or the papers lied. Al would never betray Johnny Torrio.

The door opened, and the guard led out a man she did not know.

She gasped, almost a cry, muffled by the heavy glass. She breathed in, pressed her fingertips below her eyes to hold back the tears. Trembling. Don't. Do not cry. The least you can do. The very least.

He shuffled, his body bent and flabby, skin sallow, dark circles under his eyes. His receding hair made his big face look even rounder. The gray pants and shirt hung on him.

The guard helped him to the chair across from her. A slit in the glass for them to talk.

"Thanks," Al said, looking up at the guard, but his eyes seemed vacant, his mouth slack.

The guard had to turn him toward her.

"You got a visitor, Mr. Capone. Hollywood star, few years back. Looks like you still got it, Snorky."

The tone one used for a child.

Al looked at her.

"Hello, Al."

He nodded, a half smile, not a flicker of recognition. His hand drifted to his head, smoothing some stray hair.

323

She should not have come.

Better to keep him in her mind the way he had been. Grabbing her up, carrying her, laughing. Venice Beach, the stone cabin, their desert oasis. Rolling her in his big arms across whatever bed they were in. Devouring her to his favorite opera, "Vespri Siciliani." Fishing off Todos Santos.

Tears. Impossible to stop them.

He saw.

"No," he said softly, "don't." Then he turned to the guard. "I want to go. Take me back, please." He touched the guard's sleeve, whispered something.

The guard shrugged. "Wait here, Miss Walton."

Then Al stood and shuffled through the door.

She sat shaking, tears streaming, could hardly see to grab Kleenex from her purse. Eight years. What had they done to him that he would turn from her and go back to his cell?

She took deep breaths, wiped her eyes, waited. Minutes passed. What could the guard possibly have to say to her?

She was about to leave, when the door opened.

Al walked slowly across. In his hands was the mandolin, and she remembered the shop in Tijuana, how he'd carried it in his arms like a baby.

He sat and tuned it carefully. It took several minutes.

When he looked up, he smiled. His eyes had changed. Not quite like before, but he was there.

"Remember, Gladys?" he said, "Apple Blossom Time. Listen. You'll like it." He laughed. "I've had a long time to practice."

Chapter 66

Gladys stood with the crowd at the Dearborn station, the Dixie Flyer, a regularly scheduled Pullman train, ready to take Al to the federal penitentiary in Atlanta. She held her baby in her arms, a toddler now. John John she called him, her Punkin.

A cool evening in May, she wore a light traveling suit, a hat with a short veil. People still recognized her occasionally, although she hadn't made a movie since *The Ape*, hardly a success. They would not expect Gladys Walton to be holding a child. Gladys Walton would stay forever that spunky, laughing girl, with her "virginal sexuality" and "chaste tease" smile. The Glad Girl.

The twenties were over, even the fashions had changed. Clothes fit for a Depression, as they were calling it now. May, 1932. Al had been in the Cook County jail for seven months.

John John squirmed to get down.

"No, Punkin, there's too many people." Journalists, mostly, and well-wishers. "Look, look at the big train. Choo choo, see?" She bounced him and blew against his pudgy neck, and he laughed.

How she loved his laugh. Al's laugh.

Her baby. She'd never been so happy. Rudy was right. *I cannot think more reason to stay alive.* She thought of Mabel and Nathan Andrew.

It was more than two years since she'd seen Al. When John John was born, Al was in prison in Pennsylvania - doing a year for carrying a concealed weapon. "Practically checked himself in," One Arm had said, "called a couple detectives he knew, got himself indicted and sentenced in hours."

325

It made no sense. He could've just gone to his estate in Florida.

"The other bosses wanted him out," One Arm said. "Valentine's Massacre changed everything. Guess he thought the safest place was jail."

If it weren't for One Arm, she would've had only the newspapers. Making him a monster, Public Enemy Number One.

John John was eight months old when Al got out. The Federal investigation started soon after. No, long before. It took them years to build a case. Then the trial. She'd see the front page photographs, Al in his fancy suits, each day a different color, right down to the silk handkerchief, but his eyes were different. Behind the smile he looked worn, almost sick. Afraid. The man who wanted nothing more than to be respected. Redeemed, maybe. After the Stock Market crash, he opened the first soup kitchens in Chicago.

Sirens in the distance. Gladys shifted John John to her other hip, walked to the far end of the platform. She did not want to see Al in shackles surrounded by police and F.B.I., that Eliot Ness grinning for the cameras as always, making himself the hero. "Al don't hardly know the guy," One Arm said. "Bustin' up a few breweries. Meant nothin' to Al. Those I.R.S. geeks brought him down, that's all."

U.S. marshals stood by the door to the train, his escorts. A caravan of cars pulled up. She could see the excitement shudder through the crowd as police moved the prisoner along, reporters closing in, cameras flashing. Minutes passed as Ness and his Untouchables searched the Pullman cars, afraid the syndicate would pull a rescue somewhere along the route.

Then she got a glimpse of Al's broad back. Manacled to another prisoner, they stumbled up the steps into the train. She put her hand to her mouth, fought the tears. No. Don't let him see tears. She adjusted the baby higher in her arms, smoothed his sandy hair. She lifted her veil.

Al was there in the window, smiling for the crowd. The train started to move. This way, she thought, look this way. She held John John up. "See, see the train. It's rolling. Can you wave, Punkin? It's your Papa. Wave, wave for Papa." She took his hand, showed him. And he waved on his own, laughing.

When she looked again, Al was directly across. Their eyes met. Stunned, his lips formed her name. He saw the boy and grinned, tears in his eyes. Hand to his chest, he mouthed the question. "He's mine?"

She nodded, smiling.

Then he was gone.

The next day papers reported that spectators lined the tracks at every stop all the way to Atlanta.

In August of 1934, a "secret" train transferred him to Alcatraz. A prison built mostly for him and others like him. They were wrong. There were no others like him. They had expected Al to take over in Atlanta, but he was quiet, a model prisoner. Still, they guarded that "secret" train heavily, and spectators gathered along the route west.

Alcatraz. Another word for hell. Rumors drifted out. Nine by five cells, cold and damp, isolation, weeks, sometimes months in total darkness. Al was sick. For his last year he was confined to the "bug cage."

Gladys called once. No visitors but family, and then only fifteen minutes through a tiny window.

In January, 1939 she read that they were transferring him to the Federal Correctional Institution, Terminal Island, near Los Angeles. He would serve his last year there. She called for permission, took John to Mamma's house, drove down, crossed the harbor in a small prison boat.

She sat in one of the visitor cubicles, waiting behind thick glass, the walls institutional gray. Too sick to stay at Alcatraz, the article said. Something must be very wrong for Al to give a deposition against Johnny Torrio. Either his mind was slipping or the papers lied. Al would never betray Johnny Torrio.

The door opened, and the guard led out a man she did not know. She gasped, almost a cry, muffled by the heavy glass. She breathed in, put her fingertips below her eyes to press back the tears. Shaking, she gripped her arms. Don't cry. The least you can do. The very least.

He shuffled, his body bent and flabby, his receding hair made his big face look even rounder. The gray pants and shirt hung on him.

The guard helped him to the chair across from her. A slit in the glass for them to talk.

"Thanks," Al said, looking up at the guard, but his eyes seemed vacant, his mouth slack.

The guard had to turn him toward her. "You got a visitor, Mr. Capone. Hollywood star, few years back. Looks like you still got it, Snorky."

The tone one used for a child.

Al looked at her.

"Hello, Al."

He nodded, a half smile, not a flicker of recognition. His hand drifted to his head, smoothing some stray hair.

She should not have come. Better to keep him in her mind the way he'd been. Grabbing her up in his arms, carrying her, laughing. Venice Beach, those nights in the cabin. Catalina. Fishing off Todos Santos.

Tears. Impossible to stop them.

He saw. "No," he said softly, "don't." Then he turned to the guard. "I want to go back." He touched the guard's sleeve, whispered something she couldn't hear.

The guard shrugged. "Wait here, Miss Walton."

And Al stood and shuffled through the door.

She sat shaking, tears streaming, could hardly see to grab Kleenex from her purse. Eight years. What had they done to him that he would turn and go back to his cell?

She took deep breaths, wiped her eyes, waited. Minutes passed. What could the guard possibly have to say to her? She was about to leave when the door opened.

Al walked slowly across. In his hands was the mandolin, and she remembered the shop in Tijuana, how he'd carried it in his arms like a baby.

He sat and tuned it carefully. It took several minutes.

When he looked up, he smiled. His eyes had changed. Not quite like before, but he was there.

"Remember, Gladys?" he said, "Apple Blossom Time. Listen. You'll like it." He laughed. "I've had a long time to practice."

> *How long have I been asleep in this chair?*
>
> *Barry? I try to call his name, but my voice is gone.*
>
> *Something must be wrong. Barry never lets me sleep in a chair.*
>
> *My mind fuzzy.*
>
> *Think, woman. What day is it? What year? They'll ask that at the hospital like before. Where do you live? How many children? Names, ages. I rehearse every now and then. I will not die in one of those homes. Hallways clogged with wheelchairs.*
>
> *A car in the driveway. A visitor.*
>
> *Like that young man. I remember that date exactly. April 12, 1942.*
>
> *Moment I saw him, I knew. Tall in the doorway. Crisp white uniform. Her eyes and hair. "Captain*

329

*Nathan Huxley," he said, "you were a friend of my
mother. I had to find you 'fore I shipped out."
Same Georgia voice.*

*He stayed more than an hour. I told him all he
wanted to know about Mabel. How she loved him.
And about Craig, how they would've gone to get
him. Craig never married. I told Nathan Andrew
where to find him, but I don't think he had time.*

Al's money sent her boy to the Naval Academy.

*I teased Al when he was trying to tell me his plan,
so serious. "I started as a bookkeeper, you know."
Right, Al Capone, a bookkeeper. Baltimore.*

I close my eyes, see that bare room, sawdust on the
floor, boards stacked, walls unfinished.

*His grin. Tossing me over his shoulder, sack of
potatoes... What fun, we had. "My, Mr. Capone,
what a big safe you have..."*

I hear the front door open, light floods in from the
living room. Footsteps.

I open my eyes, see him in the doorway, and know my
mistake even as I speak.

"Al."

"Mother, Linda called... your phone isn't working..."
John John looks past me to the floor. "My God! Oh, my
God!"

I follow his eyes, and then my son lifts me in his arms,
carries me to my room. Rushes to call the police.

I lie back on the pillow, still in my house dress. It
would be so easy to just sleep, let them decide. Instead I wait,
listen for my cue. Timing is everything, Mr. Baggot always
said.

Sirens, police, ambulance. Lots of commotion. John
on the phone. "We have to make arrangements, Linda. She
can't stay here alone. I don't know how she survived this."

Gladys *and* Capone, *the Untold Story*

Even without a director, you learn to anticipate the right moment for an entrance.

Or exit.

I slip out the back, never mind shoes.

How I love a detached garage. 1979, a good year for Cadillacs. The town is used to me in my big red convertible. They laugh. Star of the Silent Screen, thinks she's still a flapper. Bare breasts at her age. I heard she was Al Capone's girlfriend. Probably just a story.

If they knew.

They think I forget to wear a top. I don't forget.

I turn onto the coast road.

I ride with Valentino, scarves blowing.

The morning sun bright, a clear California sky. The blue Pacific all the way to China.

I am flying.

Standing on the wing.

"Don't look down. Keep your eyes on me."

I turn. Skeets Elliot gives the thumbs up.

I jump.

Feel the chute billowing, jerking me up, then floating. No breeze. Glorious!

I smile and wave.

Point my ballerina toes for the perfect landing.

Mazie, Queen of the Air!

My Grandson, Josh, standing at the bar within Al Capone's Suite at his West Coast Hideaway, "Fortress West" at Two Bunch Palms Resort and Spa in Desert Hot Springs, California.

Al Capone. What do you think?

GLADYS WALTON
Filmography and Musicals

After six months of grinding out fast-moving two-reel comedies for the Sunshine Comedy Company, at age sixteen, she finally got her big break and signed a contract with Universal Studios in 1919.

1920
La La Lucille, *as Peggy Hughes*
Pink Tights, *as Mazie Darton*
Risky Business, *as Phillipa*
The Secret Gift, *as Winnie*

1921
All Dolled Up, *as Maggie Quick*
Desperate Youth, *as Rosemary Merridew*
High Heels, *as Christine Trevor*
Playing With Fire, *as Enid Gregory*
Rich Girl, Poor Girl,
    a dual role as Nora McShane and Beatrice Vanderfleet
Short Skirts, *as Natalie Smith*
The Lion Tamer, *as The Lion Tamer*
The Room of Death
The Rowdy, *as Kit Purcell*

1922
A Dangerous Game, *as Gretchen Ann Peebles*
Second Hand Rose, *as Rosie O'Grady*
The Girl Who Ran Wild, *as M'liss*
The Guttersnipe, *as Mazie O'Day*
The Lavender Bath Lady, as *Mamie Conroy*

333

The Trouper, *as Mamie Judd*
The Wise Kid, *as Rosie Cooper*
Top O'The Morning, *as 'Jerry' O'Donnell*

1923
Crossed *Wires, as Marcel Murphy*
Gossip, *as Caroline Weatherbee*
The Love Letter, *as Mary Ann McKee*
The Near Lady, *as Nora Schultz*
SAWDUST, *as Nita Moore – AVAILABLE ON DVD*
The Town Scandal, *as Jean Crosby*
THE UNTAMEABLE—AVAILABLE ON DVD
—a *dual role as Edna Fielding & Joy Fielding*
The Wild Party, *as Leslie Adams*

1925
– No longer with Universal Studios, she starred in films produced by a variety of East Coast Studios.

A Little Girl in a Big City, *as Mary Barry*
Anything Once
Easy Money
Enemies of Youth
The Sky Raider, *as Marie*

1928
The Ape)

1948
The Red Shoes (1948) *uncredited as a Dancer*

NEW YORK ~ BROADWAY—A LIVE AUDIENCE
SONG ~ DANCE ~ COMEDY
Her favorite venue!

The Melting of Molly
Original, Musical, Comedy
Dec 30, 1918 - Mar 15, 1919
Gladys Walton as Miss Pierce

Shubert Gaieties of 1919
Original, Musical, Revue
Jul 17, 1919 - Oct 18, 1919

The Midnight Rounders of 1921
Original, Musical, Revue
Feb 7, 1921 - Apr 2, 1921

The Last Waltz
Original, Musical, Operetta
May 10, 1921 - Oct 29, 1921
Gladys Walton as Petruschka

The Lady in Ermine
Original, Musical
Oct 2, 1922 - Apr 21, 1923
Gladys Walton as Angelina

June Days
Original, Musical, Comedy
Aug 6, 1925 - Oct 17, 1925
Gladys Walton as Susie Rolles

As a testament to his mother, John has published a full color pictorial biography of her life. *Gladys Walton, the Collector's Edition 2009.* Now available on Amazon.com. More than 70 photos-family photos, publicity photos, movie stills, and theater lobby cards, along with photos and information on Capone's West Coast Hideaway, "Fortress West" in Desert Hot Springs, California. It includes photos of her home in Morro Bay, where she lived when "Crazy Eddie" broke in and killed her companion

3655975

Made in the USA